EARLY ARABIC DRAMA

Also by M. M. Badawi

Modern Arabic Drama in Egypt, Cambridge University Press, 1987
Modern Arabic Literature and the West, Ithaca Press, London, 1985
A Critical Introduction to Modern Arabic Poetry, Cambridge University Press, 1975
An Anthology of Modern Arabic Verse, Oxford University Press, 1970, reprinted 1975
Background to Shakespeare, Macmillan, London, 1981; reprinted 1984
Coleridge: Critic of Shakespeare, Cambridge University Press, 1973
Yahya Haqqi's The Saint's Lamp and Other Stories: a Translation with an Introduction, E. J. Brill, Leiden, 1973
Aṭlāl wa Rasā'il min London (Poems), GEBO, Cairo, 1979
Dirāsāt fi 'l-Shi'r wa 'l-Masraḥ, Dār al-Ma'rifa, Cairo, 1960; reprinted GEBO, Alexandria, 1979
Coleridge fī Silsilat Nawābigh al-Fikr al-Gharbī, Dār al-Ma'ārif, Cairo, 1958.

EARLY ARABIC DRAMA

M. M. BADAWI

Fellow of St Antony's College, Oxford

The right of the University of Cambridge to print and sell all manner of books was granted by Henry VIII in 1534. The University has printed and published continuously since 1584.

CAMBRIDGE UNIVERSITY PRESS
CAMBRIDGE
NEW YORK NEW ROCHELLE
MELBOURNE SYDNEY

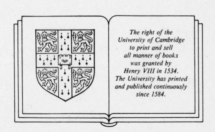

Published by the Press Syndicate of the University of Cambridge
The Pitt Building, Trumpington Street, Cambridge CB2 1RP
32 East 57th Street, New York, NY 10022, USA
10 Stamford Road, Oakleigh, Melbourne 3166, Australia

First published 1988

Printed in Great Britain at the University Press, Cambridge

British Library cataloguing in publication data

Badawi, M.M.
Early Arabic drama.
1. Arabic drama – History and criticism
I. Title
892′.725′09 PJ7565

Library of Congress cataloguing in publication data

Badawi, Muḥammad Muṣṭafá.
Early Arabic drama.

Includes index.
1. Arabic drama – Egypt – History and criticism.
2. Arabic drama – 20th century – History and criticism.
3. Arabic drama – 19th century – History and criticism.
I. Title.
PJ8211.B3 1988 892′.72′009 87-15117

ISBN 0 521 34427 1

FOR MIEKE

CONTENTS

INTRODUCTION

This book is an attempt to trace the development of Arabic drama from its beginnings in the middle of the nineteenth century until it reached its maturity in the second and third decades of the twentieth century. It is not an exhaustive history; for that a huge tome would be required if the treatment is to be more than a list of authors' names or an annotated bibliography of titles of plays. For obvious reasons the work of the pioneers receives a fuller treatment than that of many of their successors who did not contribute substantially to the development of the genre. As Arabic drama matures, however, it becomes necessary for the approach to be more selective; only major figures are chosen and their more important works treated in detail. To enable the reader to get a feel for the material I have included my translation of some extracts in the course of the discussion.

Syria (and Lebanon) and Egypt are the countries in which Arabic drama was born but it is in Egypt that it reached its maturity. There are possible reasons for this. Egypt is the only Arab country in which there seems to have been a fairly continuous tradition of dramatic or semi-dramatic entertainment going back at least as far as the Fatimid period in the tenth century when, the sources tell us, shadow plays were performed. Nineteenth-century dramatists and actor-managers emigrated to Egypt from Beirut and Damascus where they had met with opposition and hostility from the authorities and the public alike. In Cairo and Alexandria they found a much more appreciative audience. They even received encouragement from the munificent ruler of Egypt Khedive Ismail who, whatever his deficiencies as a ruler may have been in other areas, did at least officially try to encourage the arts. It is, therefore, not surprising that as this book develops it becomes largely the story of Arabic drama in Egypt. For many years to come Arabic drama was to be synonymous with Egyptian drama. Through the various visits to the rest of the Arab world by leading Egyptian theatrical troupes, as well as through the publication and discussion of the work of major Egyptian playwrights in newspapers and periodicals, Egyptian drama exercised a profound influence on Arabic drama outside Egypt. Non-Egyptian

Arabic drama can be said to have begun to make its distinct and valuable contribution only in the 1960s.

Although I hardly need to point out that fitness for stage production is a *sine qua non* for a work to qualify as good drama, my concern is with drama as part of Arabic literature; I therefore deal only with the published texts of plays. I do not attempt to provide a history of the Arabic stage or trace the fortunes of the various theatrical troupes that continued to be formed and reformed throughout this period. In this respect my book differs from Jacob M. Landau's *Studies in the Arab Theater and Cinema* (Philadelphia, 1958). It also differs from it in another important respect; in the introduction Landau writes that his book 'is intended to be a survey of the development of the Arab theater and cinema as cultural and social phenomena rather than a critical study of their aesthetic values, for which the time has not yet come'. As far as the theatre is concerned, this was an amazing judgment for a scholar to make in 1958 when so many plays of considerable artistic merit had already appeared. Unlike Landau's my approach is primarily critical, and I hope to show in the last section of this book that in Egypt, at least, plays which we can describe as good dramas without either condescension or relaxation of our normal critical standards were being written in the second decade of this century, to say nothing of the important work of subsequent dramatists such as Tawfīq al-Ḥakīm or Maḥmūd Taymūr. It is indeed gratifying to find Professor H.A.R. Gibb referring in his preface to Landau's book to the 'present maturity of the Arabic theater'.

It is obvious that there is a need for a critical survey of early Arabic drama and its subsequent development, in English, or in any other language for that matter. Nevill Barbour's articles on 'The Arabic theatre in Egypt', published in *The Bulletin of the School of Oriental Studies* 7 (1935–7), despite the many insightful comments and the generally fair judgments which they contain, provide an all too brief account. Muḥammad Yūsuf Najm's excellent study *al-Masraḥiyya fi'l Adab al-ʿArabī al-Ḥadīth* (Beirut, 1956), unfortunately stops at 1914 and therefore does not touch any of the important works which signal the coming of age of modern Arabic drama. Landau's *Studies in the Arab Theater and Cinema* attempts to cover an enormous canvas and, in spite of its extremely useful bibliography, what little literary or dramatic criticism there is in it is confined to a few perfunctory remarks. Muḥammad Mandūr's *al-Masraḥ al-Nathrī* (Cairo, 1959), valuable as it is, is not sufficiently detailed and to some extent suffers from that distinguished critic's deeply rooted prejudice against the use of the Egyptian colloquial as well as from its obtrusively didactic tone (the book consists of lectures delivered to the students of the Arab League Higher Institute for Arabic Studies). Nada Tomiche's *Histoire de la Littérature Romanesque de l'Egypte Moderne* (Paris, 1981) devotes several sections to drama, but it contains too many inaccuracies and does not even mention major playwrights such as Ibrāhīm Ramzī or Anṭūn Yazbak. The chapters dealing with drama in Matti Moosa's *The Origins of Modern Arabic Fiction* (Washington,

1983) are, as the author admits in the preface, 'much closer to being a social and literary history rather than being basically a literary criticism'. Mohamed A. al-Khozai's *The Development of Early Arabic Drama (1847–1900)* (London, 1984), on the other hand, 'attempts to evaluate and study the Arab experiment in playwriting' but clearly it stops far too early; besides, it is difficult to agree with many of the author's critical judgments particularly his wholesale dismissal of the use of the colloquial language. However, in saying that there is a need for a critical survey of early Arabic drama I wish in no way to belittle the value of important studies which have already appeared on various aspects of the subject, notably Attia Amer's *Lughat al-Masraḥ al-ʿArabī* (Stockholm, 1967), ʿAlī al-Rāʿī's *Funūn al-Kūmīdiyā min Khayāl al-Ẓill ilā Najīb al-Rīḥānī* (Cairo, 1971) and his *Masraḥ al-Damm wa'l-Dumūʿ* (Cairo, 1973) and Atia Abul Naga's *Les Sources Françaises du Théâtre Egyptien (1870–1939)* (Alger, 1972).

The absence from classical Arabic literature of drama in the western sense (i.e. the imitation on a stage by human actors of a story or situation through action and dialogue in verse or prose) is an intriguing issue which has exercised the minds of many scholars and critics, orientalists and Arabs alike. As is well known, pre-Islamic literature consisted almost exclusively of poetry, lyrical poetry which had obvious epic as well as dramatic elements but knew neither epic nor drama. After Islam, with the spread of the Islamic empire, the Arabs came into close contact with the superior civilizations of the Persians and the Byzantines, from which they gradually learnt a great deal. Much was translated, particularly in the ninth century, generally indirectly via Syriac, from Greek: science, medicine, mathematics and philosophy but hardly any Greek imaginative literature at all. Because of the extraordinarily high status accorded to the Arabic language, it being the sacred language of the Koran understood by the believers to be literally the word of God, the Arabs, who prided themselves on their tongue, seemed to feel no need to translate any foreign literature since in their view the highest degree of human eloquence could only be attained in Arabic. Whether or not the translators deliberately refrained from including Greek drama, indeed whether or not they were even aware of its existence, we can never be absolutely sure, although the latter hypothesis is more likely to be true, particularly in the absence of a living Greek dramatic tradition at the time. What is important, however, is that psychologically they were conditioned to feel self-sufficient where literary expression was concerned. Because Aristotle became a dominant influence among Arab philosophers and thinkers the desire to have him wholly available in Arabic was keenly felt. A dilemma arose over his *Poetics*; more than one attempt was made to translate it into Arabic from the Syriac in the tenth century by Abū Bishr Mattā and Yaḥyā ibn ʿAddī. From the surviving translation by Abū Bishr (d. 939) as well as from the commentaries on it by the three philosophers al-Fārābī (870–950), Avicenna (980–1036) and Averroes (1126–98), it is clear that the Arabs had no idea of the genres Aristotle was discussing in his text. The terms 'tragedy' and 'comedy' were rendered as *madīḥ* (panegyric) and *hijā'* (satire or invective) respectively, which were two accepted genres in Arabic poetry. It is true that al-Fārābī and Avicenna use the original Greek terms, but they still take them to mean 'panegyric' and 'satire'. Aristotle's *Poetics* (and *Rhetoric*) exercised some unmistakable influence on the development of classical Arabic literary theory and stylistics, but the influence remained limited to details of language and style or to the working of poetic imagination. Tragedy and comedy were never discussed later on for the simple reason that originally no one seemed to know exactly what they meant.

But why did not the Arabs themselves develop the art of drama (in the western sense)? Various explanations have been offered all of which belong to the realm of speculation, though some are patently more speculative than others. The pre-Islamic Arabs, it has been suggested, did not have a sufficiently complex mythology; as if drama of necessity could only grow out of myth. The Arabs' desert environment and their nomadic way of life, it is alleged, did not particularly help them to create drama which requires a sedentary mode of existence; as if all Arabs were nomads and no urban centres such as Mecca existed. An even more dubious explanation relates to the once much more popular generalization – the product of nineteenth-century views on race – about the so-called Arab mind. The Arab mind was held to be atomistic and excessively individualistic, and best expressed in the structure of the pre-Islamic ode, *Qaṣīda*, which used to be thought of as a collection of single, semantically autonomous lines, each ending in the same rhyme. The Arabs, so the story ran, were incapable of the sort of organization and large-scale structure essential to literary forms of some magnitude such as drama and the epic. Apart from the totally false view of the form of the pre-Islamic Arabic poem implied in it, this theory of the Arab mind conveniently overlooks such impressive monuments of large-scale intellectual structure as is found in some celebrated Islamic architecture or in the elaborate system of Islamic jurisprudence. Again, Islam has been claimed to offer a view of man which recommends total acceptance of the scheme of things, if not absolute resignation, a view which precludes the type of tragic conflict we find in Greek drama. Not to mention the crude and simplistic understanding of Islam which it involves, this explanation equates drama with Greek tragedy and only one type of Greek tragedy at that, forgetting that there is such a thing as comedy to which tragic conflict is generally irrelevant. Islam, being a strictly monotheistic religion, forbade the worship of idols and, therefore, just as it discouraged figurative arts like painting it would not have allowed drama. This is stated even though inevitably, in view of the absence of drama, there cannot possibly be an unambiguous interdiction of the theatre, and despite the fact that even figurative painting was not entirely unknown in Islamic civilization. We must indeed remind ourselves that although modern western drama may have had its roots in the medieval Christian church, as any student of the West well knows, it is uncertain that without the influence of classical Greek and Roman drama it would have acquired the form and significance it came to have in the history of western culture. One main reason for the absence of Arabic drama, one scholar argued, was that women were strictly forbidden to appear on the stage. But so they were for a long time in Christian Europe; it is easy to forget that Cleopatra and Lady Macbeth were not played by women in Shakespeare's time.

Much ink has been spilt largely by Arab authors in an attempt to disprove the allegation that there is something inherently inimical to drama in Islam or Islamic civilization. In many of the articles and even in the books devoted to the discussion of the subject, such as Aḥmad Shams al-Dīn al-Ḥajjājī's *al-ʿArab wa Fann al-Masraḥ* (Cairo, 1975), Muḥammad Kamāl al-Dīn's *al-ʿArab waʾl-Masraḥ* (Cairo, 1975), ʿAlī ʿUqla ʿArsān's *al-Ẓawāhir al-Masraḥiyya ʿind al-ʿArab* (Damascus, 1981), the attempts have been rather naive and at best no more than well-intentioned apologetics often inspired by a feeling of inferiority at the alleged absence of drama from Arabic literature. The authors of such apologetics could have been saved this trouble had they pondered T.S. Eliot's wise statement that 'the theatre is a gift which has not been vouchsafed to every race, even of the highest culture'.

The absence of drama is in no way an indication of cultural inferiority and the fact is that the Arabs did develop their own dramatic writing as well as their own epics, even though the form that these products took was different from the western form. In some pre-Islamic poems, more strikingly in the work of several Islamic poets, particularly in the love poems of ʿUmar ibn Abī Rabīʿa (d.c. 720) and later Bashshār (d. 784) and Abū Nuwās (d.c. 803), we notice a considerable use of dialogue and a specific situation is created involving the lover and his beloved. Unlike the *pastourelle*, however, this was not turned into drama by an Arab Adam de la Halle. Just as the Arabic equivalent of an epic, the romance cycles of ʿAntara and Abu Zayd al-Hilālī among others, did not develop out of poetry but were a mixture of prose and verse, so Arabic dramatic writing, as revealed in the Arabic shadow theatre, was an offshoot of the specifically Arabic forms of *maqāma*, also a mixture of prose and verse. The *maqāma*, generally assumed to be the invention of al-Hamadhānī (969–1008), is a tale told in a mixture of rhyming prose and verse dealing more often than not with the adventures of an eloquent rogue who lives by his wits. Despite its euphuistic style and its inordinate concern with manner rather than matter, particularly in the work of al-Hamadhānī's successors, the *maqāma* contained a conspicuous element of drama; its picaresque protagonist often had to resort to impersonating other characters in an attempt to eke out a living by fooling others. Formally, a typical al-Hamadhānī *maqāma* is a cross between narrative and drama, a short story and a playlet combined. In the shadow theatre the dramatic element dominates and the narrative is reduced to the words of the Presenter who introduces the characters or comments on their actions. Despite the absence of *human* actors, since the action is presented by means of leather puppets projected on a screen, I have tried to show elsewhere that in the three plays which have reached us, the work of the occulist Ibn Dāniyāl (1248–1311), we have a sophisticated form of drama which has not yet received the critical attention it deserves.

The idea of the shadow theatre may have been ultimately of Far Eastern origin, but the form of Ibn Dāniyāl's plays was clearly indigenous since it is a development of the specifically Arabic form of *maqāma*. In fact, Ibn Dāniyāl's work was referred to by the later historian Ibn Iyās (d.c. 1524) as *maqāma*. This cultural or literary self-sufficiency continued to mark Arab civilization for several centuries to come. Initially, their isolation from other cultures, particularly western culture, was justified not so much by their feeling of the superiority of their own language and literature, as by their actual military and material superiority, and this was strengthened by their mutually hostile relationship with Christian Europe. Even if they had been given the chance to see the spectacular developments of the dramatic arts in Renaissance and post-Renaissance Europe, it is doubtful if the Arabs would have been sympathetically attracted to them. As it happened, there is no indication that they were at all aware of such achievements. Their cultural contact with the West occurred much later (Napoleon invaded Egypt in 1798), at a time when they were forced to realize their own backwardness, and the West's overwhelming superiority. It was both traumatic and humiliating; the French came to Egypt and Syria as conquerors who achieved an easy victory. Despite the brevity of the French occupation (which lasted from 1798 to 1801) its impact on the Arabs' psyche and general attitude was, in the long run, tremendous. The Arabs were finally becoming more receptive to what Europe had to offer. As is well known, the process which started with Muhammad Ali's educational missions to Italy and France nearly two centuries ago was initially confined to technology and science but eventually it came to embrace intellectual and artistic aspects of life, and despite setbacks, occasional ambivalence and reluctance, the process continues. And one manifestation of it is the attempt made by Mārūn al-Naqqāsh and Yaʿqūb Ṣannūʿ to introduce western drama into the Arab world, or rather to adapt it to Arab taste. In this context it is perhaps not without significance that of these two pioneers in the field the one was a Lebanese Christian and the other an Egyptian Jew; presumably as such they were less likely to have been 'ideologically' opposed to the western way of life than their conservative Muslim compatriots.

I

THE INDIGENOUS DRAMATIC TRADITION

Modern Arabic drama is an importation from the West: it was directly and consciously borrowed in about the middle of the nineteenth century by a Lebanese writer in Beirut, Mārūn al-Naqqāsh, and two decades later by an Egyptian in Cairo, Ya'qūb Ṣannū' (Sanua). As it happened in both cases the inspiration came, apparently independently, from a sojourn in Italy and exposure to the Italian arts of theatre particularly the opera, although European dramatic arts, namely French drama and Italian opera, had periodically been performed in their original languages in Cairo from the time of the French campaign at the turn of the century onwards.

Yet dramatic representations or histrionic activities were not altogether unknown in the contemporary Arab world or even in medieval Islam. Any account of modern Arabic drama which ignored such activities would suffer from serious deficiencies, not just on grounds of incompleteness but also because it would fail to provide the necessary historical background. More importantly it would not be capable of explaining certain features of modern Arabic drama, both on the structural and the thematic levels, which are clearly the product of some deeply rooted attitudes and tendencies inherited from the past history of indigenous dramatic or semi-dramatic entertainment. The knowledge of such history is essential in order to see the manner in which the imported form was conceived and how it subsequently developed, for the imported form was in several ways determined by the local histrionic or theatrical tradition. Furthermore, traditional forms of theatrical entertainment continued to exist to some extent until the first few decades of twentieth-century Egypt and, instead of being immediately ousted by the imported western model, they overlapped with it for a considerable period of time. A word, therefore, must be said about the indigenous tradition.

I

To begin with, there were the dramatic recitations by rhapsodes (or *shā'irs*) of popular medieval romances such as Abū Zayd al-Hilālī, al-Ẓāhir Baybars or

ʿAntara, of which there is a useful account in Edward Lane's still fascinating book *The Manners and Customs of the Modern Egyptians.*[1] Lane's rather solemn and Victorian view of popular dramatic spectacle drove him to dismiss the farces he witnessed as 'low and ridiculous' and 'scarcely worthy of description',[2] despite the obvious social and political satire they might contain. Yet his reaction to the public recitation of romances was a favourable one. He thought they afforded 'attractive and rational entertainments' and commented on 'the lively and dramatic manner of the narrator'.[3] Composed in a mixture of prose and verse, these romances were 'half narrative and half dramatic'. Lane describes how they were chanted from memory by a rhapsode who specialized in a particular cycle of romances with a single chord viol and was accompanied by another musician with a similar instrument; both would be seated on a raised platform built against the front of a coffee shop, surrounded by an audience, the patrons of the coffee shop who did not pay for this entertainment. Such dramatic recitations are now a dying art, but fortunately a selection of these often very moving performances has recently been recorded and is now available thanks to the efforts of such enthusiastic students as Giovanni Canova.

II

Closer to drama proper is the religious passion play or, to be more exact, a cycle of plays known as *taʿziya* (consolation/condolence) which commemorates the massacre of Ḥusayn, the son of the fourth caliph ʿAlī, and the descendants of the Prophet Muhammad by the ruling house of the Umayyads. This type of folk drama is performed by Shiʿite Muslims (i.e. followers of the house of ʿAlī) during the first third of the Muslim month of Muḥarram, the tenth of Muḥarram being their great day of mourning as it is the anniversary of the battle of Karbalāʾ (A.H. 60/A.D. 680) in which ʿAlī's son and the Prophet's grandson, al-Ḥusayn, fell fighting against the Umayyad Caliph Yazīd. The *taʿziya* plays are generally performed in Persian but some have been done in Turkish and Arabic. In Iraq the more usual term for their performance is *shabīh* (likeness), because the actors provide a likeness, a mimesis, to the historical figures whose actions and deeds they portray. Plays are continually reworked and added to by poets who actually appear at the beginning of the performance to introduce the dramatic spectacle with appropriate verses praising and lamenting the dead. Accompanying the actors is a choir of boys playing the parts of mourning women and by gesture and sound expressing overwhelming grief. The characters themselves are numerous and they include angels (played by boys) like Gabriel and Biblical and Koranic figures such as Eve, Jacob, Mary and various prophets. Even animals are included like the lion who pays homage to Ḥusayn's head. They prophesy in detail all the ensuing events, which are told several times over, in particular the actual death of Ḥusayn. Every ounce of emotion is wrung out of the situation in order to put across the plight of the descendants of the Prophet in the manner of, but more extreme than, the Wakefield Miracle Play of the Crucifixion. Innocent children are fatally struck by arrows and young bridegrooms are slain. In the end the decapitated head of the martyr Ḥusayn is brought to the Caliph Yazīd, together with the captured women and children in a mournful procession, and the blood-stained head is made to deliver an oration.

Indeed, one authority wonders with some justice if we can apply the term drama except 'with reservation' to 'the series of sometimes 40–50 independent tableaux which constitute the performance'.[4] Structurally there are obvious problems where no particular order, not even the chronological, exists except in a very broad sense between the scenes. Nevertheless, many of the elements of drama are there. A stage is especially erected for the purpose in a public place which may even be a mosque. Specific stage properties are used such as a coffin 'with receptacles for holding lights, also Ḥusayn's bow, lance, spear and banner'. Although an appeal is made to the audience's imagination, some realistic effects are carefully sought; a heap of straw may represent the sand of the desert of Karbalā᾿ but real blood is employed. The reaction of the Shiʿite participants and the audience can be so overwhelming that violence directed against self as well as others has been known to ensue. However, despite such crude realism and melodramatic sensationalism, the sincerity of the participants was known on occasions to be such that even foreign spectators, far from dismissing it as repulsive mass wallowing in grief, were deeply moved by the sight. We recall that it was the reading of an account given by such a spectator, Comte de Gobineau (1866), that drove Matthew Arnold to write in 1871 his lengthy essay 'A Persian Passion Play' (included in his *Essays in Criticism*), an essay which incidentally despite its apparent liberal spirit is not without its Victorian commonplaces and prejudices regarding Islam.

Gobineau went as far as to claim that the *taʿziya* play he saw ranked with Greek drama 'as a great and serious affair, engaging the heart and life of the people who have given birth to it'. In comparison, he found the Latin, English, French and German drama to be 'a mere pastime or amusement, more or less intellectual and elegant'.[5] Arnold thought that a better parallel was to be found in the Ammergau Passion Play, since the plays turn entirely on one subject, namely the sufferings of the Imam Ḥusayn and his family. There is no doubt that Arnold is nearer the mark, as there is much in common between the *taʿziya* and the medieval Mystery plays produced by the guilds. Like the latter, the performance of the *taʿziya* is a corporate annual event in which people willingly collaborate and the expenses incurred, including the poet's fees, are paid by the well-to-do as an act of piety. Whoever builds the stage 'builds himself a palace in Paradise'.[6]

Yet in the study of the Arabic theatre the *taʿziya* remains of very limited relevance. Although there are no records of Persian *taʿziya* performances until the early years of the nineteenth century (the earliest example of such a performance in Tehran was noted by J. Morier in 1811), we must assume that the phenomenon must have existed at least in the late eighteenth century and that it had incorporated elements from the ancient cults of Tammuz and Adonis. Gibbon writes that 'on the annual festival of his [Ḥusayn's] martyrdom, in the devout pilgrimage to his sepulchre, his Persian votaries abandon their souls to the religious frenzy of sorrow and indignation'.[7] Nevertheless, despite its ancient origins, the form did not develop beyond the stage of crude and disorganized dramatic representation. Because of its arrested growth and its strictly confined theme and because of its close connection with religion, the *taʿziya* should, therefore, more properly be viewed as an extension of religious ritual than as drama.[8] Furthermore, because of its Shiʿite origin, sentiment and manner of presenting Islamic history, the *taʿziya* has not spread to the Sunnī parts of the Islamic world; it remains more important in Persian than in Arabic and more relevant to Iraq than to Egypt. However, a word had to be said about it here for the following reasons: first, because it explodes the commonly held fallacy that Islam as such, and not 'puritan' Islam, is incompatible with dramatic representation.[9] Secondly, it is virtually the sole dramatic spectacle of a *tragic* nature which we encounter in the Islamic world prior to its cultural contact with the West. One has to say 'virtually' because, as we shall soon see, there are references to events of a tragic character being represented in the medieval Arabic shadow theatre as early as the thirteenth century.[10] As late as the sixteenth century the hanging of Ṭūmān Bay was, according to the historian Ibn Iyās, instantly turned into the subject of a shadow play which was performed as entertainment for the Ottoman conqueror Selim.[11] Thirdly, the central theme of the *taʿziya*, the martyrdom of Ḥusayn, was to be treated later on by ʿAbd al-Raḥmān Sharqāwī in his Egyptian verse drama *al-Ḥusayn Thāʾiran wa Shahīdan* in 1969.

III

Egypt, in fact, seems to be the only Arab country with an almost continuous dramatic or semi-dramatic tradition going back at least as early as the Fatimid period. Lane was clearly not aware that what he dismissed as 'low and ridiculous' farces belonged in reality to an older tradition of dramatic entertainment which, together with mimicry and farce, included puppet shows of the Punch and Judy variety known as *Qaraqōz*, as well as the more literary type of dramatic spectacle known as *Khayāl al-Ẓill* (shadow play). As in the beginnings of Greek comedy, these predominantly comic folk dramatic spectacles had a strongly marked sexual aspect which probably originated in early fertility rites. They were held in public places such as the market or the street, on religious occasions such as fairs celebrating the birthdays of saints (*mūlids*), and significantly enough they were also performed in private on joyful occasions with sexual implications such as weddings and circumcisions. Popular music groups or bands of predominantly female dancers known as *ghawāzī*, a familiar sight in Egyptian villages, included a male clown whom the villagers call Abū ʿAggūr (lit. the man with a cucumber). In certain dramatic 'numbers' he appeared with the singers and dancers, his face like Pierrot's covered in flour, making rude comments on the dialogue of the players, raising an easy laugh by exaggerated mimicry of their female movements and brandishing his *farqala*, a lash made of plaited rope, holding its long wooden handle in overtly sexual gestures. Needless to say, the name given to him had its phallic implications. A similar function was also performed by *Khalboos*, the male servant of the slightly more respectable bands of female singers known as *ʿawālim*, of whom Lane says that 'he often acts the part of a buffoon'.[12] Another popular figure in 'low' comedy was ʿAlī Kākā who was described by the scholar and man of letters, Aḥmad Amīn, as a man 'who wore a belt from which dangled a tool shaped like a huge penis and the sight of him never failed to arouse the laughter of men and women alike'.[13] As Rushdī Ṣāliḥ has rightly observed, there is a family likeness between this kind of comic clown who appeared in popular Egyptian entertainments and such figures in the history of the western theatre as the Harlequin and Merry Andrew.[14]

Obviously such spectacles belong more properly to a primitive type of *commedia dell'arte* which relied on improvisation by the actors. No texts of such works have therefore reached us. Nor have we many detailed descriptions of these spectacles. The earliest eye-witness account of such performances is given by the Danish traveller, Carsten Niebuhr, who in 1780 saw a farce in Arabic performed in the open air in the courtyard of a house in Cairo. The story is that of a woman (played by a man in disguise), who lures one traveller after another to her tent, and who after robbing them of their belongings chases them away with a stick. Incidentally, the audience grew so tired of the repetition of this absurd situation that they forced the actors to stop their performance half way through.[15]

In 1815 another European traveller, G. Belzoni, saw a couple of farces: one representing how a pilgrim who wishes to purchase a camel to go to Mecca is cheated by an unscrupulous camel driver who, acting as a middleman, robs both the owner of the camel and the buyer. When his dishonesty is discovered he is given a thrashing and is then allowed to run away. Interestingly enough the camel is played by two men covered in cloth. The second farce shows a roguish, poor, Arab couple entertaining a European whom they comically deceive into believing that they are rich.[16]

A more detailed account is given a couple of decades later by Lane who witnessed a farce performed by players known as *Moḥabbaẓeen* before the ruler of Egypt at a festival celebrated in honour of the circumcision of one of his sons:

The *dramatis personae* were a Náẓir (or governor of a district), a Sheykh Beled (or chief of a village), a servant of the latter, a Copt clerk, a Fellah indebted to the government, his wife, and five other persons, of whom two made their appearance first in the character of drummers, one as a hautboy-player, and the two others as dancers. After a little drumming and piping and dancing by these five, the Náẓir and the rest of the performers enter the ring.[17]

The Náẓir asks how much the Fellah owed the government, and the musicians, who now act as a chorus of peasants, suggest that the Coptic clerk should be asked to consult his register. The clerk, dressed as a Copt with a black turban and carrying an inkhorn in his girdle, on being asked by the Skeykh el-Beled, says that the Fellah's debt amounted to a thousand piastres of which he has paid back only five. When the Fellah says that he has no money to pay back his debt the Sheykh orders that he is thrown down and beaten by 'an inflated piece of an intestine, resembling a large kurbág'. The Fellah screams, appealing to the mercy of the Náẓir by the honour of the horse's tail of the Náẓir, his wife's trousers and head-band etc. The beating then stops and he is thrown in jail. While he is in prison his wife visits him and is asked by him to take a gift of food to the Coptic clerk and entreat him to use his good offices to procure his release. The clerk accepts the gift and advises the wife to take some money to the village chief who, after taking the bribe, in turn advises her to entreat the Náẓir in person. She withdraws in order to adorn herself with kohl and henna, then reappears to pay a visit to the Náẓir who sets her husband free after she has given herself to him.

The farce, despite its crude elements which seem to have offended Lane, is obviously not without its satirical content, the message being to draw the attention of the ruler of the country to the malpractices of his tax-collectors. Formally speaking it has the essential elements of drama.

IV

The only texts which have been preserved for us, albeit in a very small number, are those of shadow theatre (*Khayāl al-Ẓill*), an art form generally thought to be of a Far Eastern origin. In shadow plays, which were performed in the streets and market places and occasionally also at court and in private houses, the action was represented by shadows cast upon a large screen by flat, coloured leather puppets, held in front of a torch, while the hidden puppet master, *al-Rayyis* or *al-Miqaddim*, delivered the dialogue and songs, helped in this by associates, sometimes as many as five persons including a youth who imitated the voice of women. Shadow plays must not be confused with the straightforward puppet shows of the same type as Punch and Judy which were quite popular in the Arab world and until quite recently were to be seen frequently in the streets in big cities in Egypt. The latter were known as *Qaraqōz* (in spoken Egyptian dialect: *Araʾōz*), the name of their leading character or anti-hero, which is either the Turkish Karagōz (meaning black-eyed), or a corrupt form of the name of the notoriously tyrannical, thirteenth-century Egyptian government official, Qarāqūsh.

The failure of the bulk of medieval Arabic drama to reach us constitutes a serious loss in Arab literary history, the full extent of which cannot be properly measured. However, we can form some idea of the kind of thing we have been deprived of if we examine the three earliest shadow plays that have been preserved for us, the work of the thirteenth-century poet and wit, the Mosul born Egyptian oculist, Shams al-Dīn Muḥammad ibn Dāniyāl (1248–1311). Of course, it would be rash to assume that the lost plays, written either before or after, were of the same calibre or possessed the same degree of interest, literary or otherwise, as Ibn Dāniyāl's work.[18] Nevertheless, it is clear from the introductory remarks to the first of these plays, *Ṭayf al-Khayāl* ('The Shadow Spirit'), that, far from being a solitary or even unusual phenomenon, as is sometimes assumed, Ibn Dāniyāl's plays were a rather late stage in the development of a form of dramatic entertainment. The remarks are addressed to the author's friend, ʿAlī ibn Mawlāhum, a 'producer' of shadow plays (*Khayāliy*) at whose request he composed these plays, since his friend had written to him complaining that 'people had grown tired of shadow plays and had been put off by their repetitive character'. This criticism obviously suggests that by Ibn Dāniyāl's time shadow drama had been going on for such a considerable period that it stood in danger of exhausting itself and becoming repetitive and 'mechanical'. We know, of course, from other sources that the Arabic shadow theatre had been flourishing in Fatimid Egypt. There are references to it in the tenth century, the most explicit and perhaps earliest of which is to be found in the works of the great scientist Ibn al-Haytham (born in 965 A.D.), who discusses the mechanics of it in his *magnum opus* on optics, *Kitāb al-Manāẓir*.

Shadow drama was an acceptable form of entertainment in Fatimid Egypt, even though it may not have been quite as well known elsewhere in the Islamic world at the time. There is evidence to suggest that it was not confined to farces or cheap comic shows, but probably dealt with moral, religious or historical themes with a view to pointing a moral or educating the audience. The medieval allegorical habit of mind enabled the cultivated audience to see moral or religious lessons even in dramatic entertainments such as the shadow theatre. The analogy was often drawn between the shadow theatre and man's transitory and phantom-like life on earth. The Egyptian mystic poet ʿUmar ibn al-Fāriḍ (1182–1235) found mystical significance in the shadow theatre in a major poem which, incidentally, provides us with the oldest detailed account of the themes of Arabic shadow drama that has reached us. Ibn al-Fāriḍ says that the account is not an exhaustive one, yet what he cites as examples of such scenes is sufficient to give us some idea of the themes of the shadow theatre at the time. These clearly ranged from the heroic to the common and homely: armies fighting, land and sea battles, knights and infantry heavily armed with swords, spears and arrows, seamen on the decks of ships, soldiers routed and castles destroyed. The characters also include supernatural beings of fearful appearance. At the other extreme we have fishermen catching fish with nets, fowlers spreading their gins for unsuspecting birds, benighted camels racing through the desert, ships tossed by the waves or wrecked by sea monsters, lions of the jungle, beasts of the wilderness and birds of the air preying upon one another. More peaceful scenes include birds perched in the boughs of trees and singing their delightful and moving songs.

Moreover, Ibn al-Fāriḍ describes the audience's reaction to the scenes which, judging by its deeply emotional nature, suggests that these scenes were more than mere stereotyped mechanical conventions. They must have possessed, by visual and verbal means, sufficient vividness and concrete individuality to evoke this degree of emotional response:

Thou laughest gleefully, as the most gay
Of men rejoices; weep'st like a bereaved
And sorrowing mother, in profoundest grief;
Mournest, if they do moan, upon the loss
Of some great happiness; art jubilant,
If they do sing, for such sweet melody.

Such feelings are indeed aroused by tragic or comic art. In fact, Ibn al-Fāriḍ's brief analysis of dramatic illusion is characterized by no small measure of sophistication. In the analogy he draws between it and 'sleep' and dream he is not far from the theories of dramatic illusion which began to appear in eighteenth-century Europe, starting with Lord Kames's theory of 'ideal presence' and culminating with Coleridge's famous principle of 'the willing suspension of disbelief'.

All three plays in Ibn Dāniyāl's collection begin with a short introduction in which the author briefly explains his intention. From these introductions, together with the remarks addressed to the audience by the first character to appear in the first piece, it becomes clear that like all drama, the shadow theatre was based upon a set of conventions, and it seems that by Ibn Dāniyāl's time buffoonery was one of these conventions. Buffoonery is a means to an end for 'each genre has its own method', the end being to produce good literature (*adab ʿālī*), not cheap and vulgar writing (*dūn*). This idea is reinforced by the words spoken by the Presenter (*al-Rayyis*) who claims that *Khayāl* is a literary art that can be appreciated only by *ahl al-adab* (men of breeding/literary taste), that it is not mere entertainment or pastime but is a mixture of seriousness and levity, and that it requires some intelligence to see the point of it.

However, clearly one of the conventions of *Khayāl* in Ibn Dāniyāl's age is that its characters are drawn from the lowest strata of society. In this respect it is primarily a comic art, adhering, no doubt unconsciously, to the Aristotelian conception of comedy as an art which shows men as worse than they really are. Nevertheless, the poet-dramatist does not indulge in pure fantasy for, as he says through the lips of the Presenter, 'underlying every shadow (i.e. character) a truth is to be found', a statement which suggests that Ibn Dāniyāl held a mimetic view of the dramatic art. In the introduction to the second play, *ʿAjīb wa Gharīb* ('The Amazing Preacher and the Stranger'), he says that his play 'contains [an account of] the conditions of strangers and conmen among literary people who live by their wits'. Equally, in the preface to his third play, *al-Mutayyam* ('The Love-Stricken One') he says that he has included in it something about the conditions of lovers, a little *ghazal* (love poetry) which was pure enchantment, a little about games, something about acceptable buffoonery *ṭarafan min al-mujūn alladhī mā ʿīb*. That is why Ibn Dāniyāl's plays are such a rich source of information for the social historian. Though they concentrate on certain aspects of medieval Islamic society (in Egypt) they are more deeply rooted in social reality than most *maqāma* literature by which, incidentally, they have been profoundly influenced. The characters paraded in the play *ʿAjīb wa Gharīb*, for instance, are so vividly portrayed and concretely realized that they form easily recognizable types to be seen in Cairo until the early years of the present century.

In Ibn Dāniyāl's drama we are, therefore, presented with a sophisticated art, an art which has its own established conventions and rules, and which at its best is capable of earning the respect of the literary *cognoscente*. Because Ibn Dāniyāl has been asked by his friend to write plays different from the common run which, because of their repetitive nature, had caused people to turn away from the shadow theatre, he seems to set out deliberately to compose three works each of which has its own individual form. Despite their common characteristics as shadow theatre, each of them has its own peculiar atmosphere and theme or themes. Far from being formless, random effusions in verse and rhyming prose, from which passages can be cut at will on grounds of obscenity or whatever, they are fairly well organized creations of a conscious craftsman and it behoves us to treat them with the necessary critical respect. Both in dramatic technique and in spirit they come very close to medieval European drama, to the Mysteries and Moralities as well as to the *Sotties*.

The first of the three plays, *Ṭayf al-Khayāl* ('The Shadow Spirit'), is the longest and by far the most developed as regards plot and characterization. After a short prologue, in which the Presenter or the master of ceremonies introduces the show, he calls upon Ṭayf al-Khayāl who promptly appears, a deformed hunchback. He greets the Presenter who returns the greeting and addresses a panegyric poem to him in which he ironically praises the beauty of his appearance and that of all things 'crooked' in shape such as a camel hump, a lute and a ship. Ṭayf thanks him profusely and performs a dance traditionally associated with the shadow theatre, singing verses in which he welcomes the audience, offers a pious prayer to God and expresses good wishes for the ruler and the audience in what is obviously a conventional formula. He then turns to the audience, and in a speech of rhyming prose, interspersed with colloquial expressions, describes the various aspects of sinful living in which he has been indulging. He claims that he has now repented and has come to Cairo in search of his close friend Prince Wiṣāl with whom he parted in Mosul, to find that the Sultan of Egypt, Baybars (1260–77), has waged a ruthless war on the army of Satan and that places of entertainment now lie deserted and in ruins. A messenger then calls upon Wiṣāl who also promptly appears: a soldier wearing a three-cornered head gear with unkempt, bristling moustache. After greeting the audience he proceeds to introduce himself in the rhyming prose of the *maqāma* form, but in the mock heroic style, giving sufficient information about his loose living in a manner that suggests we are in the presence of a supreme clown. He nostalgically reminisces about his wild past and recounts in the frankest language his various amorous adventures with both sexes in a lengthy poem which he concludes by advising Satan not to remain in Egypt, otherwise he will meet with severe punishment from its strict ruler.

Wiṣāl then declares his intention to mend his ways and get married. He asks for his secretary who looks after his financial affairs, typically a Copt. Since the Prince is a mock prince, his secretary too is a mock secretary and he also has a mock poet who composes panegyrics for him. In fact, we have here a topsy-turvy picture of a princely court, obviously with satirical overtones. The secretary produces the deed of investiture which the Prince has asked for and which delimits his possessions and the domains of which he is declared master, his qualification being 'his ability to dispel sorrow as efficiently as wine' and to bring joy and merriment by his wit and anecdotes. Interestingly enough, the domains assigned to him are the tombs and the ruined parts of old Cairo (obviously the connection with death is symbolically significant). The condition insisted upon for his holding these domains is that he does not leave any source of fun, however immoral, untapped. In other words Prince Wiṣāl is the Arabic *Prince des Sots* and the Lord of Misrule. He is described in the document as *fakhr al-bulh wa' l-majānīn* ('the pride of the foolish and the mad').[19]

Prince Wiṣāl confides to his companion Ṭayf al-Khayāl his intention to give up this loose living and homosexuality, to repent and find himself a wife. He asks for the marriage broker, Umm Rashīd, who promptly appears and greets the company in a manner befitting her character and profession. She informs him at once that she has available just the right person for him, a young divorced woman whose beauties she proceeds to enumerate. Wiṣāl expresses agreement and the marriage clerk, *ma'dhūn*, and witnesses are brought on the screen. The clerk makes the customary speech on such an occasion, but in rhyming prose, from which we learn that the bride's name is *Ḍabba bint Miftāḥ* (Lock, daughter of Key), a comical name with clear enough sexual implications, which also suggests ugliness, specifically referring to protruding and ill-formed teeth, thereby preparing us for the shock which Wiṣāl will receive when he sees her after the wedding ceremony and procession.

The marriage clerk's speech ends as usual with citing the amount of the bride's money, *mahr*, Wiṣāl has to pay and with the latter accepting the terms of the marriage contract. Wiṣāl's problem now is how to raise the necessary amount since we learn that he has managed to squander all his fortune on his riotous living. However, Wiṣāl withdraws and then reappears in an impressive procession riding a noble steed, preceded by candles in fine array and followed by trumpets and drums. He politely dismounts and waits for the bride who soon appears surrounded by several women waiting on her, her face veiled with an embroidered, gold-braided handkerchief. However, as soon as he lifts her veil she utters a sound like the braying of a donkey, and he is shocked to see how monstrously ugly she looks; the shock making him faint. She, in her turn, complains to Umm Rashīd that he has frightened her and her little boy (who, in fact, turns out to be her grandson, a lad that seems possessed or, at any rate, obsessed by the devil). The boy sways and writhes excitedly, then smells Wiṣāl's nose and immediately falls into a fit of coughing and farting, and when he catches his breath he recites obscene verses in very colloquial Egyptian which seem to make Wiṣāl recover his consciousness, jump to his feet and with his club assault the boy, the women and the bride, all of whom flee before him in terror.

When Ṭayf reappears Wiṣāl tells him that Umm Rashīd and her husband, Shaykh ʿAflaq, must be summoned to be thrashed as a punishment for their cheating. ʿAflaq is brought in singing and farting, an aged man who, in a futile attempt to hide his age, has had his hair dyed. He delivers a speech in verse, lamenting his lost youth and vigour, and nostalgically recounts his sexual exploits of the past. Wiṣāl threatens to have him whipped as an example to stop old women from cheating men and to give the devil a lesson. But Ṭayf intercedes on his behalf, pleading his old age. Shaykh ʿAflaq complains that his death is near and looks back sorrowfully on the wild sexual adventures of his youth, criticizes the physician, Baqṭaynūs, for being an incompetent doctor whose treatment proves ineffective and at whose hands his own wife has died. Wiṣāl is surprised to hear of Umm Rashīd's death and asks the Presenter to call Dr Baqṭaynūs to verify this. The doctor appears and gives an account of her death in a brothel, reporting her last words, which were to counsel someone present to take her place in bringing together men and women in the pursuit of love and physical union. He joins the company in lamenting her death by reciting an elegy in which he enumerates her various achievements in procuring women for men and the many aspects of her dissolute life. Like earlier poems of panegyric, this elegy is of the mock variety in which the mourner rejoices at the death of his subject: 'her loss', he says, 'is a day of festivity for me'.[20] Nevertheless, in spite of this humorous treatment as a result of her death Ṭayf repents, and Prince Wiṣāl decides to go on a pilgrimage to holy Mecca as a penitent humbly seeking to purify himself of all his past sins.

Such, in brief, is the plot of the play from which we can see that, despite seemingly irrelevant digressions, there is a clear progression and a main action that revolves around the central figure of Prince Wiṣāl, the hero or protagonist of the piece. Prince Wiṣāl arrives in Cairo at an important juncture in his life and at a particular moment in Egyptian history. Before the Prince's appearance we are given, through his friend, Ṭayf al-Khayāl, the necessary information for the larger social and political context of the action and something about the type of company the Prince keeps. From the Prince's reminiscences we learn a great deal about his past, but the action proper begins with his decision to reform and marry and develops with the preparations for the wedding, leading up to the actual ceremony. The crisis is reached upon the discovery of the marriage broker's deception and is resolved with the news of her death which results in the abandoning of the thought of marriage and the decision to undergo a pilgrimage to the holy shrine in Mecca. Making allowance for possible interpolations, the plot is on the whole reasonably well organized, and the relation between the chief episodes is more of a *propter hoc* than a *post hoc* relation.

Of course, the dramatic technique employed shows certain primitive features. For instance, characters seem to be waiting to be called upon by Ṭayf al-Khayāl, in response to Prince Wiṣāl's request. Instead of giving the impression of appearing of their own accord or happening to meet one another in a semblance of ordinary, daily business, they are simply summoned. The first to be summoned in this manner is Ṭayf al-Khayāl himself who is called by the Presenter. It is a technique which readers of the Morality Play, *Everyman*, will recognize; Everyman only needs to think of, or call upon, characters such as Fellowship, Kindred, Goods or Good-Deeds for such characters to appear at once, the author making no attempt to create a plausible situation in which characters seem to come on the stage spontaneously. Likewise, characters are directly introduced and explained to the audience either by themselves or by the Presenter. Again one can easily find similar examples of this in early European drama. For instance, in the Chester Pageant of Noah's *Flood*, God introduces himself directly by these words:

I, God, that all this worlde hath wroughte . . .[21]

However, there is nothing primitive about some of the characterization in Ibn Dāniyāl's play, particularly his portrayal of Umm Rashīd, the matchmaker. She is a cross between Juliet's Nurse and Celestina, a bawd and a female Pandarus who brings lovers together, partly deriving vicarious pleasure from the experience but also with an eye on the material advantage to be gained. She is utterly without scruples, yet richly gifted with persuasive eloquence. Compared with an early dramatic female character, such as Noah's shrewish wife in the Chester Miracle Play, *The Flood*, she is a most complex creation belonging to a different order of writing. When she appears she greets the company in a different manner from the other characters. In fact, the way dialogue is used to express the speaker's character is masterly considering the early date of the play. When Umm Rashīd asks why she has been called for in the dark of night, she uses a mode of speech totally different from that employed by the doctor when he asks a similar question later on. Each speaker expresses his character, his preoccupation and his calling in the very images used; while she employs sexual imagery, in his speech medical images abound.

In fact, Ibn Dāniyāl's mastery and sensitive handling of the Arabic language are made abundantly clear throughout the play, not least in his remarkable descriptive powers. His detailed, humorous verse accounts of Wiṣāl's poverty, for instance, never become mechanically repetitive. Equally impressive are the author's satirical powers, aided no doubt by his sharpened vision as a medical practitioner and his developed power of observation as an outsider in Cairo. A vast section of Egyptian society is mercilessly satirized here. Despite its many farcical elements, the play is by no means a cheap or crude type of popular entertainment. Admittedly sex, in all its forms, and other physical functions loom rather large. However, as Enid Welsford has shown in her classic study, *The Fool*, the absence of any sense of morality is characteristic of this type of early European literature. Commenting on 'the sheer brutality and physical nastiness of many of the buffoon stories' she says:

> This aspect of humour is important and cannot properly be overlooked. The men of those days had a robust taste in comedy, their real and their mythical buffoons were gross men of the earth, who knew well that the normal physical functions of the body have always provided the human race with an inexhaustible source of merriment.[22]

In the Fool literature physical deformity often went hand in hand with moral subnormality. Before Ibn Dāniyāl invented his hunch-backed, Ṭayf al-Khayāl, ancient Rome, for instance, had known its 'hump-backed, hook-nosed, large-jawed mime'.[23] The tricks performed by Till Eulenspiegel were often 'unspeakably gross and coarse and sometimes offensively brutal'.[24] One of the qualities that remained constant in Harlequin's character was the absence of the moral sense,[25] just as the *commedia dell'arte* was never without an element of crudity.

The connection between humour and the obscene is, in fact, a well-known feature of classical literature from the early sources of Greek comedy in the phallic dance to the more sophisticated world of Petronius' *Satyricon*. Equally, the sexual sources of humour are easily noticeable in medieval Arabic literature. Recently in his useful study, *The Mediaeval Islamic Underworld: the Banū Sāsān in Arabic Society and Literature*, which discusses the literature dealing with the confraternity of tricksters, C.E. Bosworth has reminded us that one aspect of the new themes in Arabic literature of the ninth century, poetry and prose alike, was the vogue for the erotic and near pornographic. He traces this phenomenon from its rise in the ninth century until the fourteenth century, pointing out how serious men of letters and patrons such as al-Ṣāhib ibn ʿAbbād, al-Thaʿālibī and al-Tawḥīdī, not to mention Caliphs like al-Maʾmūn and al-Mutawakkil, were keenly interested in the uninhibited jargon and the mores of the underworld.[26]

Yet the unabashed celebration of the world of the flesh is counter-balanced in Ibn Dāniyāl's play by a sense of death lurking round the corner. Death puts an end to the moral holiday and turns Prince Wiṣāl's thoughts to the holy places of Islam. Indeed, even in the midst of his obviously relished reminiscences of the pleasures of the flesh, Wiṣāl never ceases to talk about the need for repentance. To say that the Arabic shadow theatre is 'markedly secular in its themes and attitudes', as Landau does,[27] is, therefore, to miss an important component of Ibn Dāniyāl's drama. Nevertheless, it must be admitted that the two elements, the secular and religious, are no less unequal here than in, for instance, the Wakefield Second Shepherds' Play, where the greater part of the play, taken up by the comic episode of the shepherds and the stealing of the sheep by Mac and his wife Gill who disguise it as a baby in a cot, provides an ironic contrast to the religious part, about one-fifth of the total length of the play, in which the shepherds are summoned to Bethlehem to adore the infant Jesus. Here, too, there is irony in the quest for marriage of Prince Wiṣāl, whose name means 'sexual union', turning into a 'religious' pilgrimage to the holy places.

The structure of the second play, *ʿAjīb wa Gharīb* ('The Amazing Preacher and the Stranger'), is totally different from that of the first. Here there is hardly any plot at all, but after a brief prologue recited by the Presenter, the character of *Gharīb* (Stranger) appears, introduces himself as one of Banū Sāsān, the 'Children of Sāsān' (the Confraternity of Tricksters), who have been forced by historical circumstances to lead a life of wandering, living by their wits and resorting to trickery and deception in order to survive. He begins by looking back nostalgically on the past before being driven into exile, a time when all the pleasures of life were available in plenty, singling out the pleasures of drinking and sex which he describes in the detailed and uninhibited manner we have already encountered in *Ṭayf al-Khayāl.* He explains the reasons for his people's turning to trickery, namely that they had lost hope in the generosity of men around them. He then proceeds to enumerate to the Presenter some of the various professions he has assumed in order to deceive people and eke out a living. These include, among other things, the training of bears, dogs, monkeys, snake charming, quack medicine, herbalism and eye surgery, jurisprudence, grammar, philosophy and preaching. He then withdraws to be succeeded by a gallery of such characters, one at a time, beginning with the Preacher. Each character introduces himself, describes his trade which is wittily indicated or implied by his name, uses the appropriate language of the profession, and displays samples of his craft or what he has to offer. After the Preacher (who is called *ʿAjīb,* Amazing, allegedly after a certain ʿAjīb al-Dīn, a celebrated preacher of the time), the characters appear in this order: a snake-charmer, a quack-doctor, a hawker of medicinal herbs, an ophthalmic surgeon, an acrobat, a juggler, an astrologer, a trader in amulets, a lion tamer, an elephant man, a goat-trainer, a phlebotomist/prostitute, a trainer of cats (and mice), a dog trainer, a tamer of bears, a Sudanese clown, a sword swallower, a monkey trainer, a rope dancer, a conjurer with self-inflicted wounds, a torch-bearer and finally a camel driver. The Stranger then reappears at the end to provide the epilogue to the play. As Bosworth has shown, many of these roles assumed by beggars, conmen and tricksters are mentioned in the literature dealing with Banū Sāsān, both prose and poetry, from the thirteenth-century Jaubarī's *Kashf al-Asrār* to the Sāsāniyya poems by the tenth-century Abū Dulaf and Ṣafiyy al-Dīn al-Ḥillī (1278–1349?).

Although no more than sketches, these characters are so vividly drawn in Ibn Dāniyāl's play that a whole picture of a large section of the medieval Cairo market is successfully evoked. There is no interaction between the characters, we witness only a procession of grotesque figures. The total effect is not unlike that of the French *Sottie* play, as we are made aware of the fool or clown behind each character we are watching. The keynote is struck by the first two characters to appear, particularly by the Amazing Preacher, who gives what amounts to a 'fool-sermon', in which he uses the paraphernalia of religious sermons to instruct his followers in the mysteries of their trade as conmen and tricksters.[28] The whole show has many of the qualities of a *danse macabre* with the ending underlining the need for repentance and purification from the sins of this world. The mixture of the comic and religious is once more to be seen. The first character to appear (after the Stranger) is the Preacher with his mock sermon, but the last character (before the Stranger) is the camel-driver whose speech consists largely of a devotional poem he chants, in which he expresses his hope to go on a pilgrimage to the holy places of Islam. In a sense, all the characters exhibited (except for the woman and the Sudanese clown) are aspects of the same character, namely that of Gharīb. They are different roles the Stranger has had to play, as indeed he has confided to the Presenter early in the drama. At the end, after the parade of the procession of these aspects, they are reassembled back to the original character, Gharīb. The end, therefore, is perfectly logical and consistent with the beginning, Gharīb being a composite figure combining all these. The structure of the play is neatly circular and that the very last line in the epilogue consists solely of the repetition of the word *gharīb* is perhaps no mere coincidence – although it would be wrong to miss the underlying pathos in this repetition: on the literal level all the characters appear as outsiders, foreigners, who despite the satire are somewhat sympathetically drawn by our author who himself had known what it was like to be a foreigner. On another level, since the lines are addressed to God, what is meant is that we are all strangers in this earthly existence.

Unlike the second play, *al-Mutayyam* ('The Love-stricken One'), has a story and a plot. After a brief greeting delivered to the audience by the Presenter, al-Mutayyam (the love-stricken man) appears, looking distraught and worn out by his passion and amidst tears and moaning recites a poem about the agonies and suffering caused by love; it is a burlesque treatment of the conventions of Arabic love poetry, with an exquisitely comical effect. He then turns to the audience, extends a somewhat effeminate greeting to them, introduces himself, explains how he has fallen for a young man so attractive that he has spoiled the chances of lovely women, for all the men around him are madly in love with him. He adds that he fell in love with him when he saw him stripped in the public baths, looking more seductive than any woman and surrounded by a crowd of half-crazed, gazing admirers. He proceeds to recite a love *muwashshaḥ* (a strophic poem) he has composed on him.

Mutayyam continues to address the audience, telling them that he is a stranger from Mosul who only calls at the houses of the great. At this point a misshapen young man appears and while emitting unattractive noises (a mixture of snoring and farting), he claims that he is Mutayyam's old lover. He reproaches Mutayyam for turning away from him in favour of the bigger youth al-Yutayyim, and delivers a speech in rhyming prose in praise of all things small. Mutayyam replies by rebutting his argument that small is beautiful, saying that no sane man would prefer the crescent to the full moon or unripe sour grapes to the pleasurable taste of wine. (Here we note the element of medieval debate form, best illustrated in Arabic literature in the work of al-Jāḥiẓ, of which we shall see further instances in the contests between the cocks, the rams and the bulls later on in the play.) Mutayyam makes it clear to his old lover that there is no hope of their resuming their relationship, and talks to him about the present object of his passion, Yutayyim. He asks him if he has seen Yutayyim or his servant boy, Bayram, who seems to have complete control over him. He does not stop telling him of his passion for this young man and recounts in a long poem the incident in the public baths which had a powerful impact upon him. Distracted by the sight of his beloved Yutayyim walking before him as they were leaving, Mutayyam slipped and fell down on the bath floor at his feet. Yutayyim rushed to help him, knelt down to attend to him as he lay prostrate on the floor, which gave Mutayyam a chance to steal a kiss.

In response to Mutayyam's entreaties, Bayram uses his good offices and powers of persuasion and manages to soften his master's heart, convincing him that Mutayyam is genuinely in love with him, and tempting his master further by telling him that he shares with him his passion for owning performing and entertaining animals and for all manner of sports. On hearing this news from Bayram, Mutayyam is delighted, dances with joy, brings wine and glasses and proceeds to sing. Soon Yutayyim appears and joins him in singing. In turn each sings about the merits of his fighting cock. The latter challenges the former and a fight between the two cocks is arranged, refereed by Zayhūn who begins the proceedings with a speech, which, after the usual pious preamble, praises the virtues of cocks and cock-fighting, a sport, he says, enjoyed by royal and common people alike. Yutayyim's cock loses the fight and after making a splendidly humorous excuse he challenges his lover to let their rams fight. Again he loses the bet, but finally he wins when his bull fights Mutayyam's bull. All these fights, incidentally, are refereed by the same Zayhūn who formally gives appropriate speeches before each fight. Dismayed at his loss, Mutayyam tells the Presenter, Rayyis ʿAlī, that he wishes to have his bull slaughtered and a banquet to be held with all manner of food, wines, incense and merriment, to which all types of lovers are to be invited. His request is granted, and a party is given, attended by men engaged in every type of sexual activity or perversion – homosexuality, pederasty, masturbation, and gluttony – each of whom in turn gives a speech explaining his particular interest and is then plied with wine until he is overpowered with sleep and drink.

In the midst of the feasting, however, an awe-inspiring figure appears who strikes terror in Mutayyam's heart. It is the Angel of Death whose loud call rudely awakens the sleepers from their deep slumber and instantly restores their sobriety. Fortunately, Mutayyam has time to repent and he humbly asks God's forgiveness before he dies. The play ends with his funeral. Here, as in the first play, *Ṭayf*, death puts an end to the moral holiday. In fact in this respect, although the analogy must not be pursued too far, this is the Arabic variation on the theme of the Morality Play, *Everyman*.

Despite their differences these three plays have obvious features in common. They all include singing, music and dancing. They are written in a mixture of verse and rhyming prose, a clear indication that the shadow theatre, as seen in Ibn Dāniyāl's work, was a gradual development from the Arabic *maqāma* form although, of course, there is much more verse here than in the *maqāma*. Another trace of the *maqāma* is to be seen in the way stage directions are set out in Ibn Dāniyāl's plays; they are not given separately, but as an integral part of the text, thereby observing the rule of *sajʿ* (rhyming prose) which facilitates memorization. Consequently, the text of these plays reads very much like a producer's edition with all the detailed stage directions given, but because the directions form part of the text, often part of the Presenter's speeches, the work on the page looks more like narrative broken up into long speeches, than drama proper.

As has been observed by scholars, Ibn Dāniyāl uses a remarkably flexible type of Arabic, ranging from the classical to the colloquial with an admixture of obscure jargon and even gibberish when the need arises. It is this flexibility that has enabled him to make his speeches, as we have seen, so subtly and accurately expressive of the speakers, which is an important element in drama. That is why, compared with the *maqāma* literature, his rhyming prose is considerably simpler, and the balance between the phrase units is perhaps less rigorously maintained. However, this aspect of Ibn Dāniyāl's work clearly deserves serious study and analysis. After all, what gives the plays their value is in the end not so much the visual as the *literary* aspect, which relates to the particular language employed by the author, ranging from the simple device of giving characters names denoting or suggesting their qualities or trade to the more complex ability to use the 'register' and even the rhythm appropriate to the character.

Finally, two more characteristics of these plays which seem to relate them to the *maqāma* tradition deserve a comment; first, their interest in conmen, tricksters and, in general, people from the lowest strata of society who live by their wits and eloquence; secondly, the final act of repentence which characters go through after a life devoted to the pursuit of earthly pleasures (we recall that in the fiftieth *maqāma* by al-Ḥarīrī, Abu Zayd al-Surūjī repents). No doubt the link is there, but it is worth remembering that by Ibn Dāniyāl's time the realm of the shadow theatre seems to have become the flotsam of society, characters from the lower walks of life or the underworld, as he clearly says in the introductory remarks to his first play. As for the concept of final repentence which we find in all three plays, this must be related to the total vision of the Fool literature, to which these plays legitimately belong, a vision that, while celebrating the pleasures and the experiences of the flesh with all their crudities, sexual and otherwise, 'the fury and the mire of the human veins', is never totally oblivious of the fact that the Saturnalia cannot be anything other than a moral holiday and that all holidays must come to an end.

V

No other shadow plays have survived from the time of Ibn Dāniyāl until the seventeenth century, for the next texts we encounter are to be found in the imperfect manuscript known as the Manzala manuscript attributed to the authors Saʿūd, Shaykh ʿAlī Naḥla and Daūd al-Manawī al-ʿAṭṭār (the Spice-seller) and rescued by the man who contributed most to the cause of shadow plays in the nineteenth century, Ḥasan al-Qashshāsh (?–1905). Yet we know from various references that shadow drama was performed in Egypt during the fourteenth, fifteenth, sixteenth and seventeenth centuries. It is related that Sultan Shaʿbān was so fond of the shadow theatre that he even ordered a troupe to accompany him on his pilgrimage to Mecca in 1376.[29] In the following century Sultan Juqmuq, on the other hand, banned the shadow theatre and ordered the burning of all puppets in 1451, driven most probably not only by the immorality of the theatre, but also by its bitter social and political satire which spread feelings of irreverence and disrespect for the Sultan and his court.[30] That shadow drama continued to deal with contemporary events, as it had done in Ibn Dāniyāl's work, can be seen from perhaps the best known reference which occurs in Ibn Iyās's Chronicle, *Badāʾiʿ al-Zuhūr fī Waqāʾiʿ al-Duhūr*.[31] Ibn Iyās records a rumour regarding a performance witnessed by the victorious Sultan Selim one evening in 1517, at which the hanging of the defeated Sultan Ṭūman Bay at the Zuwayla gate in Cairo was represented, much to the delight of Selim who took the players with him to Istanbul to show and entertain his son.

By the seventeenth century, significant changes seem to have taken place in the shadow theatre. Ibn Dāniyāl's plays were, as we have seen, very much the work of a conscious artist who wrote on the whole in classical, albeit simplified, Arabic and who cared considerably about his style. He prided himself on producing high class literature (*adab ʿālī*). Different indeed are the later plays that have reached us; even those attributed to individual authors bear the unmistakeable marks of folk art; they are the product of several hands, and are written in the colloquial Egyptian vernacular. Instead of the *maqāma* style with its mixture of verse and prose, the medium of the later works is mainly verse, often stanzaic verse, which can easily be memorized by the performers. Texts have been transmitted largely orally from one generation of players to another, with the inevitable interpolations, additions and omissions, that usually accompany such a process. Moreover, singing now becomes predominant: the text becomes more like a libretto for a comic opera than drama proper.

According to one student of the subject 'from the death of Daud al-Manawī (who became a legendary figure in the field) until the appearance of al-Qashshāsh the shadow theatre was never quite absent from Egypt'.[32] Indeed Egyptian scholars, notably Aḥmad Taymūr (1871–1930) and ʿAbd al-Ḥamīd Yūnus, have given us eye-witness accounts of performances which they attended, some of which had been given in special, rather primitive, theatres.[33] It was only with the rise and growth of the Egyptian cinema industry that the popularity of the shadow theatre began to wane. Landau distinguishes between two kinds of shadow plays at the beginning of the century: 'the one whose exponent was Hammam is cultured and refrains almost entirely from crude language', while the second, associated with Darwīsh was 'a more popular vintage, indulging in crude jokes and ditties' designed for an uneducated audience.[34] But it is clear that the whole genre of shadow drama had suffered a sharp literary and artistic decline since the Middle Ages. Subsequently, it became a popular form of entertainment, indulged in largely by the vulgar and poor and seen by the middle and upper classes only on certain occasions like marriages, circumcisions and during the Muslim month of Ramadan.[35] The play, known as *liʿb* (play, cf. Latin *ludus*, German *Spiel* and French *jeu*), was often performed by the troupe in a noisy coffee house and would be chosen by the assembled audience themselves out of the troupe's repertoire. It was divided into acts or scenes (*fuṣūl*), the number of which could sometimes be very large indeed and which the players could alter to please their patrons. It is reported that one play *Liʿb al-Dayr* ('The Cloister Play') was sometimes performed over a period of several days.

Although artistically these plays represent a falling off from the standard of Ibn Dāniyāl's work (they are too loosely structured, they lack characterization and their style of writing is not particularly distinguished), nevertheless a word may be said here about one or two examples, since such plays formed part of the 'dramatic' scene in major Egyptian cities until early in this century. Furthermore, despite their lack of subtlety they are not devoid of social or sociological significance.

One of the most famous was *Liʿb al-Timsāḥ* ('The Crocodile Play'). The Egyptian scholar, Aḥmad Taymūr, claimed that it was regarded as particularly valuable by lovers and practitioners of this art on account of its age and the high quality of the vernacular verse (*zajal*) used in its dialogue.[36] The action takes place by the bank of the Nile. The characters or figures include the Presenter (*al-Ḥāziq*), the Clown (*al-Rikhim*), the Cat-man (*Abu'l-Qiṭaṭ*), another clown, a stock character from earlier shadow drama, a fellah named al-Zibriqāsh, his wife and child, a master fisherman (Shaykh al-Maʿāsh or Hājj Manṣūr), fishes and a whale, a black guardsman and a Moroccan magician and his companion. After a prologue in praise of the play recited by the Presenter, the action begins with the protagonist or anti-hero, an unfortunate though not altogether blameless farm-labourer, praising the Lord and asking forgiveness for his sins. He has given up tilling the soil and, having looked for some other means of livelihood, he decides to take up fishing. We are shown Zibriqāsh engaged in some dangerous attempts to catch fish. He fails, loses his fishing tackle, falls into the water and is saved from drowning by the Presenter who seems to know him well and engages him in a predominantly humorous dialogue. Through the good offices of the Presenter, a meeting is arranged between him and the master fisherman, Hājj Manṣūr, who takes pity on him and undertakes to teach him the trade, but (in certain versions[37]) on condition that they should both sing a song to entertain the audience. However, as soon as Zibriqāsh casts his rod in the Nile, a whale appears and swallows him until only his head can be seen sticking out of the whale's jaws. At this point the Clown (al-Rikhim) appears both in order to provide comic relief and to sharpen the feeling of pity for the victim through the moving dialogue between him and the fellah. Pity is further aroused by the appearance of the peasant's wife with her baby boy, engaged in loud lamentations over her husband, but she is reprimanded and driven away by Hājj Manṣūr. The latter enlists the help of others to rescue the fellah, first (and after a long comic exchange) a black guardsman, who only succeeds in getting himself swallowed up by the whale, and then by a Moroccan magician. The latter, in return for money, with the help of another Moroccan, and by offering a prayer to God and His Prophet, overpowers the whale by magic, burning incense and raising smoke, and manages to bring the fellah and the black guardsman out of the reptile's belly. The play ends with the two Moroccans marching along the screen, bearing the whale on their head and chanting a song of triumph. An enthusiastic commentator tried to attribute the popularity of the play not only to its artistic quality, but also to the social criticism it embodies, for despite the humour that pervades the entire action he finds that the image of the peasant is that of a pitiable man, though a wastrel. He also finds that the crocodile may be a symbol just as the saving of the peasant by means of magic could signify the impossibility of his salvation by means other than those of the supernatural.[38] Before dismissing this interpretation as too fanciful it is wise to recall that the play ends with these mysterious words, recited by one of the two Moroccans as the triumphal procession passes across the screen with the crocodile being carried on the players' heads:

You who wish to interpret allegories and unravel the secrets of the Shadow Play
Here are concealed mysteries, for a man does not say all that he knows[39]

Another play attributed to the seventeenth-century authors, but probably of older origins considering the nature of its subject (which is the Crusaders' attack on Alexandria), is entitled *al-Manār aw Ḥarb al-ʿAjam* ('The Play of the Lighthouse or of the War against the Foreigners').[40] Here, after a pious preamble, *al-Ḥāziq* (the Presenter) proceeds to describe in detail the beauty of the Alexandria lighthouse and the skill revealed in its construction, then engages in a comic dialogue with the Clown (*al-Rikhim* who is also called the Cat-man, *Abu'l Qiṭaṭ*,[41] in this piece). He ironically describes the Clown as a lion given to devouring the hearts of the enemy, while we are told by al-Rikhim himself that 'on the day of battle he rushes to hide behind the gate'. The Presenter then sings songs enumerating further the beauties of the lighthouse and paying homage to the art of the past masters of the shadow theatre, al-Manawī, Saʿūd and Naḥla. In a highly patriotic song he asserts the heroism and superiority of the Muslims to their Christian attackers.

The Presenter keeps urging the Clown to climb up the lighthouse and bring news of the enemy's movements. Eventually he loses his patience with him and upbraids him for his cowardice and lack of resolution. The latter says he will not climb up the lighthouse unless the Presenter sings him a song, which is an excuse for further singing, describing the lighthouse, the courage and chivalry of the Muslims and giving expression to pious sentiments praising the Prophet of God. Subsequently a Moroccan appears: he has come from Venice to warn the Muslims against the impending attack by the Crusaders and he urges them to prepare for war. Thereupon the Presenter calls on his brother Maymūn to come and lead the men to war. This is followed by comic relief with the Clown providing the comic anti-heroic element. A messenger from the Crusaders tries to persuade the Muslims to surrender in order to save themselves from the dire consequences which they would otherwise have to face. The Christian also unsuccessfully tries to tempt the Clown to defect, promising him riches as well as his daughter in marriage. Ḥirdān, a Muslim champion, is taken prisoner by the Christians who refuse to free him against a ransom offered by al-Rikhim. The prisoner begs the Muslims to try to set him free by force of arms. Eventually a battle is fought and won by the Muslims. The play ends with a song celebrating their victory and the humiliating defeat of the Christian invaders.

'The Lighthouse' is not a well-constructed play in which action moves forward in a straight line. On the contrary, there is far too much repetition.

This, of course, may be due to the possibility that the text has not reached us in good shape. There may be several versions incorporated in the body of the text, probably the work of different authors or alternative versions from which performers could choose the one they liked. But the play contains many good descriptions of the lighthouse, the sea, ships, castles and fighting. It also has the virtue of complexity arising from the irony of juxtaposing the heroic ideal propounded by the Presenter and the humorous anti-heroic Falstaffian attitude of the Clown. Although the play is written mainly in colloquial verse there is a certain amount of prose, generally confined to humorous parts of the dialogue. Among the sources of humour is the popular one to be seen in most of the plays going as far back as Ibn Dāniyāl, namely the mispronunciation of Arabic words by foreign characters. However, compared with Ibn Dāniyāl's plays the author of 'The Lighthouse' does not display much subtlety in characterization, nor does he make an attempt beyond the crudely naive one just mentioned to vary the language of different personages to make their speech match their character.

Yet, despite the undeniable drop in quality in these plays, there are obvious continuities. The prologue, praising the play about to be performed, seems to be a tradition preserved from Ibn Dāniyāl's work: it appears in later plays such as 'The Crocodile' and 'The Lighthouse'. There are also some stock characters such as *Abu'l-Qiṭaṭ* (the Cat-Man), whom we first encounter in Ibn Dāniyāl and who appears in 'The Crocodile' and 'The Lighthouse', where he seems to have become synonymous with the traditional Clown. There are also the foreigners who by their faulty and inaccurate knowledge of classical Arabic or the local vernacular provide an easy source of laughter. All these plays are basically comic in spirit; even in a play with a serious patriotic theme such as 'The Lighthouse', the serious is juxtaposed with the comic and the heroic is reduced in size as it is constantly viewed against the mock heroic and absurd. Yet despite their slapdash humour, the plays are not totally devoid of some serious content, be it social criticism and satire or a pious sentiment expressed in a religious ode or intention to perform the pilgrimage to Mecca. Finally, in all of them, singing forms an important part. This is particularly so in the later plays, where prose is virtually supplanted by vernacular verse which is meant to be chanted.

It is time now to recapitulate and state briefly what these different types of traditional entertainment have in common. In the first place, they were essentially *popular* entertainments which, with the possible exception of Ibn Dāniyāl's work, were not regarded as serious literature and were therefore ignored by literary historians and critics. It is probably for this reason that they did not develop much in form; on the contrary, their development was arrested; they did not go beyond an elementary stage of dramatic representation, with the obvious exception of some shadow plays, as we have seen in the preceding discussion. Secondly, except for the religious passion plays, *taʿziya* (of which no worthwhile written Arabic text has reached us, in any case), they were of a comic character, relying often upon rather crude methods to amuse and raise an easy laugh. However, despite their crudity and their tendency to use obscene gestures and words, they were often satirical in intent, designed to point out the excesses and shortcomings of society, at times emphasizing the injustice of those in power and the helplessness of the poor and hard-pressed peasant. Thirdly, and bearing in mind the fact that the texts that have reached us are often in an extremely imperfect and garbled condition, we can say that apart from some exceptions such as in Ibn Dāniyāl's work these plays were loosely episodic in structure, consisting often of a series of separate tableaux or pageants of social types, stock characters, vicious or grotesque conmen and tricksters and the poor and the flotsam of society. In this respect, as we have seen, the shadow plays were close to the Arabic *maqāma* form in narrative, which consisted of separate episodes revolving round a common protagonist without an overall obvious pattern linking all the episodes together. Fourthly, as in the *maqāma*, the language of some of these representations was a mixture of verse and prose. But, of course, we must remember that while the *maqāma* was regarded by Arab critics and commentators to be a superior art form, the shadow play which seemed to descend from it, was not, particularly in its later developments, in which colloquial verse became dominant and singing was an integral part. It is important to remember these common features of popular traditional dramatic entertainments because they seem to have influenced the imported foreign forms for many years.

I hardly need to point out that these traditional entertainments were too popular to be significantly affected by the performances of European opera and drama that were given in Cairo and Alexandria in Italian or French, before an audience of Europeans or a westernized local aristocratic élite who probably knew no Arabic. It is a well-known fact that during the brief French occupation of Egypt under Bonaparte (1798–1801), the French forces had their theatrical entertainment in a makeshift theatre in Azbakiyya Gardens on 29 December 1800, which was mentioned, not without some feeling of amused surprise, by the Egyptian historian al-Jabartī in his famous work *ʿAjāʾib al-Āthār*.[42]

With the growth of the European community in Egypt under the modernizing rule of Muhammad Ali and his successors, particularly Khedive Ismail, it was natural that interest should develop in local amateur productions of European plays or in promoting visits of foreign troupes. Gradually theatres began to be opened. Documents have been unearthed to show that in 1829 an amateur French theatre was opened, and shortly afterwards Gérard de Nerval gave a brief account of an evening he had spent at the Teatro del Cairo and referred to the Italian opera season.[43] By 1847 there was already an Italian theatre in Alexandria for which a set of regulations was fixed by the local municipal authorities. European travellers referred to French drama being performed in an open-air theatre in Alexandria as early as 1854. In 1868 a proper theatre called Theâtre de la Comédie was erected in Cairo to replace a wooden ramshackle structure and the famous imposing Khedivial Opera House was built in Cairo in 1869, designed as part of the celebrations which Khedive Ismail had planned on the occasion of the opening of the Suez Canal with a view to having the first performance of Verdi's *Aida* take place there. In the event the opera was not ready in time and *Rigoletto* was performed instead. While well-known European plays and operas were shown at the Cairo Opera House and the Comédie, in Alexandria foreign troupes gave their performances in a small theatre called Zizinya. It was not long, however, before indigenous or Arabic plays were presented in these theatres as well as the private theatre which Khedive Ismail had built in his palace, Qaṣr al-Nīl. The first of such plays were the work of the Father of modern Egyptian drama, the Jewish-born Egyptian nationalist Yaʿqūb Ṣannūʿ (Sanua). Significantly enough, he was dubbed 'The Egyptian Molière' by Khedive Ismail who for a while was his patron.

2

THE FATHER OF THE MODERN EGYPTIAN THEATRE: YAʿQŪB ṢANNŪʿ

The birth of modern Egyptian drama took place in Cairo in 1870 at the hands of Yaʿqūb Ṣannūʿ (1839–1912), on whose career several articles and books have been written in Arabic and in European languages.[1] Ṣannūʿ, who spelt his name Sanua, came of Jewish parents and seemed to have been a precocious child, for he claimed that at the age of twelve he could read the Old Testament in Hebrew and the New Testament in English as well as the Arabic Koran. In any case, he was capable of composing Arabic verse of such quality that when, at his father's suggestion, he recited a panegyric of his own composition to Aḥmad Yakan Pacha of the ruling house of Muhammad Ali, the Pacha was so impressed that he decided to send the thirteen-year-old boy to Italy to study at his expense. In Italy Ṣannūʿ spent three impressionable years (in Livorno), during which time he acquired such mastery of the Italian language that he is reported to have written three plays in Italian. Soon after his return to Egypt the death of both his father and his patron obliged him to earn his living for some time as private tutor to children of the nobility and well-to-do families. He was subsequently employed as school teacher at the polytechnic where he remained until his dismissal by the Minister of Education, ʿAlī Mubārak, allegedly because of his continued involvement in the Arabic Theatre.

Ṣannūʿ's interest in the theatre was developed early in his life. As a young man he regularly attended the performances of drama and opera given by visiting companies in Cairo, and not infrequently took part himself in French and Italian productions given in the open air theatre at Azbakiyya Gardens by two local European troupes, which catered for the rapidly growing number of European residents encouraged by the Khedive Ismail, as well as for the few sophisticated westernized élite among the indigenous population. Because of his passionate commitment to the stage Ṣannūʿ soon became keenly aware of the need to arouse the interest of the average, non-westernized Egyptian in drama. He was already convinced that the theatre had a vital role to play in the renaissance of modern Egypt. He held the aim of the theatre to be, as he put it in one of his plays, 'to promote civilization, progress and the refinement of manners.'[2]

In 1870 Ṣannūʿ formed his troupe of players, chosen out of a number of his old pupils, and he trained them to perform a play which, he claimed, he had written specially for them having studied works by Molière, Goldoni and Sheridan in their original languages. What that play was we shall probably never know for certain. One scholar writes that it was 'a small vaudeville show, complete with songs sung to the tune of popular melodies.'[3] On being introduced to Ismail's aide, Khayrī Pacha, Ṣannūʿ requested him to show the text of one of his plays to the Khedive and seek his support. Ismail was apparently favourably impressed and granted the young dramatist permission to perform before him at a show attended by the court, several diplomats and local dignitaries. Ṣannūʿ left us a highly colourful and dramatic account of his appearance before such a large and distinguished audience. The text of the play performed, which was obviously well received, has failed to reach us. However, we are given a somewhat detailed account of the plot by the author himself in a lecture on the Egyptian theatre which he later delivered in Paris. A European Prince bets a young Egyptian nobleman, a Pacha's son, the sum of one thousand pounds that if he is given one month in Cairo he will be able to have an amorous adventure in an Egyptian harem. By a clever trick the Pacha's son arranges for a young Syrian to disguise himself as a woman and to send a secret message with a eunuch to the European Prince, asking him to come and visit the eunuch's mistress in the harem. While the couple are embracing they are surprised by the Pacha's son, disguised as the Pacha, who orders four of his guards to tie the couple back to back, put them in a sack and drown them in the Nile. When asked to whom the sum of a thousand pounds which he has won in the bet should be paid, the Prince pleads for his life in exchange for the money. At this point the Pacha reveals his true identity and that of the mistress and apologizes to the scared Prince. The play ends merrily with a dinner party held in the palace garden.

The play, which incidentally included many songs, was meant to explode the popular, western notion about the moral depravity of the harem system. It had such a good reception that Ṣannūʿ was encouraged to reorganize his troupe and to include two women, which was a daring step to take at the time. Ṣannūʿ was, therefore, the first to introduce women onto the stage in Egypt and not, as Landau asserts,[4] the Syrian, al-Qurdāḥī, who included actresses in his troupe more than a decade later. The two women who served in Ṣannūʿ's troupe were non-Muslim Levantines whom Ṣannūʿ claims he taught to read, write and act in a matter of weeks. Ṣannūʿ was subsequently invited to perform before the Khedive again and it was on one such occasion, during a performance given in the Khedive's private theatre at Qasr al-Nil, that the Khedive is alleged to have conferred upon him the title 'The Egyptian Molière', partly in recognition of what Ṣannūʿ was doing and partly, no doubt, out of a desire to compare himself with Louis XIV, Molière's illustrious patron. On that evening Ṣannūʿ's troupe put on three plays: *Ānisa ʿala'l-Mūḍa* ('A Fashionable Young Lady'), *Ghandūr*

Miṣr ('The Egyptian Dandy') and *al-Ḍurratayn* ('The Two Rival Wives'). All three comedies were obviously satirical. Of the three, the text of only the last one has reached us which will be described later. However, the author does provide us with a brief account of the first play where he launches an attack on the blind imitation of western manners and superficial aspects of westernization; a young woman spoils her chances of marriage by flouting social custom and indulging in excessive freedom in dealing with young men copying the behaviour of western women. It is reported that 'The Two Rival Wives', which is an outspoken attack on the practice of polygamy, incurred the displeasure of the Khedive who felt that it was directed against a practice followed by himself as well as by members of the court.

It does not seem, however, that it was this play that brought an abrupt end to Ismail's patronage of Ṣannūʿ in 1872. The reasons for the Khedive's closure of Ṣannūʿ's theatre are not clear. Many have assumed that it was because of the dramatist's political criticism. Yet, of the plays which have survived belonging to that period, not a single one can be construed as a political attack on Ismail, although many contain outspoken social criticism. Landau was certainly wrong in saying that most of Ṣannūʿ's plays 'directed resentment against the Khedive',[5] a statement which clearly shows that he could not have seen or read the plays. Admittedly, we do not have the texts of all the plays actually performed, which at one point were assumed to number thirty-two (a figure which has proved to be somewhat exaggerated). Nevertheless, the extant plays of that period, far from being anti-Ismail, are not devoid of fulsome praise for the Khedive's achievements. It was only later on, when he resorted to satirical journalism and political activity, connected with nascent Egyptian nationalism, that Ṣannūʿ published his virulent attacks on Ismail. Ṣannūʿ himself blamed the British for inciting the Khedive to close down his theatre, which they warned him fostered dangerous political criticism of his government, Ṣannūʿ's rather weak argument being that he had painted an unsympathetic picture of them in his drama. Another reason he offered was the resentment on the part of Draneth Bey, the Director of the Khedival Opera and the Comédie Française, who regarded Ṣannūʿ as a dangerous rival.

Whatever the real cause, Ṣannūʿ's theatrical activities, which lasted barely three years, came to an end, and his relations with the Khedive became strained. Having gone through periods of ups and downs, he was finally exiled in 1878, after launching an attack on the Khedive in his satirical newspaper *Abū Naḍḍāra Zarqā* (The Man with Blue Spectacles). Ṣannūʿ went to France where he resumed his political journalism, issuing a series of satirical periodicals in which he published a large number of short, dramatic dialogues, called *Muḥāwarāt* (dialogues) or *Luʿbāt*[6] (scenes or playlets), full of bitter political and social satire directed against Ismail's rule and that of his successor Tawfīq. These dialogues or dramatic sketches are of considerable interest to the student of modern Egyptian politics and journalism, but hardly contain any merit as plays. They are too brief to possess any dramatic structure, too caricature-like to allow for any characterization or deep psychological insight, too directly political to be works of art. The interesting thing about them, however, is that early on Ṣannūʿ developed within them a crude kind of symbolism in his *dramatis personae* whereby *Shaykh al-Ḥāra* (the Quarter Chief) stood for Ismail, *al-Wad al-Ahbal* (the Foolish Boy) for Tawfīq, *Jamʿiyyat al-Ṭarāṭīr* (the Assembly of Clowns) for the Council of Ministers, *Abū Shādūf* (the one with Shadoof)and *Abū ʾl-Ghulb* (the Man of Misery) for the Egyptian peasant, etc.

It is now time to turn to the longer plays, some of which fortunately became available in 1963 thanks to Professor Najm's edition. Najm's collection contains eight works in all: 'The Tourist and the Muleteer', no more than a two-page dialogue, 'The Two Rival Wives', a very short play and the remaining six considerably longer but averaging only about half the length of a normal play.

Burṣat Miṣr ('The Cairo Stock Exchange'), the first in the collection, is basically a comedy of manners and intrigues; it is clearly the work of someone who, as Ṣannūʿ himself informed us, had read the work of Molière, Goldoni and Sheridan before trying his hand at writing Egyptian drama. The main theme is the rivalry between two suitors for the hand of Labība, the daughter of a rich banker, Salīm, and the success of Yaʿqūb, the victorious suitor, through the intrigue of his agent/servant, Yūsuf, in contrast to the failure of the other suitor, Ḥalīm, who is only after her money.

There is also a comic sub-plot, consisting of the hopeless passion Farag, a humble Egyptian servant in Salīm's household, develops for the much higher class maid-servant or housekeeper, the Armenian Teresa, and his unsuccessful proposal to her. The events take place against the background of the Cairo Stock Market. The play consists of two acts: Act I takes place at, or near, the Stock Market while the setting for Act II is the home of the rich banker, Salīm. Each act ends with a song.

The dangers and the excitement attendant upon monetary speculation are well described here. By choosing his main characters among the rather westernized, Levantine middle class, the author makes it possible to have a modicum of social intercourse between the sexes. On the whole these characters are reasonably well-defined and distinguished from one another, although the characterization is somewhat crude, except possibly in the case of the servant Farag who is lively enough. In the manner of the Roman comedy and its modern descendant in artificial European drama, the servants are shown to be eager and willing to help their masters in the pursuit of their interest, amorous and otherwise, but always with their eyes fixed on the material advantage that may thereby accrue to them. Because he uses spoken Arabic in the dialogue the dramatist manages to use language as a further means of characterization. For instance, he attempts to give a realistic picture of the language of money-dealers and workers at the Stock Exchange, whose speech is studded with Italian phrases. The Nubian servant speaks Arabic in a Nubian accent.

Ṣannūʿ's satirical intent in this play is abundantly clear. Apart from the dangers of monetary speculation at the Stock Exchange, the butt of the author's social criticism is the foolish imitation of western manners by Egyptians in an attempt to impress outsiders as well as one another. Similarly, the playwright attacks prearranged marriages and the failure of parents to take into consideration their daughters' wishes or feelings. He also condemns the contemptuous attitude towards the Egyptian working class which dismisses them as mere *fellaheen*, as exemplified in Teresa's manner of treating the servant, Farag.

Yet the play is not merely a didactic exercise; it is lively, dramatic entertainment, despite the fact that, not surprisingly, the technique is occasionally somewhat primitive. For instance, there is an inordinately large number of scenes. Act I contains no fewer than eleven short scenes, while there are seven in Act II, the obvious reason for this being the author's feeling that the mere entry of a fresh character on the stage automatically constitutes a different scene. There is also excessive use of soliloquy by the first character to appear on the stage. The servant, Farag, imparts directly to the audience the necessary amount of background information. Likewise, signs of carelessness are visible: the list of *dramatis personae* does not include all the characters in the play: for example, Ḥalīm and Antoine are missing from the list. Furthermore, there are links with popular, traditional, dramatic entertainments. The humour sometimes arises from the traditional linguistic sources, i.e. mispronunciation of Arabic by foreigners or the comic effect of dialect, such as the use of Nubian in the reported speech of the Nubian doorman at the Stock Exchange.

Like 'The Cairo Stock Exchange', *al-ʿAlīl* ('The Invalid') turns on the successful attempt of a young couple to achieve a marriage union after overcoming obvious obstacles, in this case, instead of disparity in wealth the impediment being the mysterious illness of the young woman's father. Whereas the action of the former play takes place against the background of the Stock Market, in 'The Invalid' the context is medical practice in contemporary Egypt, particularly in the newly established sanatorium at Hulwan. Ḥabīb is suffering from severe depression as a result of the shock of hearing of his brother's sudden death in Istanbul. He has been receiving treatment from several doctors but without success, much to the chagrin and near despair of his unmarried, young daughter, Hanum, who is looking after him. Mitrī, a young friend of the family who is in love with Hanum, has been calling on the patient every day and giving her much moral support. He informs her of his intention to ask her father for her hand in marriage, but she advises him to wait until her father's health has improved. In the mean time the manservant, Jawda, who after many years in their service has grown closely attached to the family, manages to persuade them against their better judgment to allow a Moroccan medicine man, Hājj, to visit the patient and prescribe treatment by magic. Hājj prevails upon Ḥabīb to make a solemn vow to give his daughter in marriage to the person who manages to bring about his cure. However, a young, properly qualified physician, Zakī Effendi, calls, correctly diagnoses the ailment and prescribes an immediate course of treatment by the waters of Hulwan. Accompanied by Mitrī the family moves to Hulwan (where Act II takes place).

At Hulwan Mitrī finds that the sanatorium is run by his friend Dr Kabrīt and he at once confides to him his plight concerning Ḥabīb's vow. Kabrīt agrees that should he be able to cure the patient he would give up the daughter in favour of his friend Mitrī. In the mean time another friend of Mitrī, Ilyās, turns up at the sanatorium suffering from a severe stammer. Ilyās's speech impediment is so comical that Ḥabīb has a fit of laughter from which he faints and when he comes round has recovered from his depression. Assuming that his cure was brought about by Ilyās he promptly offers him his daughter, despite her loud protestations. To complicate matters, Ilyās, who has taken a fancy to Hanum, jumps at the offer and comes to blows with his friend Mitrī over her. The noise of the quarrel brings Dr Kabrīt to the scene and he soon resolves the problem by stating that the sick man's cure was the direct result of the hot baths and the special treatment administered by himself. Consequently, he becomes entitled to the daughter whom, according to plan, he gives up at once for his friend Mitrī. The play ends with a song celebrating the benefits of the Hulwan sanatorium and praising the ruler of Egypt for his having given the order for its establishment.

Once more the humour, which becomes more striking when the scene shifts to Hulwan, relies largely upon language: the faulty Arabic used by the European doctor, Kabrīt (whose name, incidentally, means sulphur), and Ilyās's stammer, which is so skilfully employed by the dramatist that the effect in certain places is to this day extremely funny. Also amusing is the appropriate language of the Moroccan. Here again echoes of the traditional shadow plays can be heard. As in the previous play, the minor characters of the servants, both in Ḥabīb's household and at the sanatorium (e.g. Saʿīd) are memorable, lively sketches. The underlying social criticism is directed not only against quack medicine but also against the foolish practice of arranging the marriage of daughters without their consent.

The third play in the collection *al-Sawwāḥ wa' l-Ḥammār* ('The Tourist and the Muleteer') need not detain us long. It is no more than a brief dramatic dialogue (covering a couple of pages), between an English tourist, who insists upon speaking faulty and ungrammatical, classical Arabic, and a muleteer who complains that it would have been considerably easier for him had the tourist spoken English to him. It is a mildly amusing scene, where again the humour arises from the popular, traditional use, or rather misuse, of language.

A much more substantial work, *Abū Rīda wa Kaʿb al-Khayr* ('Abu Rīda and Kaʿb al-Khayr'), a play in two acts, opens with a song by the black man-servant, Abū Rīda, who is madly in love with the black maid, Kaʿb al-Khayr. After complaining of his passion in an amusing speech, which is addressed to the audience and which derives its humour partly from the Nubian mispronunciation of Arabic and partly from the colourful imagery he uses, he bursts into song again, extolling the merits of his beloved. When by chance the mistress of the house, the rich, young widow, Banba, learns of his passion he implores her to help him and use her influence with her maid in obtaining her agreement to marry him. Banba soon discovers that the maid, convinced that Abū Rīda is really after the neighbour's maid, cannot bear him and would rather see the back of him. Banba, however, assumes that Kaʿb al-Khayr is only jealous of the neighbours' maid and she therefore promises to further the cause of Abū Rīda.

Parallel to this theme of the servant's love for the maid is that of the eligible cloth merchant Nakhla's love for the young widow, Banba; here we find an interesting inversion of the usual practice of making the servants' love a sub-plot to the main theme of love between their masters and mistresses. And just as Banba undertakes to bring the servants together, so the professional matchmaker-cum-saleswoman, Mabrūka, assiduously endeavours to promote the cause of the marriage union of Banba and Nakhla, in the mean time earning quite a bit of money from both sides. A somewhat tenuous link between the two themes is created by the mistress's vow to bring about the marriage of her servants before her own wedding. As it happens, the engagement of the mistress proves a lot easier to bring about than that of the servants, for the Nubian maid turns out to be as obstinate and as mule-like as the Nubian stereotype is popularly supposed to be. Despite the various tempting offers made to her in the way of money and expensive clothes she categorically refuses Abū Rīda, and agrees to marry him only at the end of the play when he seriously threatens to commit suicide in her presence.

Within its largely self-imposed limitations this play has many merits, and is certainly one of Ṣannūʿ's plays which deserves to be revived on the stage. It is a competent piece of dramatic writing, far superior to anything one would expect of a nascent theatre. It is reasonably well-constructed and moves forward fairly smoothly, with enough action to sustain the audience's interest. Except for the opening speech in which Abū Rīda tells us about his passion for the maid, whatever information is necessary to follow the action of the play is given to us indirectly through dialogue. The dialogue is witty and lively, and exploits to the full the colourful potentialities of the extremely expressive, colloquial language; each character is given a distinct type of language in keeping with his temperament, sex and station in life. The author once more derives much humour from dialect, mispronunciation of Arabic and amusing malapropisms (e.g. the Nubian servant's calling the matchmaker, Mabrūka, by the name Mafrūka with its slightly obscene suggestions). There are at least two memorable portraits: the Nubian servant, Abū Rīda, and the matchmaker Mabrūka. But it is in Mabrūka that we have a masterly portrait of the traditional figure of the matchmaker in Egyptian society, a picture that in some respects reminds us of Ibn Dāniyāl. At once sly, materialistic, vain and persuasively eloquent, she is not entirely without concern for the happiness and well-being of her clients whom she, nevertheless, because of her mature understanding of human nature, manages to manipulate skilfully, getting them to do exactly what she wishes, while giving them the impression that she is only trying to please them and that she is utterly without a thought for her own advantage, material or otherwise. She flatters, cajoles and is not averse to telling a lie or to inventing an imaginary rival in order to gain an extra couple of pounds.

Al-Ṣadāqa ('Fidelity'), a one act play, also begins with a song sung by one, Najīb, who proceeds to give, in a soliloquy too, the necessary background information to the audience. He tells of his sister Warda's love for her cousin, Naʿūm, who has been away studying in England for the past six years and whose return she is anxiously awaiting so that they may get married. Najīb himself, we learn, is in love with Tiqla, the daughter of the prosperous Syrian merchant, Niʿmat Allah, who, in turn, has been courting the rich widow, al-Sitt Ṣafṣaf. Ṣafṣaf, in whose house in Alexandria the action of the play takes place, is the aunt of Najīb and Warda who have been in her care since they were orphaned; they live with her and she has provided for their education and even managed to find employment for her nephew, as a bank clerk.

The action becomes a little complicated when a certain Englishman by the name of Hincks appears on the scene and expresses an interest in Warda (he is, in fact, none other than her cousin, Naʿūm, returned from England in disguise in order to test the strength of her constancy and love for him). In the mean time, partly because she has not received any letters from her cousin and partly because she is told that Naʿūm got married to an English girl, Warda is urged to marry Hincks, especially as the latter is thought to be wealthy and well-connected and is, therefore, likely to be of great use to Niʿmat Allah's business. However, resolved in the end to be faithful to her love for her cousin despite his apparent deception, Warda refuses the Englishman, preferring to remain unmarried. Her incensed aunt threatens to turn her out of the house, and just as she is about to leave, she is stopped by Hincks, who, convinced of her absolute fidelity to him, reveals his true identity and explains the reasons for his strange course of action. Everything ends happily not only for Warda and her cousin, but for all three couples.

As is clear, the play is a variation on the Griselda theme. It is a very lightweight piece, despite the lively dialogue and the typical Ṣannūʿ humour which arises from the usual linguistic sources: the broken Arabic of Hincks and the Syrian dialect of Niʿmat Allah. Not much social criticism is attempted here. The play ends, just as it begins, with Najīb's singing.

Far more serious is *al-Amīra al-Iskandaraniyya* ('The Alexandrian Princess') which, like the previous play, is also set in Alexandria. Unlike 'Fidelity', which is designed largely as entertainment, 'The Alexandrian Princess' is obviously satirical in intent. It is perhaps the first extant Arabic play to launch a frontal attack on the negative aspects of superficial westernization, the problem of the blind imitation of the outward forms of western life in Egyptian society.

Maryam, the wife of a wealthy Alexandrian merchant of humble origins, is a social climber and a snob who gives herself airs and graces. Having fallen under the spell of France and all things French, she forces her reluctant but henpecked husband, Ibrāhīm, to agree to her adopting a French way of life at home, and even makes him take her to Paris every summer for holidays. In Alexandria she goes for rides, accompanied by her husband, in the afternoons, takes her daughter, ʿAdīla, to the theatre in the evenings, she employs European, French-speaking servant-maids and is attended by a European doctor. She will not hear of her daughter marrying Yūsuf, the decent young man who is in love with her, because he is a mere Egyptian and a common man, for she has made up her mind to marry her off to Victor, whom she believes to be a titled Frenchman on a visit to Egypt, and the son of a French aristocrat whom she and her husband met in Paris during their summer holidays the previous year. Her fondness for France and her scorn for Egypt have driven her husband to apply for the family to become French citizens, protected by the local French Consul, instead of their remaining Ottoman subjects.

The plot of the play, which is basically a comedy of intrigue and impersonation, influenced to some extent by Molière's *Le Bourgeois Gentilhomme* and *Georges Dandin*, describes the course of action adopted by the young couple to fool the mother and circumvent her opposition to their marriage. By an ingenious stratagem Yūsuf pretends to be Victor, the son of the French nobleman (whom Maryam has not seen in Paris as he had been on a visit to England at the time). He forges a letter of introduction from his assumed father and engineers a meeting one evening at the theatre with the mother and daughter to whom he subsequently pays his attentions. When he comes to ask for the daughter's hand in marriage, the mother is naturally delighted and only after the couple have actually been married does the mother learn the truth about the impersonation from the real French nobleman who unexpectedly visits Alexandria. The shock of the discovery makes her faint, but being powerless to do anything about it she gradually learns to accept the *fait accompli*.

The action of the play revolves around two axes: the sexual battle between husband and wife (which the husband seems to lose except at the very end, when the unexpected twist proves the wife to be the loser) and the absurd idealization of all things western. The humour arises largely from the ridiculous, blind attempts to ape western manners, ranging from the habit of interlacing Arabic conversation with French phrases, the wife's absurd lying in order to cover up the fact that her husband speaks no European language (falsely explaining this by claiming that a severe attack of fever has caused him to forget all the European languages he had previously known), the hopeless attempts to get the unsophisticated, local servant, Ḥasanayn, to adopt western ways (for instance, when asked to ring the gong to announce dinner, Ḥasanayn brings the gong into the drawing room, holds it above his mistress's head and starts banging it). The play is, in fact, rich in such laughable details, quite apart from

Ṣannūʿ's usual device of poking fun at European mispronunciation of Arabic, as seen in the speech of Yūsuf when impersonating Victor, the maid, Carolina, and the physician, Dr Kharalambo.

Moreover, the play is cunningly constructed: the very opening scene is in a sense a harbinger of the main theme of the play; the juxtaposition between the Egyptian and the European as seen in the comic dialogue between the Egyptian servant, Ḥasanayn, and the European maid, Carolina, and the former's infatuation with the latter's beauty. The audience's interest and suspense are maintained because the audience is not told of Yūsuf and ʿAdīla's plot until very late in the course of the play; to add to the credibility of the action the dramatist makes the husband equally ignorant of the plot, so that his comments on the strange course of events become a vocal expression of the views of the audience. In short, 'The Alexandrian Princess' is no primitive drama; it makes its point concisely, competently and without at any moment ceasing to be entertaining. Interestingly enough there are no songs in this play.

Equally satirical in intent is the play that apparently aroused the Khedive's displeasure, *al-Ḍurratayn* ('The Two Rival Wives'). It is a short play, about one-third the length of 'The Alexandrian Princess', and is in no way as good a play as the longer work. There are four characters: Aḥmad, who has been married for fifteen years to Ṣabḥa, takes on a second wife, Faṭṭūma, who is barely sixteen-years-old and the sister of Aḥmad's boon companion, Baʿgar, with whom he spends his evenings smoking hashish. In an attempt to reconcile his first wife to the idea of sharing her home with her rival, he slyly tries to tell her that the only reason for his taking a younger woman for a wife is to relieve her of the chores of housework. Far from being convinced by her husband's specious argument, Ṣabḥa, who entertains no illusions about the fickleness of her husband, is resolved to make his life and that of the new wife such a misery that he will be forced to divorce her. Equally, the new wife is determined to get rid of the old. The result is that the rival wives become involved in a violent quarrel, during which the new wife's brother sides with his sister and kicks the first wife. In the ensuing *mêlée* the younger woman plucks the husband's beard and the older woman threatens to gouge out his eyes unless he divorces the newcomer immediately. The unhappy but foolish husband divorces both women at once and, in a speech addressed to the audience, he bitterly attacks the practice of polygamy. In the end, however, he allows his first wife to come back but apparently only to please the audience.

'The Two Rival Wives' is clearly a skeleton of a play, and not a full length drama. It is also more primitive in technique, although as usual with Ṣannūʿ his mastery of dialogue already reveals itself, particularly in the speeches given to the first wife, whose character is briefly sketched out but in an exceedingly vivid manner. The fighting scene is rather crude and the humour arising from it is of the cheap, horse-play variety. The play may have set out to criticize a serious social custom, bigamy, but dramatically speaking it is basically no more than a farce, in which the author seems to resort to the Punch and Judy-like effects of puppet shows of *qaraqōz*.

The last play in Ṣannū''s published collection is of a different nature and style. It is the only play of a reasonable length which he published in his lifetime; it came out as late as 1912. This is *Molière Miṣr wa mā Yuqāsīh* ('The Egyptian Molière and What He Suffers'). Until Professor Najm published his collection of Ṣannū''s plays in 1963, thereby making them available, Ṣannū', the dramatist, had to be judged solely by this play. How erroneous and distorted would be our view of Ṣannū''s dramaturgy if it was based on this work alone. Although there is an allusion in the dialogue to the fact that the play was performed during the second year of Ṣannū''s theatrical activities in 1871,[7] and that it ran for two months, there is ample evidence to suggest that the author had subsequently interfered with the text and that the play as it was published in 1912 is in no way the original version.[8] Indeed, the passages quoted in it from the other plays of Ṣannū', the texts of which we now have, differ substantially from the original texts. For one thing, unlike the earlier versions, they are written in rhyming prose. Furthermore, the author's attitude to his themes suffers considerable change: for instance, the savage attack on the Stock Exchange in the passage allegedly quoted from the play, 'The Cairo Stock Exchange', is absent from the original play. One must therefore assume that Ṣannū' rewrote this play for publication forty years later.

'The Egyptian Molière and What He Suffers' has been likened to Molière's *L'Impromptu de Versailles* by which, as Najm rightly says, it was generally inspired,[9] although we must not exaggerate what some scholars see as 'the unmistakable influence'[10] of the French play. The only thing in common between the two plays is that they both deal in part with the difficulties faced by the dramatist/director *vis-à-vis* his company of actors and actresses in rehearsing for a performance. But the differences are much more significant. Molière wrote his play to avenge himself on his professional rivals, in particular Boursault who had attacked him in the play *Le Portrait du Peintre*, and also to defend himself against the charge of having drawn the characters of particular persons in *L'École des Femmes*. That explains why in his play, *L'Impromptu*, Molière provides an intelligent discussion of the nature of comedy and of his own comic art. It is true that Ṣannū' does refer to an attack on his plays by an Italian critic, who condemned him for his use of the colloquial language in his dialogue, and that Ṣannū' defends himself on the grounds that drama is meant to be about what people actually say or do, and that in real life nobody speaks classical Arabic. However, Ṣannū''s play deals primarily with Ṣannū' himself and the efforts he made to establish Arabic drama in Egypt, the envy he aroused, the opposition to him by 'Alī Mubārak, the Minister of Education at the time and the everyday difficulties he encountered in matters like paying his troupe.

Molière's play ends with the King excusing the troupe from performing, while Ṣannūʿ concludes his with the patching up of the quarrel between members of the troupe and their getting ready to perform.

Although it is not an entirely reliable account of the beginning of the Arabic theatre in modern Egypt, largely because of the author's predilection for exaggeration and perhaps because of his unreliable memory after the passage of such a long time, the play nevertheless provides considerable interest as it sheds some light on the early Arabic theatre. For instance, we know from it that it was Ṣannūʿ's practice to put on more than one play (usually two plays) the same evening which, to some extent, may explain why Ṣannūʿ's plays are so short. We also learn from it (as well as from other sources) that there were actresses on the Egyptian stage right from the beginning of the early 1870s. We are given the titles of many plays by Ṣannūʿ not all of which, alas, have been retrieved. From the list of the *dramatis personae* who represent the actual members of his troupe we can deduce the basic types who formed the groundwork of his characters: Mitrī is described as an actor known for his imitations of fellaheen, Ḥabīb for his imitations of merchants, Isṭifān for imitating dandies, Ḥunayn for imitating Europeans, etc.

But from the dramatic point of view the play represents a sharp decline in Ṣannūʿ's art. The mere use of rhyming prose (*sajʿ*) for dialogue, despite the comic use to which he occasionally manages to put it,[11] has robbed the author of one of his greatest gifts: the ability to produce convincing dialogue which expresses the speakers' characters, thereby interrelating dialogue and characterization. The result is that, compared with the earlier plays 'The Egyptian Molière' is weak in characterization. Why Ṣannūʿ used rhyming prose in this play is an intriguing question. It could be due to the influence of modern Arabic drama outside Egypt (in Syria and Lebanon) which, as we shall soon see, employed this style of writing. It could even be atavism, as we have seen in the early medieval Arabic plays where rhyming prose was generally the medium chosen, although we must remember that Ṣannūʿ did use rhyming prose in some of the short pieces he published in his satirical periodicals. Whatever the reason it marked a retrogressive step in Ṣannūʿ's dramatic art. There is no doubt that the abrupt end to his theatrical activities in 1872 was a calamitous event, not only in the dramatic career of Ṣannūʿ, but also in the history of modern Egyptian drama.

3

THE SYRIAN CONTRIBUTION

MĀRŪN AL-NAQQĀSH

Between 1872 and 1876 little seems to have happened in the world of Egyptian drama (apart from the publication in 1873 of the superb Egyptian adaptation of Molière's *Tartuffe* by Muḥammad ʿUthmān Jalāl which will be discussed later). Four years after the closure of Ṣannūʿ's theatre a Syrian company headed by Salīm al-Naqqāsh (d. 1884) moved into Egypt, attracted by what had become known of Khedive Ismaíl's munificence and encouragement of the theatrical arts. Salīm al-Naqqāsh arrived in Alexandria with a company consisting of twelve actors and four actresses, and a repertoire of plays, of which the first to be produced was *Abū'l-Ḥasan al-Mughaffal* ('Abū'l-Ḥasan the Fool'), the work of his uncle Mārūn al-Naqqāsh, the author of the very first play in Arabic and hence the father of modern Arabic drama.

Mārūn Mīkhā'īl al-Naqqāsh (1817–55) was a prosperous and cultured businessman in Beirut who knew several foreign languages, including French and Italian. His business interests caused him to travel widely and it was during a visit to Italy in 1846 that he fell under the spell of the Italian theatre and opera just, as we have seen, Ṣannūʿ did later. In 1847 he wrote and produced, with the help of his family in his own house, the first modern play in Arabic, *al-Bakhīl* ('The Miser'). Encouraged by the favourable reaction of his invited audience, which included local notables and foreign consuls, he went on to produce, again in his own house, his second play *Abū'l-Ḥasan al-Mughaffal* (in 1849–50), a short account of which was left to us by the British traveller, David Urquhart. Subsequently al-Naqqāsh managed to obtain an Ottoman decree to allow him to have a theatre built close to his house, in which he produced his third and last play *al-Salīṭ al-Ḥasūd* ('The Sharp-tongued, Envious Man') in 1853. His dramatic career, however, was not to last long for in 1855, while he was away from home, he caught a fever and died.

For obvious reasons al-Naqqāsh felt the need to introduce his production to his audience, many of whom had never seen such a thing before, with a speech in which he tried to explain the nature and function of the theatre in Europe and to describe the various kinds of dramatic entertainment available. Two things are important in this speech: first, al-Naqqāsh's deep awareness of the civilizing influence of the theatre, the moral functions of drama and its attempt to promote virtue and to discourage vice through the examples shown on the stage: second, the author's deliberate choice of the dramatic forms which rely upon singing, the reason for this being not only his personal preference for opera and musicals, but also his strong conviction that his people would find the musical theatre more to their taste.[1] We have seen that Ṣannūʿ also emphasized the didactic, civilizing function of the theatre and tended to introduce singing into his drama, although by no means on the same scale as al-Naqqāsh whose plays were either entirely musical or partly so. Singing, in fact, was to become an indispensable part of Arabic plays for many decades to come.

Probably because of the similarity of its title, it was wrongly assumed for a long time that al-Naqqāsh's first play, 'The Miser', was a translation or adaptation of Molière's *L'Avare*[2]. But a cursory look at the Arabic play is sufficient to show that it is indeed an original although, as in the rest of al-Naqqāsh's work, one can detect in it an echo of Molière as well as the *general* pervasive influence of his drama. Bearing in mind the fact that it is the very first modern Arabic play it is for the most part a remarkably competent work. The plot is relatively simple. Attracted by his wealth, al-Thaʿlabī wants to marry his young and beautiful, widowed daughter, Hind, to the ugly and elderly miser, Qarrād. Ghālī, al-Thaʿlabī's son, is horrified at this prospect and tries in vain to persuade his father to consent to Hind's marrying instead his friend, ʿĪsā, a relation of her deceased husband, whom Hind loves. The action of the play consists in the young people's successful attempt to get rid of old Qarrād and marry Hind to ʿĪsā. In brief, knowing what a miser he is, they arrange that Hind should pretend not only to agree to marrying Qarrād, but also to show him how eager she is to be his wife because she is looking forward to spending his money extravagantly on clothes, finery, jewels and gracious living. At once Qarrād, who is himself after what he believes to be Hind's money and inheritance, is alarmed and declares that he is no longer interested in the marriage, but Hind will not release him without financial compensation. In the mean time, al-Thaʿlabī is persuaded by the young people that Qarrād intends to kill him in order to seize the money which Hind would inherit on his death. Shocked and disgusted by his behaviour, al-Thaʿlabī turns Qarrād out of his house and consents to marry Hind to ʿĪsā. Besides these main characters, there are a handful of minor ones whose function it is to help the plot along: al-Thaʿlabī and Qarrād are given amusing men servants while there is an old and cunning maid in the Thaʿlabī household who is supposed to look after Hind. There is also a chorus who occasionally comment on the action, but not in a wholly impartial fashion since they are supposed to be the friends of the two young men and they help them to achieve their ends. As has been observed by scholars,[3] the play could quite easily have ended at the close of Act III, when Hind has been saved from Qarrād and her marriage to ʿĪsā has been approved of by her father. However, the author chooses to expand it to five acts, filling the extra two acts with the young people's machinations to punish Qarrād and extract as much money as possible from him. Ghālī disguises himself as the Turkish governor with ʿĪsā pretending to be his Egyptian clerk while al-Thaʿlabī's servant, Nādir, dresses up as a police sergeant. Qarrād complains to the governor of his ill-treatment at the hands of the family and asks for financial damages and to be released from his obligation to marry Hind. He is falsely promised help and is given a taste of the beating that he is assured will be inflicted on Hind. He ends up being outwitted by them and made to part with all his money, although, when they reveal their true identity, he surprisingly forgives them and the play ends with all the characters singing 'Let this be a lesson to all misers'.

The dialogue is written entirely in verse (of a rather indifferent quality and not altogether metrically regular), which is meant to be sung to the tune of well-known Arabic songs indicated in detail by the author (as well as the tunes of two Arabized French songs). Although the language employed is largely classical Arabic, the author introduces a measure of humour by using dialects and foreign accents as a means for further characterization. For example, the maidservant, Umm Rīsha, uses Lebanese dialect, the disguised Egyptian clerk uses Egyptian dialect and the Turkish ruler and sergeant speak broken Arabic with a Turkish accent. Equally, the names of some of the characters are meant to be an indication of their disposition or physical appearance, as is pointed out by the chorus at the opening of the play: Qarrād from *qird* (monkey) and Thaʿlabī from *thaʿlab* (fox). But the characters remain wooden and lifeless, apart perhaps from Qarrād and Hind, though the former is more of a caricature with his comical antics such as fits of fainting every time he hears Hind explain how she is planning to squander his money, or his subsequent attempts to put her off by pulling faces to make himself look even uglier and by exaggerating his decrepit, old age. Hind certainly comes to life when she acts the part of the spoiled woman of the world.

Just as the play could have been shortened without serious loss to its main theme, likewise the dialogue could have been purged of some extraneous matter such as praise of the reigning Ottoman Sultan (p.15)[4] and a discussion of the moral function of the theatre in Europe (p.16), which the author could not refrain from putting in. Such detail, of course, helps date the play, but although the events are supposed to take place in nineteenth-century Lebanon the social content of the play is very thin indeed. Apart from one or two allusions to the practice of not allowing a woman to appear alone before her male suitor (p.14) and the father's anger on being told by his daughter that she is in love (p.28), contemporary social reality is conspicuously absent.

In his second play, 'Abū'l-Ḥasan the Fool', Naqqāsh went for his inspiration to the fantasy world of the *Arabian Nights*, thereby setting an example which subsequent Arab dramatists were to follow to this day. The story of the play is based on the tale by Sheherazade entitled 'The Sleeping and the Wakeful' (tale no.153), which describes how, disgusted with the ways of the world and the fickleness of friends, Abū'l-Ḥasan wishes he could be given sole sway over the world even for one single day in order to set things right. Overhearing him the Caliph Hārūn al-Rashīd, who happens to be on one of his usual nightly inspection tours of the city of Baghdad, disguised, and accompanied by his executioner, decides to grant him his wish to see how far Abū'l-Ḥasan will be able to change the world. He has him drugged and transported to the palace where he wakes up to find himself Caliph. When his time as Caliph is over, Abū'l-Ḥasan discovers to his dismay that he has been able to achieve little of his good intentions, having spent all his time in the pomp and distractions of royal office, which blurred his vision and affected his judgment.

The obvious point of the *Arabian Nights* tale, namely the gap that separates intention and action, the result of the inherent imperfection of man, is clearly not what Naqqāsh has in mind for the central theme of his play. The action of the Caliph here is motivated mainly by his desire to amuse himself and make fun of the gullible simpleton, Abū'l-Ḥasan. We are first introduced to Abū'l-Ḥasan's household. He is unhappy because he has become bankrupt due to the dishonesty of the trustee and (although he doesn't admit it) to his own foolish extravagance. His close friends have now deserted him. He wishes he were the Caliph in Baghdad, so that he could punish the corrupt trustee and his false friends by death. When his servant ʿUrqūb hears his master express such a wish aloud he asks him jokingly to appoint him vizier if he should become Caliph. Abū'l-Ḥasan agrees on condition that the servant obeys him and helps him in his plans to get his daughter Salmā to consent to marry ʿUthmān, since, unless he marries her, ʿUthmān will not allow his sister Daʿd to marry Abū'l-Ḥasan who is besotted with her. ʿUthmān, we learn, is in truth not serious about his promise to Abū'l-Ḥasan, since Daʿd is in love with Abū'l-Ḥasan's younger brother, Saʿīd, who reciprocates her feelings. He knows that there is no chance of her agreeing to marry Abū'l-Ḥasan who is clearly a fool yet he continues to deceive him. We also learn that Abū'l-Ḥasan's mother who is unhappy at the way her foolish son has squandered his and his younger brother's fortune on drinking and riotous living, has gone on a pilgrimage to the Holy Places.

As for the Caliph Hārūn al-Rashīd and his vizier, Jaʿfar, they go round the streets of Baghdad disguised as a pair of dervishes, in order to see for themselves the conditions in which the ordinary citizens live. They appear here as regular visitors to the house of Abū'l-Ḥasan, whose company amuses them, particularly on account of his singing at which he seems to be skilful. They shower him with presents, thus enabling him to continue to indulge his pleasures with them as his boon companions. They plot to make him Caliph for one day, curious to see what misadventures he would be involved in, since they have often heard him wish he were the sole ruler of the country even for one day. Before they execute their plot of drugging his food at a banquet they hold for him on the bank of the Tigris, they witness a quarrel between him and his younger brother over Daʿd and the Caliph takes a dubious part in it, clearly favouring the younger brother. When he regains consciousness, Abū'l-Ḥasan finds himself in the splendid surroundings of the court, where he is told he is Caliph and his erstwhile servant, ʿUrqūb, stands next to him dressed as his vizier. Although bewildered at first, he soon begins to enjoy his new life enormously. While he is Caliph he is tricked by Hind, a court concubine he grows fond of, into issuing a decree enabling the two young couples to marry and thus to give up his claims to Daʿd. He does manage, however, to order that his enemies, namely the dishonest trustee and his disloyal friends, should be punished. The true Caliph, still in the guise of a dervish, also makes him believe that the Persians are amassing huge armies in order to invade Baghdad. Scared at the prospect of having to go to war, Abū'l-Ḥasan unsuccessfully tries first to sell the Caliphate and then to escape from the palace disguised as one of the concubines. However, his day as Caliph comes to an end, and he is once more drugged and brought back to his humble dwelling. He wakes up confused, thinking he is still Caliph, beats his mother when his wishes are thwarted, and realizing that he has lost both Daʿd and Hind, becomes unable to distinguish between reality and dream. At first he believes what he is told by the disguised Caliph, namely that he has been under the influence of magic which his brother has used in order to avenge himself on him. But later the truth that he has been the victim of a diabolic trick, in which his own servant took an active part, is revealed to him. His mind for a while is unhinged, not knowing what to believe and what not to believe. But in the end when the Caliph Hārūn and his vizier, Jaʿfar, reveal their true identity, everyone is rewarded with purses of money and Abū'l-Ḥasan, towards whom the Caliph has mixed feelings of guilt and pity, is given money and is promised the concubine Hind in place of the wife whom he has divorced at the Caliph's instigation. The play ends with the irate Abū'l-Ḥasan beating his servant, while the latter is busy picking up the dinars from the floor with which the Caliph has showered everybody.

This is by far the most accomplished of al-Naqqāsh's three plays, particularly as regards characterization. The author has managed to give us two memorable portraits: those of the simpleton Abū'l-Ḥasan and of his servant, ʿUrqūb. It is perhaps an exaggeration to suggest (as Najm and, following him, Moosa seem to do)[5] that al-Naqqāsh aims at portraying the character of a day-dreamer in Abū'l-Ḥasan. Najm even describes him as schizophrenic. Vivid as he is, Abū'l-Ḥasan is not really a very complex creation. He is in many ways, as the title of the play suggests, a simpleton, a foolish man and a wastrel who has squandered his fortune and that of his family on his pleasures and on feasting a number of sychophantic flatterers who desert him when his money is gone. He is described by ʿUthmān as 'naive and easily led' (p.79) and he is very suggestible; although healthy, he takes to his bed when he is told by his friends he is sick; and he claims that he divorced his wife at the instigation of others. He cannot add or tell the day of the week, nor is he fully articulate. Despite his abysmal ignorance of history he still tries to parade his ill-digested scraps of knowledge with ludicrous results. When prompted by Jaʿfar he mispronounces names and is guilty of several comic malapropisms. He is even given to crying a great deal (pp. 101, 103).

Apart from his singing, it is his naivety which mainly attracts Abū'l-Ḥasan to the Caliph and explains why the Caliph chooses to put him on the throne for one day: the Caliph finds amusing the prospect of watching how this foolish man, who 'like a child is easily deceived', is going to behave (p.106). In fact, no other clear motive can be detected for the actions of the Caliph. When he finds him quarelling with his younger brother over the young woman they both love and want to marry the disguised Caliph, under the pretence of trying to reconcile them, resorts to lying and deception and deliberately makes fun of Abū'l-Ḥasan. Again it is the Caliph who, disguised as a dervish with some knowledge of magic, reads Abū'l-Ḥasan's fortune and predicts an invasion by the Persians who are marching on Baghdad in huge numbers like locusts (p.120), producing the desired effect of scaring Abū'l-Ḥasan out of his wits. Almost until the end of the play the Caliph pursues this sadistic line of action with Abū'l-Ḥasan; he deliberately misleads him by telling him that all his recent misadventures and troubles are due to magic worked on him by the magician, Bahrān, whom his rival brother, Saʿīd, has employed to avenge himself on him, with the result that he becomes thoroughly incensed with Saʿīd. It is no wonder that from the start Abū'l-Ḥasan takes a dislike to the disguised Caliph and that when he momentarily loses his reason the Caliph is not without some feeling of guilt and responsibility for the sad turn of events and tries to make amends (pp.174, 183).

In many ways the servant, ʿUrqūb, is the opposite of his master. He is by far the liveliest and most consistent and amusing character in the play. Despite his age he is full of zest and vitality. He is a most plausible rogue, prepared to plot with anybody for or against his master in order to line his own pockets. (Critics noted some similarity between him and Scapin, and the valet in the classical French comedy.[6]) In his soliloquy (p.88) ʿUrqūb admits that he deceives everybody, goes along with everyone in the pursuit of his aims while himself enjoying the gifts and favours bestowed upon him by everybody. He pretends to accept gifts most reluctantly (p.108) while all the time stretching out his hand for payment. The most important plot he takes part in, the one which brings him the greatest monetary reward, is that in which he collaborates with the Caliph and his vizier to realize his master's oft repeated wish to be Caliph for one day. When the drugged Abū'l-Ḥasan wakes up in the palace and thinks that he is either dreaming or else he has died and, having lived like a good Muslim, is now in Paradise, it is his plausible servant, ʿUrqūb, who, dressed as the Caliph's vizier,

Jaʿfar, reassures him that he is now Caliph in reality, and that his wish to become Caliph was granted by God four years previously on the Night of Power (*Laylat al-Qadr*) (p.113), when it is believed that such miracles can occur, and that his promise to make ʿUrqūb his vizier was also fulfilled. He is most skilful in allaying his master's doubts and fears while the latter reiterates the words 'I must have been transformed by magic, or else my mind has been unhinged' (p.117). Because of his endless charm, ʿUrqūb's greed and love of money are not felt to be offensive. His manner of selling the post of vizier to Jaʿfar is most amusing and no less amusing is his attempt to rob Daʿd of the four purses containing thousands of dinars given to her by the Caliph (pp.135–9).

Structurally, the two themes of Abū'l-Ḥasan's Caliphate-of-a-day and the love interest are not separately treated but are inextricably intertwined in a fairly subtle manner. However, the resolution of the complicated plot, which takes up the whole of the third and final act, takes far too long, as the author is clearly suffering from prolixity of writing. Echoes of Molière can also be found here. For instance, in Act I Scene xv we are reminded of *L'Avare* when Abū'l-Ḥasan asks his brother Saʿīd what he thinks of Daʿd as a possible wife for himself without realizing that Saʿīd is his serious rival in this matter; in the brawl which ensues the brothers exchange very expressive abuse in which Abū'l-Ḥasan uses a most colourful language which still sounds comical today (p.93). Yet it cannot be claimed that the dialogue accurately and sensitively reflects the characters of the speakers; it is a mixture of rhyming prose and verse, both in some kind of classical Arabic. Unlike the first play the dialogue here is not wholly sung.

The events of the last play by al-Naqqāsh, *al-Salīṭ al-Ḥasūd*, take place in nineteenth-century Beirut, although very little social reality is, in fact, portrayed in it. Here is an outline of the story. Abū ʿĪsā, a teacher of Arabic language and literature who has moved into Beirut from Damascus, owes a large sum of money to a handsome young man, Samʿān, the sharp-tongued, envious man of the title of the play. Samʿān gives him an ultimatum, either to consent to his marrying Abū ʿĪsā's attractive young daughter, Raḥīl (who, unbeknown to her father, is in love with him), or else pay him back the money owed to him. Since Abū ʿĪsā is in no position to discharge his debt he reluctantly agrees to the marriage and is overheard by the maid, Barbara, who hastens to inform her mistress. Abū ʿĪsā is about to break the news to Raḥīl when he is interrupted by Bishāra, the servant of a certain prosperous merchant from Jerusalem called Isḥāq who wishes to make his acquaintance. Abū ʿĪsā goes to see Isḥaq who asks for Raḥīl's hand in marriage and offers him a pearl necklace as a present for her. Abū ʿĪsā is impressed by Isḥāq's pleasant character and when he is offered enough money to pay back his debt to Samʿān, he has no hesitation in going back on his promise to Samʿān and accepting Isḥāq as his future son-in-law instead. He asks his daughter's opinion on the marriage and is promptly informed that she is prepared to accept the man her father has chosen for a husband, being convinced that it must be Samʿān. In the mean time, Samʿān discovers what has happened and rushes to see Raḥīl, accusing her of fickleness and lack of sincerity. In vain does she try to make him realize that she is an innocent victim who is as shocked by the news as he is. He breaks down and cries, then goes off contemplating suicide, but his courage fails him. So instead he decides to get drunk to muster up sufficient courage to face the situation. At the same time Raḥīl plans to elope, accompanied by Barbara, in order to join Samʿān, fetch a priest to marry them and to marry Barbara to his servant, Jabbūr, with whom Barbara is in love. They don't go far before they run into Samʿān and Jabbūr. As usual Samʿān distrusts Raḥīl and accuses her of hypocrisy; she is deeply hurt because of his doubting her love for him. Then ensues a scene of mutual recrimination of the lovers, parodied by the parallel mutual recrimination of the servants written in a comic vein. The two women hasten home when they hear Abū ʿĪsā approaching; he has been alerted by his pupil, Jirjis, as to what they are up to.

Thinking that she has gone to Isḥāq, Samʿān rushes to challenge him to a duel. The two frightened women watch Samʿān and Jabbūr fighting Isḥāq and his servant, Bishāra, Raḥīl nearly fainting, and they ask Jirjis to stop them, but Jirjis will not risk interfering on behalf of his cousin, Samʿān, who has always ill-treated him. We then learn that the duel ends with Samʿān's defeat; Raḥīl is married to Isḥaq, whom she grows to like, especially after becoming thoroughly fed up with Samʿān's constant suspicions. Samʿān, apparently reconciled to them, even acts as best man at their wedding and gives them a splendid wedding present. But Raḥīl doesn't trust him and her suspicions are justified, for he tries to murder the couple by giving them a box of poisoned sweets for the wedding feast. The plot, however, is thwarted by his servant, Jabbūr, who reveals the secret of the poisoned sweets and is rewarded by being allowed to marry the servant girl, Barbara. The disappointed Bishāra, to whom Barbara was promised, avenges himself by trying to steal his master's silver plate, but is surprised in the act and he jumps out of the window. After a series of amusing disguises Jabbūr challenges his master with his villainy, but surprisingly enough Samʿān is forgiven at the end, for as Abū ʿĪsā says 'forgiveness is the best policy' (p.291).

Al-Salīṭ al-Ḥasūd is probably the most symmetrically structured of al-Naqqāsh's plays. The plot which deals with events connected with the marriages of Raḥīl is paralleled in the sub-plot, the theme of which is the marriage of Raḥīl's servant maid. Just as there are two suitors for Raḥīl, Samʿān and Isḥāq, there are also two suitors for Raḥīl's servant, Jabbūr and Bishāra, the servants of Samʿān and Isḥāq respectively. (And, of course, just as Raḥīl has her servant, so has each of her suitors.) In the list of *dramatis personae* Isḥāq is described as a gracious young man, while Samʿān is given the epithets, jealous and envious. Conversely, Samʿān's servant is described as a charming young man but Isḥāq's servant is referred to as tedious. Samʿān, the 'misanthropist', is morose but he is given a cousin who is described as insensitive and lacking in charm. In reality, however, Jirjis is a clown and a comical figure with a slight stammer and a tendency to show off the garbled, linguistic and prosodic knowledge he possesses and to make a fool of himself by grotesque attempts at eloquence. On the whole, this symmetry or parallelism has a damaging effect in that it enhances the impression of artificiality the play produces, although it can sometimes be a source of humour, as in the scene in which Raḥīl sings of her love for Samʿān and Barbara of her passion for Jabbūr (pp.222–3); or that in which the mutual recrimination of the lovers Raḥīl and Samʿān is parodied by the recriminations of the servants Barbara and Jabbūr (pp.245ff), where language is used to suit the character and status of the speaker.

Other instances of humour arising from the interplay of character and the language of dialogue can be found in the course of Abū ʿĪsā's attempt at teaching his pupils. Curiously enough, the lesson he chooses to give them is in Arabic prosody. The pupils are made to read aloud from a mnemonic poem explaining the details of Arabic versification, which the audience must find somewhat boring. Certainly the malapropisms which occur in the speech of the dim-witted Jirjis, as he unsuccessfully grapples with the terminology of Arabic prosody, would have been much more comical had the subject been of a less technical nature. In despair his teacher advises him to learn prose instead, and like Monsieur Jourdain in Molière's *Le Bourgeois Gentilhomme* (Act II Scene IV) Jirjis is surprised to learn that he has been using prose all his life without knowing it (p.206). Echoes of Molière's *Precieuses Ridicules* (Act I, Scene IX) can also be heard in the amusing exchange of words between the servants Jabbūr and Bishāra (p.242), and when Jabbūr, pretending to be a gentleman, introduces himself to Bishāra as the Chief of the Damascus Guilds of Merchants, only to be met soon afterwards by his master who proceeds to upbraid him in forthright language for his misbehaviour. Jabbūr, in fact, is one of the livelier characters of the play.

But it is the character of Samʿān that has impressed critics and scholars; clearly, and as Najm has noted, it was inspired by Alceste in Molière's *Le Misanthrope*, but it has become thoroughly Arabized in the process. He is a handsome but conceited young man who looks down upon the rest of mankind, yet he is at the same time consumed with envy. He is jealous of the schoolteacher, Abū ʿĪsā, because of the respect shown to him by his pupils and cannot forgive him for transmitting his learning to them, thereby removing their ignorance and consequently their inferior status. Because the poor teacher owes him a large sum of money, Samʿān feels he can be overbearing, rude and generally uncivil towards him even in Abū ʿĪsā's own house and in the presence of other people. He insensitively reminds the teacher's daughter, Raḥīl, whom he is supposed to love, of his acts of generosity and kindness to her family and of the help he has given them (p.210). He hates and despises his cousin, Jirjis, whom he constantly belittles. His jealousy is such that he even accuses Abū ʿĪsā of having promised to give his daughter's hand in marriage to Jirjis, who is really no more than a clown. He searches Raḥīl's quarters for possible undesirable visitors and is jealous of all the young men who go for their lessons to her father's house, and urges him to put an end to their visits. And we have seen how he forces Abū ʿIsā to consent to his marrying Raḥīl by giving him an ultimatum either to let him marry her or else pay back his debt. Strangely enough, Raḥīl is very much in love with him (p.211) and is prepared to elope with him, but even she later on changes her attitude to him on account of his pathological jealousy and totally unreasonable behaviour. It is true that when Abū ʿĪsā goes back on his word and allows Raḥīl to marry Isḥāq instead, Samʿān breaks down and cries in despair and even thinks of committing suicide. Professor Najm feels that he becomes a tragic figure at this point and he even finds in him some similarity to Hamlet (p.32). Indeed, it would be wrong to dismiss the whole of Mārūn al-Naqqāsh's work as not forming part of the Arabic literary heritage, as does the distinguished critic Muḥammad Mandūr,[7] but, nevertheless, Najm's judgment seems to be a gross exaggeration. For one thing, Samʿān's subsequent attempt to poison his friends with whom he has recently been reconciled clearly shows he is far from being a sympathetic, let alone a tragic, figure. Furthermore, he is a coward at heart. On the dark, wintry night when he resolves to kill himself he is easily frightened by the night-watchman and decides to get drunk first to give himself sufficient courage to commit suicide. There is an amusing scene when, in the dark and unable to see one another, he and the servant Bishāra threaten to kill each other, using the most horrific language while they are both trembling with fear (p.234).

Like *Abū'l-Ḥasan*, this play is written in a mixture of rhyming prose and verse, and it is not entirely sung. Again, on the whole, the language of the dialogue does not express the character of the speaker, except in a few scenes some of which have already been cited. There are far too many moral precepts, general remarks and wise sayings, particularly in the verse speeches, not to mention the long passages dealing with Arabic prosody which serve no useful dramatic purpose. Once more the author inserts in the dialogue irrelevant material such as a discussion of the theatre, this time all three plays of al-Naqqāsh himself (pp.274–5). In fact, the work could quite easily have been cut down to half its length with profit. One interesting feature of al-Naqqāsh's drama, however, to be seen here too is the use he makes of the chorus. While occasionally commenting on the action, the chorus changes its character, playing several roles at different moments in the play ranging from pupils to night-watch-men and ordinary male and female citizens.

It may be useful at this stage to pause and ask, what did the two pioneers of modern Arabic drama have in common? It is interesting that, although both dramatists clearly followed their paths independently and a gap of twenty-three years separate their first plays, Ṣannūʿ and Mārūn al-Naqqāsh share a number of features. In the first place their work betrays the influence of Italian opera; they both emphasized the role of singing in drama, albeit in different degrees. Secondly, both were clearly inspired by Molière, whose influence was crucial in shaping the early attempts at writing Arabic plays. The plays we have been discussing owe an obvious debt to the artificial comedy of intrigue; they have complicated plots, in which servants are no less involved than their masters, with disguises and mistaken identity as obvious sources of humour which also arises from malapropisms, dialect and misuse of language. Among the dominant themes in the work of both dramatists are love and marriage, money and greed. Where the plot requires mixing of the sexes, non-Muslim characters are introduced. It is interesting that both playwrights confined their work to comedy and farce; even when complications threaten to take a sad turn a happy end is never in doubt. Here and in the particular kind of comedy they wrote, Naqqāsh and Ṣannūʿ determined the course of Arabic drama for generations. It is noteworthy that few serious attempts at writing tragedy were later made and these tended to belong more to melodrama than to tragedy proper. The result is that Arabic tragedy did not develop to the same extent as comedy. For tragedy the Arabic theatre generally turned to translations from European dramatists, particularly Shakespeare, Corneille and Racine.[8]

Yet there are important differences between Ṣannūʿ and al-Naqqāsh, both in the content and the language of their plays. Ṣannūʿ's work reflects contemporary social reality much more intimately than al-Naqqāsh's, which, as we have seen, tends to be set either in a social vacuum or else in the fantasy world of the *Arabian Nights*. Likewise, unlike Naqqāsh, Ṣannūʿ did not hesitate to use spoken Arabic in his dialogue, and with the exception of his last play he refrained from the employment of traditional rhyming prose.

From the point of view of stagecraft no significant advance was made on the work of these two gifted pioneers in the dramatic productions of their immediate successors which, despite their interest, were on the whole little more than pale imitations.

SALĪM AL-NAQQĀSH

Together with his uncle's three plays, Salīm al-Naqqāsh brought to Egypt another five works which he had adapted or loosely translated. These were *ʿĀida* adapted from Verdi's opera *Aida, Mayy aw Horace* ('Mayy or Horace') based on Corneille's play *Horace, al-Kadhūb* ('The Liar') based on Corneille's *Le Menteur, Gharā'ib al-Ṣudaf* ('Strange Coincidences') and *al-Ẓalūm* ('The Tyrant'), the last two obviously adapted from European plays which have not yet been identified. All five plays were performed in Egypt and (except for *al-Kadhūb*) continued to be acted by the leading theatrical companies of the day, in Cairo and Alexandria as well as the provinces, well into the second decade of the twentieth century. Three, in particular, namely *ʿĀida, Mayy* and *al-Ẓalūm*, enjoyed great popularity and should therefore be discussed, albeit briefly, here. The first two were called tragedies, while the last, *al-Ẓalūm*, was described as a dark comedy *daʿjā'* or a tragi-comedy.

Clearly Salīm al-Naqqāsh brought with him his version of *ʿĀida* to please

Khedive Ismail of Egypt who had hoped that his newly-built, opulent Cairo Opera House would open with Verdi's opera. (In the event *Aida* was not finished in time and *Rigoletto* was performed instead, although *Aida* still had its first performance in Cairo in 1871.) Al-Naqqāsh based his work on Ghislanzoni's libretto and turned the opera into an operetta mainly, but not wholly, sung to popular Arabic tunes of the time. The dialogue is a mixture of verse and rhyming prose and it is not at all clear why, in the same speech of a certain character (p.17)[9], some sections are in verse while others are in prose. Moreover, much of the verse is irregular and unmetrical. The speeches tend to be declamatory or lyrical rather than dramatic. The poetry, though not particularly distinguished, tends to fall into two, time-honoured, traditional Arabic categories: either conventional love poetry or equally conventional poetry of *ḥamāsa* and *fakhr* (martial boastfulness). Lovers express their emotions in the traditional Arabic idiom, just as warriors praise their own valour and courage in the conventional Arabic heroic manner. There is hardly any characterization; the main character, the Egyptian soldier and lover, Rādamīs, takes major decisions affecting his as well as other people's lives, without his motivation being made psychologically convincing, as the author makes no attempt to show any character analysis or development. The last two lines of the 'play' with which Amīnarīs concludes her elegy on the two dead lovers, refer to ʿĀida and Rādamīs as *shahīdā gharām* (love's martyrs), thereby placing the story of ʿĀida within the context of traditional, Arabic love poetry and presenting ʿĀida and Rādamīs as figures of traditional *ʿudhrī* (idealized) love. This may help to explain why the play attained such popularity in Egypt and indeed in the Arab world (as it was performed by Abū Khalīl al-Qabbānī several times in Damascus).[10] The theme of a young man giving up everything – military glory, the offer of marriage to the royal princess who is madly in love with him, the prospect of the throne of Egypt and even life itself, for the sake of the woman he loves – was found captivating by the Arab audiences who were also charmed by tunes of popular songs, later to be replaced by the work of one of the most popular singers of the day, Salāma Ḥijāzī.

The same use of the non-dramatic, traditional poetry of love and boasting is found in *Mayy aw Horace*. The theme of the play is, of course, love and war, and the inevitable conflict (which ensues) between love and duty. Horace, the Roman, is married to Malaka who comes from Alba and whose brother, Curiace, is betrothed to Horace's sister, Mayy. When war breaks out between Rome and Alba the men have to fight one another in single combat. Horace kills Curiace much to Mayy's horror and, shocked at the unpatriotic reaction of his own sister, he kills her in a fit of uncontrollable anger, but is pardoned in the end by the King in recognition of his heroic services to his country.

It is clear that the story outline of Corneille's play is kept and with it the main (historical) characters: King Tulle, Horace's father and son and Curiace. However, the King is given a vizier by al-Naqqāsh; the names of some characters are changed: Valère becomes Qayṣar, Sabine and Camille are Arabized becoming Malaka and Mayy respectively and their confidante, Julie, becomes Rogina, a servant in the household of Horace's father. The Alban soldier, Flavian, is dropped and Procule, the Roman soldier, appears as Iskandar. Al-Naqqāsh also adds a chorus consisting of the King's retainers, but they hardly say anything until towards the end of the play when they join in singing a hymn of praise for the King and vizier in the true Arab manner.

As in *ʿĀida* the love interest is dominant. Unlike the original Valère, Qayṣar, who is Curiace's somewhat unprincipled rival for the affection of Mayy, makes his feelings abundantly clear, pesters Mayy with his unwelcome attentions and challenges Curiace to two duels. In spite of the emotionalism and sentimentality of much of the love poetry, the dialogue tends to be excessively formalized and cold, the use of stichomythia abounding as in the farewell scene in which the young warriors, Horace and Curiace, take leave of their mistresses before going to battle (p.113). But, of course, we must remember that much of the dialogue is meant to be sung which has an adverse effect on its dramatic quality and naturalness.

In *ʿĀida* and *Mayy* the lovers die in tragic circumstances but this is not so in *al-Ẓalūm* ('The Tyrant'), which, despite its happy ending, has much in common with *ʿĀida*. The King's son, Iskandar, the tyrant of the play's title, falls in love with Asmā, the orphaned commoner, who does not requite his love because she has lost her heart to Salīm, the nephew of Lubnā, the dead Queen's midwife. Salīm is offered riches by Iskandar in return for giving up Asmā, but he refuses the offer and prefers to endure jail and torture for his love. Likewise, Asmā rejects the attentions of the King's son and chooses to suffer in jail instead. Iskandar does not hesitate to employ all manner of dirty tricks to achieve his end. He lies and tells each of the lovers that the other has been killed by him as punishment for their obstinacy, and each of the lovers tries without success to get the jailer to buy them poison, under cover of medicine, in order to commit suicide. Realizing her true intention Asmā's jailer brings her some harmless powder. Salīm also escapes death as the King, unaware of his son's actions, orders him to be set free. Iskandar does not give up and proceeds to plot to kill Salīm, but after a series of complications, wild adventures and improbable events all ends happily. It is discovered that none of the young people are who they are assumed to be. Asmā is revealed to be the King's daughter, Salīm, the vizier's son, while Iskandar turns out to be the midwife's nephew. The lies about their identity were invented to please the dead Queen, who, having given birth to a baby girl, decided to swap her for a boy in order to give the King greater pleasure. The midwife, who was the only person who knew the truth, keeps it secret until she decides she can reveal it at this stage. In the end all are forgiven. Salīm marries Asmā and they are both proclaimed heirs to the throne.

In its rather primitive structure, its complications and improbabilities, the work has many of the ingredients of a popular medieval romance. The characters are painted in black and white: Iskandar, the tyrant, is all bad while Salīm and Asmā are idealized lovers (in fact the play was known also as *Salīm wa Asmā*). Again, despite the abundance of melodrama, the dialogue is full of traditional, non-dramatic poetry in which the speakers complain of the pangs of love, of the wickedness of tyrants or the harshness of fate.

Like *al-Ẓalūm, Gharā'ib al-Ṣudaf* ('Strange Coincidences), known also as *Ḥifẓ al-Widād* ('Faithfulness') is a tale of love, adventure, improbabilities and coincidences, as the title suggests, but is set against the background of a nationalist uprising in India. Thanks to the miraculous interference of a grateful Indian all ends happily for the European characters, English and French alike. The dialogue is mainly in prose interspersed with verse, but interestingly enough the prose here is generally free from the fetters and artificialities of the customary *saj*ʿ.

As for the last play, *al-Kadhūb* ('The Liar'), it did not prove successful after its first performance. As has been said, it is based on Corneille's play, but unlike Dorante in *Le Menteur*, Dīb does not in any way gain our sympathy but is a thoroughly evil man who deserves punishment for his wicked lies. The play ends with the moral, uttered by all the characters on the stage and addressed to the audience, that lying is a wicked vice and that a liar is bound to fail.[11]

It is clear from the preceding account that Salīm al-Naqqāsh's contribution is in no way an improvement upon the work of his uncle from the point of view of dramatic structure or characterization, although it sheds considerable light on the type of plays the Arab audiences saw and which helped to form their taste. Several things become clear: the dominance of love themes, the romantic quality of events, the passion for singing as well as the overtly didactic and moral function of drama. Like his uncle, Salīm believed that drama was meant to portray virtue in an attractive light, thereby encouraging people to follow it, and to show clearly the disastrous consequences of vice so that they could avoid it.[12] But the moral function of drama is conceived rather crudely; as we have seen, it often takes the form of moral precepts explicitly stated in a direct address to the audience at the end of a play.

AḤMAD ABŪ KHALĪL AL-QABBĀNĪ

In Egypt, Salīim al-Naqqāsh enlisted the help of his fellow Lebanese friend, Adīb Isḥāq, who had already translated Racine's *Andromaque* (in the usual mixture of prose and verse with songs added) at the suggestion of the French Consul in Beirut. Isḥāq joined him in Alexandria where for a while they co-operated in theatrical activities but soon (in 1877) they turned away from the theatre becoming engrossed in political journalism. However, one of the actors in Salīm al-Naqqāsh's company, Yūsuf al-Khayyāṭ, took over the management of the company in 1877 and began his productions at the Zizinya theatre in Alexandria, and in 1879 moved to Cairo where his company produced 'Abū'l-

Ḥasan the Fool' at the Cairo Opera House before the Khedive and his court. It is reported that a subsequent performance of 'The Tyrant' had incurred the wrath of the Khedive who imagined that the play implied a criticism of his own tyrannical rule of Egypt.[13] Khayyāṭ withdrew from Cairo but he did not give up the stage; after a checkered career, during which he gave performances in Alexandria and Cairo as well as in provincial towns such as Zagazig, Tanta, Mansura, Damanhur, Damietta, Benha and Meit Ghamr, he seemed to cease acting in 1890.

In 1882 one of the actors in Khayyāṭ's troupe, Sulaymān Qurdāḥī, decided to set up a troupe of his own in Alexandria. He had several successful seasons in Alexandria and Cairo, performing at the Zinzinya theatre and at the Cairo Opera House, winning the admiration of the distinguished audiences, particularly in Cairo with his productions of Arabic translations as well as original plays. He too toured the provinces both in Lower and Upper Egypt: Assiuyt, Mansura and Tanta, Zagazig and Mahalla al-Kubra; he even took his troupe to North Africa: Tunisia, Algeria and in Tunisia he founded the Arabic theatre. His activities came to an end with his death in 1909.

Many of the plays which Qurdāḥī's repertoire included were the work of the Syrian actor/dramatist Aḥmad Abū Khalīl al-Qabbānī (1833–1902), who is regarded as the father of the Syrian theatre. Al-Qabbānī, a product of traditional Islamic education, knew no European language. Probably inspired by the example set by Mārūn al-Naqqāsh in Beirut, he tried to establish Arabic theatre in Damascus sometime during the 1870s.[14] Together with works by Mārūn and Salīm al-Naqqāsh, he produced plays of his own which were derived from Arab and Islamic heritage and folk tales and contained much singing, music and dancing of which he was very fond. He first met with some success and was even encouraged by the authorities, particularly the Turkish ruler, Midḥat Pacha, who commissioned Iskandar Faraḥ to form a theatre troupe in Damascus of which al-Qabbānī was to be an important member. However, after a while al-Qabbānī was opposed by extremist religious and puritanical factions who forced him to close his theatre and to bring his activities to an end. In 1884, encouraged by an Alexandrian/Syrian friend, he moved his troupe to Alexandria where he began to produce his plays at the Zizinya theatre and Danube café. Soon he was able to act in Cairo, even at the Opera House and subsequently in the provincial towns of Egypt. He continued to be active until 1900 when, after the burning of his own theatre, he returned to Damascus where he retired on a state pension.[15]

According to one authority,[16] the number of plays performed by al-Qabbānī totals thirty-one. Of these fifteen were his own work, while the rest were either written by other Arab authors ranging from Mārūn al-Naqqāsh to Najīb al-Ḥaddād or freely translated from plays by European playwrights, notably Corneille, Racine, Victor Hugo and Alexandre Dumas. Interestingly enough they include one play, based on a contemporary or recent important event in

Egyptian history, the ʿUrābī revolution, entitled *ʿUrābī Pacha* written by Muḥammad al-ʿAbbādī, now unfortunately lost.

The first play which al-Qabbānī wrote is entitled *Nākir al-Jamīl* ('The Ungrateful Man'). He revived it no fewer than six times in his acting career, yet it shows remarkably little dramatic insight, being both episodic in structure and excessively verbose in dialogue, a dialogue which consists in the main of inordinately long monologues full of conventional wisdom sayings and general observations. The theme is the ingratitude of a destitute young man named Ghādīr to Ḥalīm, the vizier's son, who, against the advice of his mentor Nāṣir, befriends him, adopting him as his intimate companion and sharing his wordly possessions with him. Ghādir plots Ḥalīm's murder because he resents being bound to him and feeling subservient to him, but his plot misfires and by mistake he kills Ḥabīb, the King's son, instead. He simulates deep grief and regret at what he has done and persuades Ḥalīm to help him, and in order to turn suspicions away from himself he gives him the dagger he has used. In the mean time he treacherously convinces the King that his son's killer is Ḥalīm since the blood-stained dagger is found with him. The aggrieved king orders Ḥalīm's execution and is led to believe that the order has been carried out but later, in his sleep he sees a vision from which he learns of Ḥalīm's innocence and Ghādir's villainy, when he is visited by the ghost of Ḥalīm who has come to trouble his conscience for the unjust sentence. The King tells the executioner he wishes he could see Ḥalīm again, whereupon the executioner, who has been bribed by the vizier to spare his son's life, promises to bring Ḥalīm alive before the King. The contrite King is delighted to see Ḥalīm again, and recompenses him with the offer of his own daughter as a wife. To the astonishment of all, Ḥalīm pleads with the King on behalf of Ghādir, who is then forgiven by him.

The play is written in a mixture of verse and rhyming prose, which is meant to be sung. The characters are crude types whose names suggest their dominant quality. Ghādir means 'treacherous', Ḥalīm 'forbearing and forgiving', Ḥabīb 'beloved', Nāṣir 'supporter' and so forth. There is no attempt at psychological analysis and despite the excessively long and wordy speeches, characters do not even begin to explain their motives. They inhabit the world of folk tales, where verisimilitude is rather irrelevant. For instance, Ḥalīm is forgiving to the point of utter folly, but because he is called Ḥalīm this doesn't seem to matter. Equally, the action takes place in a timeless world of nowhere in particular. In fact, it did not require much effort for the first publisher of the play to turn it into a narrative work (so undramatic is the quality of the writing), for it was first published not in the form of a play but as a short novel.[17] Like other plays by al-Qabbānī, 'The Ungrateful Man' ends with praising the Sultan and the local ruler.

Despite the Arabic names of its characters 'The Ungrateful Man' may well have been derived from the plot of a western original. In the next play, *Ḥiyal al-Nisā'* ('The Trickeries of Women'), known as *Lūsiya* ('Lucia'), it is safer to assume that the source is European, judging at least by the European names of characters as well as the setting. Lucia, the wife of Count Frederick Governor of Messina, is in love with her husband's nephew, Jean, who does not requite her feeling but is in love with her stepdaughter, Eugène. His rival for Eugène's love is the Count's secretary, Emile. The Count proceeds to marry his daughter Eugène to Jean as they are deeply in love with one another. The frustrated Lucia and Emile plot to destroy the young married couple, but fail in their attempts and are punished by the Count who puts them in jail. In the mean time, Eugène (who has fled for her life from her stepmother), her accomplice and her baby son, together with her husband, hitherto assumed to have drowned in the sea, all miraculously run into each other in the wilderness and are united with the Count. The Count is prevailed upon by his daughter to forgive the wicked Lucia and Emile.

Like 'The Ungrateful Man', this play, which starts reasonably well, soon develops into a popular romance full of improbable events and ends happily with the unbelievable forgiveness of the wicked characters and a prayer for the Sultan. One interesting addition is the introduction of four drunken clowns who appear from nowhere just at the time when Emile is about to murder Eugène, thereby saving her life and forcing him to listen to their joking and singing.[18]

A similar, obvious intrusion of singing and drinking occurs in *ʿAfīfa* ('The Chaste Woman'), where two whole scenes (Act IV, Scenes I, II)[19] are taken up by a drinking party at which songs including bits from well-known, classical, Arabic poems and *muwashshaḥāt* (strophic poems of Andalusian origin) are sung. The only justification for these scenes is to provide an excuse for the singing which the audience loved so much. *ʿAfīfa* is al-Qabbānī's version of the theme of *Geneviève*, although the European original has not yet been precisely identified.[20]

ʿAfīfa, an ex-slave girl is freed by her master, Prince ʿAlī, who subsequently marries her, but their blissful married life is interrupted by the Prince's decision to go to war to rescue a fellow Prince in trouble. Before his departure he appoints his trusted friend, Salīm, as his deputy to run the state and to look after his wife in his absence. Salīm falls in love with ʿAfīfa who repulses his unwelcome attentions in disgust and indignation. Realizing that she is absolutely incapable of having an adulterous relationship with him, the frustrated Salīm puts her in jail and sends a message to the Prince saying that she has been unfaithful to him and that the fruit of her adultery is a baby son. The Prince promptly tells him to put both mother and child to death at once. However, when he returns victorious from war, Prince ʿAlī is shocked to find his erstwhile, trusted friend drunk and he then learns the truth about his faithful wife. Fortunately as the death sentence has not been carried out she and her child are rescued in the nick of time and reunited with the Prince who shoots his false friend.

Despite the emotionalism and tearful scenes, the play is not dramatic enough. It is episodic in structure and lacks convincing characterization. Many of the speeches sound like sermons. For instance, on discovering that Salīm, who has been entrusted by her noble husband to run the country in his absence, is lusting after her and wants her to commit adultery with him, ʿAfīfa gives us a soliloquy, which, far from describing her feelings at the moment, is in effect a sermon on good and evil.[21] Similarly, the play ends with a speech by the Prince in which he emphasizes the need to follow virtue and avoid vice, by learning from the good example of his faithful wife and the bad end of his false friend.

A similar combination of love, treachery and war is to be found in *Lubāb al-Gharām aw al-Malik Mitridāt* ('The Quintessence of Love or King Mithridate'), which is al-Qabbānī's version of Racine's tragedy, *Mithridate*. Since al-Qabbānī knew no French he must have relied upon a translation, written or oral, of the French play. Here is an outline of Racine's play. The aged Mithridate, King of Pontus, infatuated with a young Greek Princess from Ephesus, Monime, who having accepted his gift of a royal diadem, has agreed to marry him and comes to his court. Before Mithridate has the chance to consummate the marriage he is obliged to go away to fight Pompey. He is defeated and falsely reported dead, whereupon his son, Pharnace, tries to force Monime, with whom he is in love, to marry him. Monime who hates him refuses and appeals for help to his half-brother, Xiphares, whom she loves and who returns her love. A quarrel ensues between the brothers in the middle of which Mithridate unexpectedly returns and is furious to learn of Pharnace's conduct. To test him he explains his plan to invade Italy and to marry him to a Parthian Princess in order to obtain Parthian support. Pharnace refuses to go and is promptly arrested; so he reveals that not only he but Xiphares too loves Monime. Through sheer cunning Mithridate discovers that Monime returns Xiphares's love and that she now prefers death to marrying the King. Incensed, Mithridate orders her death by poison. In the mean time, Pharnace rebels and leads a Roman army against his own father who sensing defeat stabs himself. Xiphares, however, crushes the Romans, rescues his father who, before he dies, manages to save Monime and to bless her marriage to Xiphares. In its essentials Racine's plot is followed by al-Qabbānī, except that contrary to historical fact he kills Pharnace. He also invents a prison scene in which the two brothers and the young woman are shown locked up, and railing against Fate. Events are rushed through with little sense of dramatic plausibility as Abul Naga puts it:

> In the space of twenty-four hours Monime arrives in Pontus, after which Mithridate declares war on the Romans, marches to the encounter, engages in battle, loses it, escapes and then recovers his land. He imprisons his sons and his betrothed (fiancée), pardons Pharnace who joins the enemy forces and returns to the palace where he meets with his death. The King engages in another battle, tries to commit suicide while the Romans are defeated by Xiphares whom they proclaim King of the Romans as well as the Greeks![22]

Unlike the original, the Arabic play, as the title indicates, makes love the dominant interest, reduces the tragic inner-conflict, flattens characters and provides a happy ending in which not only are the lovers united and the good son, Xiphares, crowned, but the wicked Pharnace is killed. The two outstanding characters in Racine's play, Mithridate and Monime, are simplified to the point of distortion. Monime, who is a mixture of charm, modesty, pride and courage, is reduced to a weak and tearful female, lamenting her pitiable fate. As for Mithridate, he appears as a selfish tyrant who is in no way torn between his tender feelings for his own children and his passion for the young woman. The author has largely turned the plot into a number of situations in which, in conventional lyrical verse, characters either complain of love or Fate, or else boast of their military prowess. After a detailed comparison between Racine's tragedy and al-Qabbānī's play, one scholar arrived at the conclusion that in the latter 'instead of character analysis we have songs and sermons, instead of sentiment violent emotion, and tragic fear is replaced by terror. In short tragedy is demoted to melodrama'.[23] It was precisely because of these factors, namely its lack of complex characterization, the dominance of singing and its melodrama, that the play proved so popular with the semi-literate Arab audience of the time.

It is time now to turn to the published plays which al-Qabbānī derived from traditional Arab sources to see if they are different from his adaptations of western drama. *Hārūn al-Rashīd maʿa Uns al-Jalīs* ('Harūn al-Rashīd with Uns al-Jalīs'), which is based on the forty-fifth night of the *Arabian Nights*, seems to have been one of his most popular plays. Between 1884 and 1890 it was revived twenty-three times. Al-Muʿīn ibn Ṣāwī, the vizier of Prince Ibn Sulaymān of Basra, becomes jealous of his colleague al-Faḍl Ibn Khāqān because he is convinced that the latter is the Prince's favourite and he therefore plots his downfall. A chance presents itself when al-Faḍl allows his son ʿAlī Nūr al-Dīn to marry Uns al-Jalīs, the beautiful and accomplished slave girl whom al-Faḍl has been commissioned to buy for the Prince, and with whom ʿAlī has fallen desperately in love. At the instigation of al-Muʿīn, who forges a letter from the Caliph ordering the death of al-Faḍl and his son, the incensed Prince imprisons al-Faḍl, seizes his property and is about to put him and his son to death when at the eleventh hour the Caliph intervenes for, by a series of adventures, ʿAlī and his wife Uns al-Jalīs have been able to see him and impress him with the justice of their case. Muʿīn and Ibn Sulaymān are punished by life-imprisonment, al-Faḍl is promoted to the post of Governor of Basra and the young couple are generously recompensed by the Caliph.

Contrary to what Professor Najm claims,[24] the story of the play varies from the *Arabian Nights* version in some important details designed largely to make the character of ʿAlī more sympathetic, while the events are telescoped in order to render the work somewhat more dramatic. Nevertheless, the play is not dramatic enough and once more it is largely an excuse for singing. However, while it shares with other plays the jail scenes which provide ample opportunity for tear-jerking, self-pitying verse, it differs from most of them in that it is not mainly about love; al-Muʿīn's destructive jealousy is certainly an important component, even though the author does not allow himself sufficient room to portray it in a convincing manner.

The theme of love and the ensuing improbable adventures are dominant again in the other published plays of al-Qabbānī. In *Hārūn al-Rashīd maʿa'l-Amīr Ghānim ibn Ayyūb wa Qūt al-Qulūb* ('Hārūn al-Rashīd with Prince Ghānim ibn Ayyūb and Qūt al-Qulūb'), he derives the story from the fifty-second night of the *Arabian Nights*. Ghānim, a Syrian merchant just settled in Baghdad, finds himself locked out of the city at night and takes refuge from robbers in an outlying cemetery. He climbs up a tree to hide when he sees some black slaves approaching carrying a box which they deposit in a cave. Ghānim decides to examine the box and finds a drugged woman in it whom he rescues and takes to his house. He later learns that she is none other than Qūt al-Qulūb, the favourite concubine of the Caliph Hārūn al-Rashīd, whom the Caliph's jealous wife wanted to get rid of. The Caliph is told that she has died, but while mourning her death he is informed by one of the female slaves that she is still alive and living in the house of the young Syrian merchant, Ghānim. The incensed Caliph orders that the young couple should be arrested and put to death. Ghānim escapes, while Qūt al-Qulūb is put in jail, but just as she is about to be executed, the Caliph discovers that she has not been unfaithful to him, for as soon as Ghānim learnt of her relationship with the Caliph he overcame his love for her and refrained from touching her. The Caliph immediately forgives them and sets her free so that she can search for Ghānim in order to marry him. Prior to that on the Caliph's orders, Ghānim's house in Syria had been raided and his possessions confiscated by the police. Ghānim's mother and sister, now destitute, set out on a desperate journey looking for Ghānim. By a series of miracles, Ghānim, who has been roaming the land as a fugitive falls ill, is picked up and nursed by a good Samaritan named Ṣāliḥ, and is finally reunited in Ṣaliḥ's house with his mother and sister, and also with his beloved Qūt al-Qulūb. The Caliph himself appears at the moment of their reunion and the play ends happily not only with the marriage of the lovers, but also with the Caliph marrying Ghānim's sister.

Clearly, this is not real drama, but a popular tale linked together by improbable events; the story is narrated by several voices and concluded happily when virtue is rewarded. Even the figure of the scheming old woman-servant of the traditional folk-tale is there in the form of the maid who helps persuade the Caliph that Qūt al-Qulūb has died and who, incidentally, is punished by death on the Caliph's orders. There is no proper dialogue, but only set speeches. Characters address the audience directly in the form of soliloquies in which they give the necessary information about themselves or render an account of what has happened.[25] There is no real characterization; characters do not develop or interact. They change their feelings too quickly, are too soon persuaded or shift their positions suddenly without any attempt to provide adequate motivation. For instance, when the enamoured Ghānim courts Qūt al-Qulūb she does not respond to him saying that she belongs to another man, the Caliph, yet in the same scene she falls for him and woos him only this time it is his turn to resist the temptation. Another example is seen when the Caliph suddenly forgives Qūt al-Qulūb at the very moment his executioner is ready to kill her, simply because she tells him that she has not been unfaithful to him. Again, the action of the play is a scaffolding for the main object of the work which is clearly singing.

The same features of popular tales are found in the play *al-Amīr Maḥmūd Najl Shah al-ʿAjam* ('Prince Maḥmūd, son of the Shah of Persia'), which was revived by al-Qabbānī no fewer than eleven times. Prince Maḥmūd falls hopelessly in love with the picture of a beautiful woman and, disregarding the advice and even the threats of his father, sets out on a journey to look for the original of the picture. His travels take him to India where by chance he learns of an impending Persian invasion. Using his influence, the Prince stops the invasion and in gratitude the King of India offers him the highest military office in the land and his own daughter in marriage. However, the Prince declines and explains the nature of his quest. He is enabled by a clever device to discover the identity of the woman who turns out to be the daughter of the King of China. The grateful Indian King gives him 'supernatural' assistance to enable him to go to China where he kills the genie who forced the King of China to offer him his daughter for a wife and ends by marrying her himself amidst celebrations attended by the Kings of Persia, India and China, their viziers and courtiers, as well as the grand magician of India, who has managed to remove all the obstacles in their path.

Once more the play is about love, with the subject of war occupying only a few lines; interesting additions, however, are the elements of magic and the supernatural which, together with the folk theme of falling in love with the picture of a woman, put the work securely on the level of the popular folk-tale. There is also humour provided by the low life characters: beggars, impecunious Shaykhs frequenting the free public baths and singing about the sumptuous dishes they are dreaming of eating: an element of relative realism in a work otherwise of pure fantasy and utter improbability.

Magic also features in the last play to be considered here *ʿAntar Ibn Shaddād* ('ʿAntar Ibn Shaddād') which was revived by al-Qabbānī fifteen times between 1884 and 1890. Based upon the popular medieval romance, it treats a period in the life of the semi-mythical hero, the black slave ʿAntara and describes his victory over his rival, the tribal chief, Masʿūd, who insults ʿAntara by proposing to his wife ʿAbla with whom he has fallen in love and who, he claims, was married against her wishes to ʿAntara. There is an amusing scene in which Suʿād, the wife of Masʿūd's tribesman, uses black magic to bewitch ʿAbla, by raising four genii (Act II, Scene I) to accomplish her designs. Her magic works for a moment but the spell is broken by the counter-magic of a friend of ʿAntar's who kills her with his sword.[26]

This is perhaps the least satisfactory of al-Qabbānī's plays. No fewer than twenty-five characters appear in the list of *dramatis personae* in what is, after all, one of his shortest plays. There is plenty of ranting and much complaining about the pangs of love, but there is hardly any characterization and the events of the play are not sufficiently developed; wars are waged, fought and won in the space of a few lines. Once more we are presented with the world of the popular tale where songs about love and war abound.

It is clear that as far as dramatic technique is concerned, neither Salīm al-Naqqāsh nor al-Qabbānī (despite Muḥammad Mandūr's enthusiastic remarks about his work[27]) advanced a great deal beyond the art of Mārūn al-Naqqāsh or Yaʿqūb Ṣannūʿ. Their contribution, however, consisted in strengthening certain aspects of theatrical activity and what became the dramatic tradition in Egypt, namely: singing and music, the predominance of the theme of love and emotionalism both in the plays with happy endings and those (fewer in number) which end tragically. Al-Qabbānī, in particular, because of the great musical talents he employed in the production of his plays, helped to popularize musical drama in Egypt and the whole Arab world. Moreover, because of his more traditional, cultural upbringing and background and his greater command of the Arabic language, he also played a considerable role in establishing the tradition of regarding the cultural and literary heritage of the Arabs, including the *Arabian Nights*, as a constant source of inspiration for Arab dramatists.

THE LEGACY OF THE SYRIAN PIONEERS

Al-Qabbānī's collaborator, Iskandar Faraḥ, accompanied him when he moved to Egypt and continued to give him administrative and moral support for several years, until he decided to set up a company of his own in Cairo in 1891. The company proved a success, partly because of its varied repertoire and partly on account of the distinguished and popular actors and actresses which it included. These, in the course of Faraḥ's long career in the theatre from 1891–1908, included Salāma Ḥijāzī (1852–1917) and later Najīb al-Riḥānī (1891–1949).

Salāma Ḥijāzī, who came from a thoroughly traditional Islamic background, had from his early youth developed a passion for singing mystical *ṣūfī* songs and chanting and reciting the Koran. His outstanding voice, which later became almost legendary, enabled him to embark on a career first as a singer, then as an actor in Yūsuf al-Khayyāṭ's troupe and subsequently as an actor in Qurdāḥī's and Faraḥ's troupe. In 1905 he formed a troupe of his own and his performances, as Rādamīs in *ʿĀida* and as Romeo in Najīb al-Ḥaddād's translation of

Shakespeare's *Romeo and Juliet* (which in Arabic was given the title *Shuhadā' al-Gharām*, 'Love's Martyrs') became the talk of the town, in particular his excellent singing in these roles. He suffered a stroke in 1909 and after recuperating joined the company of Jūrj Abyaḍ (1880–1959).

With Abyaḍ we enter a new phase in the history of the Egyptian theatre. For the first time we encounter an Arab actor who received a proper professional training and who, for a while at any rate, produced plays without the intrusion of singing. Born in Beirut, he was educated at the Ḥikma school where he used to act in the annual school play. In 1898 he moved to Alexandria where he had the opportunity to see the Arabic productions of the troupes of Iskandar Faraḥ and Salāma Ḥijāzī, and to join an amateur dramatic society. In 1904 he managed to obtain a bursary for theatre studies at the Conservatoire in Paris at the expense of Khedive Abbas. After a long training, reportedly supervised by the celebrated actor Sylvain, he returned to Egypt in 1910 with a French troupe which put on *Tartuffe, Horace* and *Andromaque* among other French plays. In 1912, Abyaḍ turned to Arabic acting and at the request of Sa'd Zaghlūl, who was Minister of Education at the time, he formed a troupe which became noted for its productions of several western classics in good, literary translations such as Sophocles's *Oedipus* (translated by Faraḥ Antūn), Shakespeare's *Othello* (translated by the distinguished poet, Khalīl Muṭrān), Molière's *Tartuffe* (in the superb Arabized version *al-Shaykh Matlūf* by the gifted 'Uthmān Jalāl). Abyaḍ's troupe was later amalgamated, first with that of 'Ukāsha (1913), and then with Salāma Ḥijāzī (1914). The troupe continued to produce translations or adaptations of old classics as well as modern plays set in contemporary Egypt.

Other troupes appeared, one of the most important of which was that of 'Azīz 'Īd, who joined Iskandar Faraḥ in 1905 before setting up his own troupe in 1907, and began a distinguished career both as actor and as producer. He tended to specialize in comedy and encouraged particularly the efforts of local playwrights in writing modern Egyptian drama dealing with problems of Egyptian society faced by Egyptian characters. In fact, the closing years of the nineteenth century and the first two decades of the twentieth century witnessed the rise of a large number of theatrical companies and these now included many Egyptian actors and playwrights. Some of these companies proved short-lived and not all performed in proper theatres built specifically for the purpose, but at times performances were given in cafés. Apart from notices in newspapers and other periodicals, there are several contemporary allusions to the proliferation of theatres and theatrical companies. In a play written in 1913 by 'Abbās 'Allām *Asrār al Quṣūr* ('The Secrets of Palaces') we learn from one character that the number of theatrical troupes in Egypt at the time was 'as much as could be counted on the fingers of both hands'.[28] Clearly the theatre had come to stay; from now on it was to become a permanent feature of Egyptian, urban life.

Indeed as early as 1900 the Egyptian theatre had already become a political force of some significance. Original plays dealing with recent political events such as *ʿUrabī Pacha* ('ʿUrabī Pacha') (1900) or *Dinshawāy* ('Dinshawāy') (1906) were at times banned by the censor. In 1908 a play entitled *Fī Sabīl al-Istiqlāl* ('For the Sake of Independence') written by Ibrahīm Salīm al-Najjār, was for a while intercepted because it portrayed Muhammad Alī and the Turks unsympathetically. Translated plays were also treated with suspicion by the British authorities if they contained matter which could be regarded as capable of inflaming nationalist feelings: an example is Victorien Sardou's *La Patrie* which was given the significant title *Shuhadā' al-Waṭaniyya* ('The Martyrs of Patriotism') by the translator, Zakī Mabrū (1900). Some plays, however, were allowed although they still dealt with contemporary events: for example, *Patriotism* (1900), *The Heroes of Freedom* (1908) and *Musṭafā Kāmil* (1908).[29]

The list of theatres which Professor Najm gives in his valuable study of Arabic drama (and we must remember that the study is limited to the period up to 1914)[30] contains no fewer than twenty-eight theatres which at some time or other existed in Egypt mainly, but not exclusively, in Cairo and Alexandria. In these theatres were performed not only musicals, translations and adaptations of western drama and serious, original Arabic plays, but also farces which were a development of the traditional, crude *faṣl muḍḥik* (comic act) which we encountered in Chapter One, and which at the same time betrayed the influence of the Italian *commedia dell'arte*. Prominent actors, particularly Egyptians, began to appear in increasing numbers, forming their own troupes or merging with those of other actors. One of the most distinguished was the rich, young Yūsuf Wahbī who, having received his training in Italy, returned to form Ramsīs troupe (1923) and for a while he merged with Abyaḍ. Even Muslim women began to enter the world of acting, such as Fāṭima Rushdī, who came from a traditional Muslim background with no knowledge of a European language. Like Abyaḍ and Wahbī, who tended to play tragic or melodramatic and historical parts, the comedians ʿAlī al-Kassār and Najīb al-Rīḥānī attained great fame not only in Egypt, but throughout the Arab world.

Jūrj Abyaḍ was only an actor, albeit a memorable one. He popularized Arabic translations of western drama, notably Sophocles's *Oedipus Rex*, Shakespeare's *Othello* and Casimir Delavigne's *Louis XI*, his favourite plays, but he neither wrote plays himself, nor did he create any stage characters. Yūsuf Wahbī (1896–), on the other hand, who dominated the Egyptian stage for more than four decades, adapted a huge number of French melodramas and wrote some himself, including one which attained unprecedented popularity, *Awlād al-Fuqarā* ('Children of the Poor'), a tear-jerking melodrama with an exceedingly complicated plot, revealing the inhumane treatment of the poor and even their poor relations, by the rich. It includes all the social horrors and heart-rending situations imaginable: seduction, illegitimacy, deception, shooting for revenge, imprisonment, drug addiction, drunkenness, prostitution, venereal disease, the chance meeting of long-lost relatives, repentance and mercy killing.[31] ʿAlī al-Kassār specialised in revues which attracted a large audience, particularly from the lower classes, with his presentation of the character, *al-Barbarī* (the Blackie), a Nubian clown who made fun of every social type in Egypt, Arab and non-Arab alike. A much more subtle creation was the character of Kish Kish Bey, invented and played by al-Rīḥānī also in the review theatre; Kish Kish Bey was a village headman (*ʿumdah*), whose innocence and weakness (especially his susceptibility to female charm) exposed him to a series of misadventures in the capital city of Cairo, where he fell an easy prey to conmen. He 'reflected the commonsense attitude of the simple man to all matters concerning world developments, state affairs, social conditions and morals'.[32] Al-Rīḥānī continued to use Kish Kish Bey in one sketch after another as a symbol of the little man surrounded by a corrupt world whose falsehood, materialism and greed were brought into focus more sharply when set against the little man's basic goodness. Working in close co-operation with Badīʿ Khayrī, al-Rīḥānī borrowed his stories from French drama and used much of the technique of the French farce, but the atmosphere and character he Egyptianized so thoroughly that Kish Kish Bey became a much better known figure to Egyptians and other Arabs than most characters from Arabic drama. His art is shown at its best in his most popular work, which he wrote in his more mature period in 1943, again in collaboration with Khayrī, *Ḥasan, Murqus and Cohen*, a hilarious comedy, inspired by Tristan Bernard's *Le Petit Café*. Here al-Rīḥānī lashes out at his favourite target, the spread of hypocrisy and materialism, by showing how their common greed and love of money drive a Muslim, a Christian and a Jew to conspire together to rob an unsuspecting innocent man. Al-Rīḥānī, generally regarded as the greatest comedian to appear on the Egyptian stage, was the last in the tradition of the revue entertainer/actor/manager/author, who successfully combined the methods of the French farce with the traditional Egyptian forms of popular, comic entertainment arising from the age-old *faṣl muḍḥik*.

4

THE SEARCH FOR EGYPTIAN IDENTITY

ADAPTATIONS: ʿUTHMĀN JALĀL

The student of Arabic drama will notice that a large proportion of the plays performed in Egypt during this early stage in the development of the Egyptian theatre consisted of translations from western drama, which were predominantly French at first, but were later to include English plays, mainly Shakespeare's. However, even when the original European play was a well-known classic, the Arabic version was almost always a free adaptation rather than a faithful translation. It was considerably later that the classics of European drama were performed in anything like their original form. This is not at all surprising, particularly in view of the fact that drama in its western form was not known in the Arab Middle East. Even in cultures which had a strong dramatic tradition of long standing, the work of a foreign dramatist was, as a rule, first performed in adaptations of varying degrees of freedom. The study of the fortunes of, for instance, Shakespeare outside the English-speaking world has shown that what happened to his work in Arabic was not altogether dissimilar to the treatment it had received in India or even France or Poland.[1] Foreign plays had to be fully Arabized and made palatable to the tastes of the local audience and public.

Furthermore, in Egypt the birth of modern drama coincided with the rise of national consciousness, and this provided an incentive not simply to Arabize, but to Egyptianize foreign works as well. It is no accident that the father of Egyptian drama, Yaʿqūb Ṣannūʿ, no less than other prominent figures in the early history of the Egyptian theatre such as Salīm al-Nāqqāsh, Adīb Isḥāq and ʿAbdallah Nadīm, turned to political journalism and became active in the Egyptian nationalist movement. The very slogan 'Egypt for the Egyptians' was attributed to Ṣannūʿ himself.

As is to be expected the attempt to give western plays a local colour often produced very amusing results, for it went beyond the occasional, simple device of giving characters Arabic names such as calling Othello, ʿ*Aṭallah*, or Caliban,

Ghalbān. Here are two interesting examples, both from translations of Shakespeare. The first is to be found in *Romeo and Juliet* which was presented in 1890 under the sub-title *Shuhadā' al-Gharām*. In the translation written by the voluminous translator and playwright, Najīb al-Ḥaddād (1867–99), in a loose mixture of verse and prose and posthumously published in 1901, we find that instead of giving us Shakespeare's opening scene, the translator makes Romeo come on the stage looking lovelorn and addressing the moon in a poem which answered all the requirements of traditional Arabic love poetry, and which is still remembered to this day because of the mellifluous voice in which the actor/singer Salāma Ḥijāzī sang it. The translator has provided a typical situation for the recitation of conventional, Arabic love poetry: the pining lover, unable to sleep at night, complains of his love pangs to the moon, the beauty of which reminds him of the face of his beloved. The plot is simplified, emphasizing the themes of love to the extent of excluding other important elements such as the feud between the two families which provides the background of social disorder against which the tragedy of the young lovers takes place. Consequently, the action does not begin with the street brawl, but with the meeting of the lovers in the Capulets' orchard. Similarly, the play does not end with the restoration of order in the form of the reconciliation of the old generation, but with the suicide of Romeo and Juliet and the additional suicide of Friar Laurence, much against the spirit of the play. After its action has been telescoped in this fashion and some of its characters such as the Montagues, omitted, the play emerges as a simple love story with a sad end and a number of melodramatic situations giving rise to fairly traditional poems on lovers' courtship, reunion, parting and death.[2]

The second instance occurs in an early translation of *Hamlet* (1901) by Ṭanyūs ʿAbduh who deemed it necessary to alter the end of the play in order to satisfy the taste of his audience who, he believed, would revolt against the unjust death of such a good and heroic character as the Prince of Denmark. The play, therefore, ends not with the death of Hamlet, but with the appearance of the ghost who commands him to ascend the throne. We are also given this stage direction: 'Hamlet ascends the steps leading to the throne while looking admiringly at his father's ghost. The ghost looks at Hamlet as it descends into the depths of the earth. The curtain falls slowly while singing is heard from within'.[3]

Yet, it must be pointed out that when the adaptation is truly successful its contribution to the technique and language of Egyptian drama cannot be exaggerated. The supreme example of this is the Egyptianization of Molière's comedies achieved by Muḥammad ʿUthmān Jalāl (1829–94), a product of the Bureau of Translation set up by the pioneer of Egyptian enlightenment, Rifāʿ Rāfiʿ al-Ṭahṭāwī. Jalāl published *al-Shaykh Matlūf* (his version of *Tartuffe*) first in a separate volume in 1290 H/1873, then together with his translation of three other comedies of Molière in 1889: *Les Femmes Savantes, L'Ecole des Maris* and

L'Ecole des Femmes. Seven years later *Les Facheux* was translated. He also published in 1311 H/1893 his translation of three tragedies by Racine; *Esther, Iphigénie* and *Alexandre le Grand*. A short, one-act play of his own *al-Khaddāmīn wa'l-Mukhaddimīn* ('Domestic Servants and their Agencies') was published posthumously in 1904. All of these plays Jalāl rendered into *zajal*, verse in the Egyptian spoken idiom.[4] As critics have noted[5], it was certainly a daring thing to do at the time, even to contemplate translating the august, French tragedies of Racine into the Egyptian colloquial. It must be admitted, however, that on the whole the attempt was not half as successful in Racine's tragedies as it was in the comedies of Molière, particularly in the case of *Tartuffe* which, contrary to Landau's assertion,[6] was a tremendous success, a *tour de force* almost, in which the reader is hardly aware, except in very few, almost unavoidable, details, that he is reading a non-Egyptian work. Unfortunately the first of these comedies to appear on the Egyptian stage was not *Tartuffe*, but *L'Ecole des Femmes* which was produced by Qurdāḥī in Alexandria in 1895, and because of the lack of relevance of its subject to Egyptian society at the time, it did not have much appeal for the Egyptian audience.

Different indeed was *al-Shaykh Matlūf* which, since its first production in Cairo by Jūrj Abyaḍ in 1912, has been a favourite with Egyptian audiences to this day. For instance, during the very successful season of 1958–9 of all plays performed by the Egyptian National Theatre Troupe, it drew by far the largest audience.[7] No doubt one reason for its popularity is the subject it deals with, namely the unmasking of the hypocrisy of professional men of religion, which is one of the recurrent themes in modern Egyptian literature in all its genres both in the literary and in the colloquial idiom, as we can see in works by writers as different as Muḥammad Ibrāhīm al-Muwayliḥī, Ṭāhā Ḥusayn, Muḥammad Ḥusayn Haykal, Tawfīq al-Ḥakīm and Bayram al-Tūnisī. But surely it is the complete Egyptianization of the French play, in language and in spirit, which accounts for its almost phenomenal success. One enthusiastic scholar wrote that in its splendid colloquial verse, its great poetic spirit and the degree to which it truly reflects the popular spirit of the Egyptian people, it stands equal to Molière's play.[8] It is not simply that Jalāl often manages to find the exact Egyptian equivalent to the French text but that he has thoroughly adapted the text, taking considerable liberties with it, faithfully following not its letter but its spirit and filling it out with significant details from Egyptian life, so much so that the final result can be described as a truly creative and inspired rendering of the French play. That is why it occupies such a distinguished place in the history of the Egyptian theatre, providing subsequent playwrights with an example to follow, not only of Molière's mature, dramatic techniques, structure and characterization, but also of the translator's subtle and skilful use of the Egyptian colloquial Arabic for finer comic ends. We have already seen how Ṣannūʿ made use of the potential of the Egyptian colloquial at about the same time, and indeed the language used by the maid, Bayhāna, in *al-Shaykh Matlūf* is just as colourful and as expressive of the speaker's character as that employed by the matchmaker, Mabrūka, in Ṣannūʿ's play *Abū Rīda*. But Ṣannūʿ's plays were unfortunately not performed after the demise of his theatre and indeed to all intents and purposes were not retrieved from oblivion until 1963, whereas Jalāl's work continued to appear on the stage and, therefore, to influence the course of Egyptian drama.[9]

Yet it is puzzling to find that when he came to write his own play, 'Domestic Servants and their Agencies', Jalāl seemed not to realize the need for dramatic structure. This short play, if it can be called that, consists of two brief acts. In Act I a gentleman goes to an agency to find a good, honest and reliable servant; a servant is found whom he fits out with a new set of clothes but when he takes him to his house, he discovers that the corrupt agent has given the servant instructions as to how to cheat his new master and share with him his ill-gotten gains, so he promptly dismisses him. Act II is taken up with the gentleman's attempt to employ another servant through another agency who turns out to be just as corrupt, and his plan to report the agency to the police. The play ends with the gentleman's decision to submit to the Khedive a French-inspired project of setting up responsible agencies in order to provide protection for employers under the law of the land. This brief, biting satire lacks all sense of drama, being merely episodic in structure without even sufficient length to build up to a climax. Yet the play has the same versatile use of colloquial verse, the same lively dialogue and Egyptian sense of humour as that which we find in Jalāl's adaptations. It also shares with them the same wealth of social detail, clearly the result of a great power in observing Egyptian social reality.

FARAḤ ANṬŪN

The need for drama to deal with the reality of Arab and indeed Egyptian society was stressed by articulate drama critics and theoreticians who also happened to be dramatists themselves: Faraḥ Anṭūn (1874–1922), Ibrāhīm Ramzī (1884–1949) and Muḥammad Taymūr (1892–1921). Faraḥ Anṭūn was one of the best informed and well-read journalists and men of letters of his generation; he contributed greatly towards freeing Arabic prose from the shackles of rhyme and similar artificial, rhetorical devices by his insistence upon the primacy of meaning and ideas in style. He published a number of articles on drama and literature in general and the specific needs of the Egyptian theatre in particular in several periodicals, including the magazine *al-Jāmiʿa* (1899–1906), which he edited himself.[10] Far from supporting the kind of play which aimed merely at entertainment, he advocated a serious type of drama which clearly set out to instruct and improve its audience, since he was a passionate believer in the morally didactic and civilizing force of the theatre and its role in character-building and in promoting respect for civic virtues, qualities which he felt the modern Arab needed more than anything else, and which, he felt, it was the duty of modern Arabic literature to provide.[11] Although later on in life, after his return from an unsuccessful sojourn in North America, he was driven by financial considerations to produce musical comedies, the drama which *al-Jāmiʿa* constantly asked for, he explained in his editorials, was social drama, what he called *al-riwāyāt al-ijtimāʿiyya*, or plays which dealt with the problems and issues of the age. He felt that even historical plays were something of a luxury as far as the Arabs were concerned, and in their usefulness to them could not be compared with those which treated matters of relevance to contemporary society.[12] If history had to be introduced into drama it should be treated as a subsidiary element since a play should revolve round social ideas and principles.

Indeed Faraḥ Anṭūn did write historical drama himself: *al-Sulṭān Ṣalāḥ al-Dīn wa Mamlakat Urshalīm* ('Sultan Saladin and the Kingdom of Jerusalem', 1914), but his object here was clearly to point out the need for the Egyptians to unite in order to get rid of the western imperialists. He showed the courage and magnanimity of the Arabs as compared with the deceit and materialism of the Crusaders in an attempt to encourage the moral rehabilitation of his contemporary audience through appealing to their glorious past. In this respect Anṭūn was following a fairly common trend in the Arab theatre of dramatizing glorious events from Arab and Islamic history; Najīb al-Ḥaddād had already treated the same subject several years earlier in a play inspired by Walter Scott's *The Talisman* entitled *Ṣalāḥ al-Dīn al-Ayyūbī* ('The Ayyubid Saladin'). However, Anṭūn's attempt is marked by a greater degree of seriousness and was of such obvious relevance to contemporary political reality that his play was banned by the censor who insisted on drastic cuts and omissions in the dialogue.[13] Anṭūn had no doubt whatsoever that the main effort in the modern theatre should be devoted to issues of contemporary Egyptian society. He had similar reservations about translations of western plays as he had about historical dramas. It is not that he disapproved of such translations; on the contrary, he himself translated serious plays by ancient and modern dramatists like Sophocles, Sardou and Alexandre Dumas, which were all performed by the talented Jūrj Abyaḍ; but he did not think it was healthy for the nascent, Egyptian theatre to rely so heavily upon translations or adaptations.

Faraḥ Anṭūn's main contribution in this context is his play, partly inspired by Emile Zola, *Miṣr al-Jadīda was Miṣr al-Qadīma* ('Egypt, New and Old', 1913), together with the critical discussion this play gave rise to, particularly on the issue of the language of dialogue. The play is difficult to summarize because it attempts to deal with several, perhaps too many themes at once, probably in part due to the fact that while writing it the author seems to have been influenced by naturalism and the slice-of-life school.[14] According to his own account, Anṭūn's play is 'in truth four interrelated plays'. The first is about Fu'ād Bey, the hero of New Egypt, and is based on the idea of strength of will power, work and serious application, self-discipline, defence of virtue and family values. The second revolves round Almaz, the modern, liberated and educated woman, who comes from a reputable family but goes too far in her search for freedom from the moral and social restrictions and norms of her society, ending up as a singer/artiste of doubtful virtue. The third deals with Christo, the Greek owner of the largest casino in Egypt, who deals in white slaves, amasses a fortune from encouraging gambling, drinking, sex and from money lending at exorbitant rates of interest. The fourth concerns Muhafhaf Pasha and a group of wealthy heirs who waste away their fortunes and their lives in the endless pursuit of physical pleasures, which drives their high class wives into getting together and thinking up a scheme to bring their menfolk back to the straight and narrow path. That is how Anṭūn himself described his play on the occasion of its performance by the troupe of Jūrj Abyaḍ at the Opera House on 5 April 1923; 'The fundamental idea upon which the play is constructed [is] the force of the will to work and the work of the will',[15] as Fu'ād Bey says to the other characters in the play *quwwat irādatt al-ʿamal wa ʿamal al-irādah*.

Briefly, this is illustrated by the story of Fu'ād Bey, a married man with a daughter who falls in love with the liberated singer Almaz who returns his love and, despite Christo's pressures, is prepared to sacrifice her career to be his wife, but on learning of his marriage she decides to give him up. He, in turn, tries to save his marriage and decides to go away on a business trip to the Sudan where he succeeds in making a fortune. In the mean time, we see Fu'ād in various melodramatic situations; for instance, trying to save the young and innocent French maid brought to Egypt by an unscrupulous French couple, with the secret intention of using her as a prostitute for the likes of Muhafhaf Pacha in collaboration with Christo. Christo and the other morally corrupt characters are meant to stand for Old Egypt while Fu'ād Bey represents New Egypt which, by sheer will-power, overcomes all temptations and pursues the path of virtue, self-reliance and success.

The play is overtly didactic in tone and the symbolic significance of the characters is too crudely obvious with the result that they lack warmth and lifelike individuality; but it has several lively scenes with details of life in modern Egypt faithfully reproduced. The problems are likewise identifiably Egyptian. In fact, in many ways the main subject that the playwright treats is one of the major and recurrent themes of modern Egyptian literature, namely the impact of western civilization on modern Egypt and the need to sort out the damaging effects from the positive results of this impact. It is the theme of so many works, beginning with al-Muwayliḥī's *Ḥadīth ʿIsā ibn Hishām* ('The Story of ʿĪsā ibn Hishām').[16] In its celebration of the value of will-power the play belongs squarely to the general reformist movement in modern Egypt which owes much to Shaykh Muḥammad ʿAbduh and his neo-Muʿtazilite position. Although Faraḥ Anṭūn was a Christian, he can still be regarded as forming part of the anti-fatalistic, rationalist approach of the predominantly Muslim, modern Egyptian reformers.[17]

Because of his insistence upon the need to write about contemporary

Egyptian reality, Faraḥ Anṭūn had to face the problem of the language of dialogue which is one of the serious and perennial problems of modern Arabic drama, caused by the enormous gap that separates the colloquial, spoken language (*al-ʿāmmiyya*) from the classical or literary, written language (*al-fuṣḥā*). And it must be admitted that Anṭun's perception and analysis of this issue of the diglossia are remarkably acute, especially when one considers the early date of his discussion. Starting from the assumption that what we see on the stage is meant to be an imitation of real human beings, he concludes that it is permissible to use the literary language for translated plays since these plays are meant to imitate the condition or state of people whose language is not Arabic and we should, therefore, feel free to choose any language we see fit for such an imitation. The case is different, however, when the plays are not translations but original writings dealing with the affairs of people whose language is spoken Arabic. If in such a case the literary language is used, then we deviate from nature which drama is meant to imitate and depart from the form and outward appearance of reality thereby destroying one of the fundamental principles of acting. How can a foreigner like Christo in the play, 'Egypt, New and Old', for instance, speak in classical Arabic, he asks, and what would the audience of that play think if they heard classical Arabic uttered by chorus girls in the dancing hall, newspaper boys, servants, Nubians and tottering drunkards or even ladies at their private gatherings? At the same time Anṭūn was not happy at the prospect of neglecting the beauties of literary Arabic and certainly did not want to be guilty of contributing towards the weakening of the *fuṣḥā* which he believed was the only medium fit to express the grandeur and nobility of sentiments and ideas. So he resorted to the use of three levels of language: the spoken (*al-ʿāmmiyya*) for the lower class characters, the written or literary (*al-fuṣḥā*) for the higher strata of society which, however, had to use the spoken when conversing with the former category, and a middle language, which he called reduced *fuṣḥā* or heightened *ʿāmmiyya* for the ladies to use among themselves.

It is indeed fortunate that this cumbersome solution was not followed by many dramatists, although the problem of dialogue continued to face Egyptian dramatists for generations to come and it is a tribute to Faraḥ Anṭūn that he was aware of its dimensions so early in the century. Underlying his position is, of course, the commonly-held assumption that the colloquial is not a fit medium for sublime tragedy or elevated emotion and the not-so-commonly accepted view that for serious comedy, dealing with contemporary events, the colloquial is the most natural and suitable medium.

IBRĀHĪM RAMZĪ

Like Faraḥ Anṭūn, Ibrāhīm Ramzī (1884–1949) did not hesitate to employ the colloquial in his social comedy and satire, but except for one part of the play, *al-Fajr al-Ṣādiq* ('True Dawn'), written in 1937,[18] he wrote his comedies in spoken

Arabic throughout, while using the classical language only in his historical plays and his serious drama (*bourgeois drame*). Like Anṭūn too, Ramzī was a well-educated man; he had first-hand experience of European dramatic productions in England, where he went in 1907 to study medicine but, in the event, ended up doing social sciences in London. His first venture in playwriting was a historical drama he produced sometime after his return from England called *al-Ḥākim bi Amr Allāh* ('al-Ḥākim bi Amr Allah', 1915), which deals with the controversial Fatimid Caliph who seemed to fascinate Egyptian dramatists, and not, as was thought for a long time even by eminent scholars and critics such as Muḥammad Yūsuf Majm and Muḥammad Mandūr, *al-Muʿtamid ibn ʿAbbād* ('al-Muʿtamid ibn ʿAbbād', a historical play about some dramatic events in a late period of Muslim history in Spain, written in 1893 by our author's namesake, another Ibrāhīm Ramzī, who was also a dramatist and translator but of an older generation, his dates being 1867–1924).[19] Apart from the obvious need to distinguish between these two writers for the sake of historical accuracy, and to avoid the unnecessary surprise at the enormous difference in standard between their work, it is important to note the fact that *all* our author's plays, whether historical drama or social comedy, are set in Egypt and deal with themes connected with Egypt's past or present. This was no doubt in part an expression of Ibrāhīm Ramzī's desire to create *Egyptian* drama.

Ramzī was a prolific writer, a dramatist, a novelist and an adaptor and translator not only of plays, but of works in history, sociology, ethics and even science. Among the dramatists he translated were Shakespeare (*King Lear* and *The Taming of the Shrew*), Sheridan (*Pizarro*), Bernard Shaw (*Caesar and Cleopatra*) and Ibsen (*An Enemy of the People*). When we consider that he was also employed as a full-time civil servant in several ministries and engaged for a while in journalism, we realize that he must have produced some of his writings with remarkable alacrity. In fact, he was gently censured by his gifted contemporary playwright and critic, Muḥammad Taymūr, for the speed at which he was turning out works below his usually high level of writing.[20] Much of Ramzī's rich and varied output was lost (including an Arabic/English dictionary of the Egyptian colloquial)[21] and a great deal (including two novels and five plays) is still unpublished.[22]

Besides the plays he adapted or translated, Ramzī wrote six historical plays, four social comedies and two serious dramas. The historical plays were, apart from *al-Ḥākim bi Amr Allāh* (1915), *Abṭāl al-Manṣūra* ('The Heroes of Mansura', 1915), *Bint al-Ikhshīd* ('Ikhshīd's Daughter', 1916), *al-Badawiyya* ('The Bedouin Maid', 1918, about a girl from Upper Egypt with whom the Fatimid Caliph al-Āmir bi Aḥkām Allah had fallen in love), *Shāwir ibn Mujīr* ('Shāwir ibn Mujīr', 1938?, the minister of the last Fatimid Caliph) and *Ismāʿīl al-Fātiḥ* ('Ismail the Conqueror', 1937). Except for the last-mentioned play which deals with nineteenth-century Egyptian history, in particular with the conquest of Sudan by Ismail, all the plays are about Fatimid, Ikhshīdīd or Mamluk Egypt.

The social comedies, satires, farces and serious dramas include *Dukhūl al-*

Ḥammām mish Zayy Khurugūh ('Admission to the Baths is a lot less Difficult than Coming out of them', 1915–16), *ʿUqbāl al-Ḥabāyib* ('The Same to You, Friends'), and *Abū Khawanda* ('Abū Khawanda'), both still unpublished but written in 1931. They deal with topical issues such as the rising cost of living, the disastrous temptations to which naive country folk are exposed in the city and the tricks played upon them by city people, especially by the traditional figure of the female matchmaker (*al-khaṭiba*). The serious dramas include *Ṣarkhat al-Ṭifl* ('The Baby's Cry', written in 1923 but published in 1938), and two unpublished works, *Bint al-Yawm* ('The Woman of Today', written in 1931), and *al-Fajr al-Ṣādiq* ('The True Dawn', 1937). 'The Baby's Cry' concerns a childless woman with no work to do, who is married to a lawyer completely absorbed in his job, and who has an affair with her husband's cousin, but her marriage is saved in the end. The theme of the play is the trials of modern marriage arising from the underemployment of young Egyptian wives neglected by their husbands. 'The True Dawn' is a plea for parity, particularly in age, between husband and wife, using as a subject the infatuation of a young, educated Iraqi woman with a liberated, Egyptian university professor and their eventual realization that, despite their common intellectual interests, their marriage would be an unwise step on account of the large gap in age between them. 'The Woman of Today' tackles similar issues, namely the problems created by the changes in the position and expectations of women in modern Egypt and the conflict between women's desire for freedom and the rules and conventions of Muslim society. The story is that of a young woman anxious to exercise her newly acquired freedom but who comes into conflict with her rich, conservative husband from the country. In the end the rebellious wife comes to terms with her life and both husband and wife escape from the temptations of the city to the peace and safety of the countryside. Because the dialogue in this play is in the colloquial the author manages to make it more expressive of the speaker's character with the result that it is perhaps more dramatic and less artificial than the other plays which similarly deal with the problems of contemporary Egyptian society.

The two plays which reveal Ramzī's dramatic powers at their best and most clearly show the extent of his contribution to the development of Arabic drama in Egypt are the one-act comedy, 'Admission to the Baths is a lot less Difficult than Coming out of them', and the historical play, 'The Heroes of Mansura'; both of which seem to have been written around 1915. They are the plays which I propose to discuss in detail.

'Admission to the Baths', which has been described with justice, as the first, fully-fledged, truly Egyptian social comedy,[23] is set in Cairo under Khedive Ismail, but it is clearly about the First World War period, when the cost of living had soared in Egypt and the poor sections of the community were badly hit. The action takes place in the poor quarter of Bulaq, in the public baths run by Abū Ḥasan, who lives with his wife, Zaynab, on the premises, with the help of his assistant, Nashashqī. The first thing that strikes us about the play, a feature which we encounter in other works by the same author, is the highly detailed and full stage directions; suddenly we meet with a surprising level of sophistication; everything that can help a producer on the stage is provided by the author: for instance, the description of the public baths is given in the minutest detail, such as the quality and means and manner of lighting and the blue and red colours of the bath towels hanging from the ceiling. It is not unlikely that in this matter Ramzī was influenced by Shaw whom he translated into Arabic.

The play opens with Abū Ḥasan sitting on his dais at daybreak, smoking a nargila, depressed and fulminating against the evil days he has fallen upon. He tries to rouse his assistant from the slumber into which he has fallen due to boredom caused by lack of custom. Abū Ḥasan suddenly decides to sell some of his bath equipment to raise money and he is impatiently ordering Nashashqī to collect the towels, nargilas and other effects. Alarmed at the prospect of losing his job, Nashashqī tries to dissuade his boss, who angrily and noisily tells him to do as he is told. The shouting brings Zaynab to the window who asks what is going on. Abū Ḥasan tells her to shut up and mind her own business, but undaunted she insists upon being told why he is selling the towels. He is apparently planning to buy himself a cashmere shawl and a new pair of shoes and put on the kaftan and gown, stolen from a previous rich customer, and an expensive fez, to smarten up his appearance so that he can work as a *shāhid zūr rasmī* (an official false witness in the *Sharia* court of law) since this has proved to be a lucrative business. At first both his wife and his assistant show concern at the prospect of Abū Ḥasan transgressing the law, returning to a life of crime and exposing himself to danger, but in the end they give in having obtained his consent to let them run the baths in his absence and try their luck.

Soon after his departure, a village chief (ʿUmdah), Abū ʿUways, and his bailiff, ʿUwaylī, newly arrived from the country, come into the baths partly attracted by Zaynab's singing. The ʿUmdah has just been paid a handsome sum for his cotton crop and he and his bailiff have decided to wash themselves before going to visit the minister to thank him for his help in bestowing the title 'Bey' upon him. Delighted to see some customers at last, Nashashqī makes a move to kiss the ʿUmdah's hands, but the ʿUmdah, who has heard much about the ways in which wily townsmen trick rich country folk, suspects him of trying to rob him and orders his bailiff to give him a thrashing. This does not, however, deter the desperate Nashashqī who is resolved not to let them go without using the baths. At the uproar caused Zaynab appears and welcomes the ʿUmdah who, at first, because of a particular expression used by Nashashqī, superstitiously fears she might be one of the evil spirits who haunt public baths, but she soon reassures him, in the most seductive manner, that she is human and uses her female wiles to charm him. At last he consents to let the bailiff go first with Nashashqī to have a bath while he stays behind ostensibly to guard his clothes but in truth to chat with the lady. Zaynab tells him that she is the daughter of the manager of the baths and that her father will not be back until late in the afternoon. She also explains that she is married but that her husband, whom she still loves dearly and whom the ʿUmdah uncannily resembles (so much so that she took him for her husband when she first saw him), mysteriously left her seven years previously. Flattered by her words, the ʿUmdah makes advances to her, comparing her favourably with the uncouth women of his village. He is, however, gently but coquetishly pushed away and told that he can enjoy her only as his lawful wife. As she is still legally married to another they agree that they should go to the Judge and that he should pretend to be her husband come back after his long absence and now prepared to give her the necessary divorce so that she can marry Abū ʿUways. At this point Abū Ḥasan conveniently arrives, dressed in his newly-acquired, elegant clothes and accompanied by Zaynab's brother who works as usher in the law court. Zaynab leads Abū ʿUways to believe that Abū Ḥasan is the Judge who has come to the baths as he sometimes does, and that they might just as well get the necessary divorce paper from him on the spot. In the mean time she has a word in secret with her husband explaining her scheme to him which he proceeds to help her implement. She grabs hold of the ʿUmdah and appeals to the 'Judge' to grant her divorce from the man who has deserted her for more than seven years. Abū Ḥasan lends a sympathetic ear to Zaynab's story and grants her a divorce. She also asks for the delayed portion of her dowry, for alimony and maintenance for the whole period of her husband's absence and, in the end, claims such a huge sum of money that Abū ʿUways has to part not only with the price of his cotton crop, but also with the new clothes he has just purchased in Cairo. It gradually dawns on him that what began as play-acting on Zaynab's part is now developing into an earnest attempt to fleece him. However, when he begins to deny that he is her husband the Judge (Abū Ḥasan) threatens him with the dire punishment of being thrown into the boiling waters of the baths if he is found guilty of perjury. The alarmed ʿUmdah at once swallows his words only too grateful to be allowed to escape alive. He flings his new clothes to Zaynab and one shoe hits Nashashqī who has been asking for a tip. Abū ʿUways is horrified at the thought that he has been tricked by a Cairene woman while all the while he has been on his guard against such trickeries. He rushes out of the baths accompanied by the bewildered bailiff who has just emerged clean, happy, contented and singing the praises of those marvellous baths. The play ends with a song which explains that in such hard times the poor have to live off fools.

This is an extremely well written play in which not a word seems out of place. Although exceedingly funny most of the time, the author does not lose sight of his satirical intention; among the butts of his criticism are the inflation caused by the War which drives people to resort to crime and deception in order to survive, the malpractices at the courts of law, and the army of 'official false witnesses' who are prepared to testify to anything for a small consideration

(Abū Ḥasan refers to someone he knows who has amassed a considerable fortune in this way and it is for this reason that he decides to take it up as full-time employment). Such witnesses are hired by dishonest trustees, legal guardians and rich divorcees who, in an attempt to avoid paying alimony to their ex-wives, turn up in court barefoot and dressed in rags (p.95).[24] Abū ʿUways says that in his village he has in his pay some thirty or forty men ready to bear false witness at any time, in any case, he wishes (p.105). The author also pokes fun at the way judges apply laws mechanically, however absurd and irrelevant to the circumstances of the case. Zaynab claims that she is pregnant and, therefore, she asks for, and is granted by the Judge, maintenance costs for the unborn child from her divorced husband, even though she says that he has deserted her for several years! But apart from the difficulty of obtaining divorce from an absent husband[25] the major object of satire is the well-known phenomenon of the village chief (ʿUmdah) who, after selling his cotton crop, goes to the metropolis to have a good time and ends up being cheated of his money by every type of smooth and plausible urban conman lurking to swoop on such an easy prey. In prose fiction we have already encountered him in the vivid portrait created by Muḥammad al-Muwayliḥī in *Ḥadīth ʿĪsā ibn Hishām* (1907).

The play which is supposed to take one hour and a quarter in performance is not divided into acts or scenes. The events are so carefully organized and the plot so tightly knit that the audience is well prepared for the turn events will take. All the necessary information is imparted to us indirectly in the course of the dialogue which sounds natural and spontaneous. We are given a hint of Abū Ḥasan's unscrupulous past (p.98) to prepare us for his subsequent fraudulent behaviour. We are also told that he has forced Zaynab to cheat a wealthy customer in the past (p.96), so we do not find her behaviour towards Abū ʿUways totally inexplicable. When Abū Ḥasan puts on fine clothes he looks so impressive that even his assistant, Nashashqī, thinks he looks like the Judge (p.98); it is, therefore, not unbelievable that Abū ʿUways should be prepared to accept Zaynab's assertion that he is the Judge. At the same time, in an attempt to impress her new client, Zaynab tells Nashashqī to go and prepare the special, private closet normally used by the Judge when he visits the baths for Abū ʿUways and his companion, as it is still too early in the day for the Judge to come, with the result that Abū ʿUways is ready to believe Zaynab when later on she claims that the Judge has arrived with his usher.

The few songs we find in the play are strictly functional; we have now moved away from the world of musical comedy where action provides an excuse for singing. The play contains no more than three songs, two of which are very brief. The first and longest occurs early in the story at the point where Nashashqī is left alone on the stage thinking of his unhappy lot; in his song he complains of the bad times, the high cost of living, his poverty and hunger, and offers a prayer to God to relieve the hardship. The second song, a five-line stanza, is sung by Zaynab; it is the lament of a woman who has been deserted by her lover for more than seven years. Abū ʿUways hears her singing and, in his innocence, thinks it is the mellifluous voice of the famous singer, Almaz, and is therefore encouraged to go into the baths hoping to see the great Almaz herself. At the same time Zaynab makes use of the song by telling him that she has been singing of her own sad plight in having been deserted by her husband for so long. The last song occurs right at the end of the play; it is a brief summing up of the situation by Zaynab, Abū Ḥasan and his assistant and a comment upon the action, namely, that in these bad times the poor survive only by preying on the foolish and the gullible.

The humour of the play arises from a rich variety of sources ranging from character, situation, word play, malapropism and overall irony. Abū ʿUways is anxious to an almost pathological extent not to be duped by any trickster from Cairo and yet he falls an easy prey to the wiles of a Cairene woman who spots his fatal weakness, turning his susceptibility to female charms to her complete advantage, thereby robbing him of the several hundred pounds he has on him:

NASHASHQĪ: Welcome, Your Excellency. Let me kiss your hand.

ʿUWAYS: Keep off, you rogue! We won't have any hanky-panky here. I suppose you are after my signet ring.

ʿUWAYLĪ: Keep your hands off His Excellency, young man! We don't want any of your tricks.

ʿUWAYS: They seem to think here that we are only country folk, easy to fool. Dreadful people, these Cairenes!

NASHASHQĪ: Why, Your Excellency? What have I done? I only wanted to welcome you by kissing your hand; God knows how delighted I am to see you here.

ʿUWAYS: Keep your distance, you rogue! Stay where you are!

NASHASHQĪ: As you wish, Sir I crave your pardon. Let me kiss your head instead, to show you that no offence was meant.

ʿUWAYS: This rogue is up to no good. Thrash him soundly, ʿUwaylī!

ʿUWAYLĪ: [*Striking him with his cane on his back, which is covered with towels*]: Don't you touch His Excellency, thief!

NASHASHQĪ: What a terrible business this is! Dear God, don't you ever send us anything good without making us pay for it?

ʿUWAYS: Look at him ʿUwaylī! Look! This rogue is intent on stealing my brand new turban, which I've just bought at the Faḥḥāmīn market. I suppose you take me to be one of those simple village headmen you see around these days!

NASHASHQĪ: I do beg your pardon, Sir! Let me kiss your foot instead. Whatever you say. Just go in and take your bath, I implore you! (*About to kiss* ʿUWAYS's *knee.*)

ʿUWAYS: ʿUwaylī! Help!

ʿUWAYLĪ: (*hitting* NASHASHQĪ *on his back*): Let go of his shoes, you son of a bitch! We've just paid a whole silver half-crown for them.

NASHASHQĪ: Oh, my God! Help me, please! I appeal to you, People of the House [the Holy Family]!

ʿUWAYS: People of the house? Are these baths inhabited by spirits?

NASHASHQĪ: I'll do anything, anything you like, my dear Sir! I ask your forgiveness. (*He pats* ʿUWAYS *on the shoulder.*) Only please go in and have your bath. What a morning! Never mind, just go in and have your bath! Go and take off your clothes! There is a closet over there for Your Excellency to use.

ʿUWAYS: Go in and take off my clothes over there? Why can't I remove my clothes where I have my bath? Amazing! Don't you have a stool next to the bath tub? Or even a metal bowl where I can put my things? Is it a bath you have, or a mere pond?

NASHASHQĪ: We simply don't want your clothes to get wet or damp because of the steam rising from the bath tub. Since when has there been any need for stools in the baths?

ʿUWAYS: Better for them to get wet than to be stolen, together with the entire proceeds of the sale of the cotton crop. Don't you agree, ʿUwaylī?

NASHASHQĪ: My dear Sir, I'm telling you, we're not thieves here. We're common, decent people, working for our living. Here is the key to the valuables chest where you can put anything you like for safe-keeping.

ʿUWAYS: Amazing! (*to* ʿUWAYLĪ.) You see how the rogue is trying to fool us.

NASHASHQĪ: Whatever makes you think so, Your Excellency?

ʿUWAYS: Supposing someone comes along and steals the chest with all its contents.

ʿUWAYLĪ: You think you can trick us, don't you, you rogue? You'd better look out! We can trick a dozen chaps like you.

NASHASHQĪ: My dear Sir, I swear to you the chest is safe! It cannot be removed, it is built in underneath the dais. All right, don't put your belongings in the chest, let that gentleman sit on them while Your Excellency is having a bath.

ʿUWAYLĪ: Sit on them, like a hen brooding on her eggs? Mind your language, boy!

NASHASHQĪ: I'm sorry, Sir; no offence was intended. I only meant that you could yourself sit by the clothes to guard them, while His Excellency has his bath.

ʿUWAYLĪ: Can't you see that I too want to have a bath? It's I who's brought His Excellency here. We can't afford to be late for the Pacha who we want to catch before he leaves his office, can we?

ʿUWAYS: Of course not. I can't go to see him alone.

ASHASHQĪ: All right then. Why don't you go in first and His Excellency can keep an eye on your clothes.

ʿUWAYS: You impudent wretch! You want me to keep an eye on my bailiff's clothes? Have you no manners or respect? Oh, if only you were in my village, then I could show you your place and teach you a lesson you'd never forget.

NASHASHQĪ: Heavens! Help me, please, all you Muslims, be you men or spirits! My patience has run out!

ʿUWAYS: He isn't summoning the spirits of the baths, is he? I heard him a while ago calling upon them. Come on, ʿUwaylī, let's go, otherwise we'll come to no good. The people here are not to be trusted; they keep the company of genii. I know that these baths are always inhabited by spirits.

NASHASHQĪ: (*holding them by their clothes*): Please don't go away! Why don't you go in and have your bath, like ordinary folk? I'll fetch stools for you from the nearby café, if you like. Just go in and have your baths. I don't want the boss to laugh at me when he comes back.

ʿUWAYS: I think we've had it, ʿUwaylī, boy. We've had it all right. It's too late now, I can hear the spirits of the baths walking about and opening doors, can't you? (*Listens*)

ʿUWAYLĪ: I can hear some noise all right. I wonder if it is a spirit?

(ZAYNAB *emerges from the door, wrapped in a light cloak.*)

ʿUWAYS: It looks like it, by God's Prophet! Here she comes! Here she comes! Heaven protect us! In the name of God, the most Compassionate, the most Merciful!

(*Both men rush and hide behind the sofa. When* ʿUWAYS *sees* ZAYNAB*'s figure, he keeps bobbing up and down, peeping at her from behind the side of the sofa, while* ʿUWAYLĪ *is in a state of panic.*)

ZAYNAB: Good day to you, gentlemen!

(ʿUWAYS *remains silent.*)

ʿUWAYLĪ: Please answer her, your Excellency, the ʿUmdah, we don't want her to do us any harm.

ZAYNAB: Good day to you, Your Excellency, the ʿUmdah!

ʿUWAYS: She seems to be a Muslim genie.

ZAYNAB: Good day to you, Your Excellency, the ʿUmdah! What on earth is the matter with him? Why doesn't he speak?

NASHASHQĪ: Answer her, man!

ʿUWAYLĪ (*in panic*): Please answer her, Your Excellency.

ZAYNAB: Why don't you answer? Perhaps you think that I eat men. (*She laughs while* ʿUWAYS *keeps peeping at her. She goes up to him and takes him by the hand.*)

Come here, and don't be afraid!

ʿUWAYS (*appearing from behind the sofa*): Good day to you, Lady! I beseech you, don't do me any harm! I'm a man with a large family. I've come to Cairo only to meet the Pacha, the Governor, to thank him for the title of Bey that has been conferred upon me. And I've come here to have a bath and perform the necessary ablutions after what happened last night. You know it is improper to meet a ruler when one is in a state of impurity.

ZAYNAB (*laughing gently*): But why don't you want to get into the bath so that you'll be in time to see the Pacha?

ʿUWAYS: I was afraid of this rogue here. I am carrying on me the price of the cotton crop and he may be tempted to steal it or something.

ZAYNAB: God forbid! This would be most improper. He wouldn't dare. He knows I would go for him with my slipper.

ʿUWAYS: My lady, he was intent on stealing my signet ring and my turban and my shoes.

ZAYNAB: Aren't you ashamed, you wretched boy, to behave like this towards such a great and noble ʿUmdah on our own premises?

NASHASHQĪ: I swear to God, dear lady, that I only wanted to kiss his hand and feet to show him how delighted I was to see him. I wanted to kiss his head to ask his pardon, and to do what was necessary.

ʿUWAYS: Do what was necessary? What do you mean, do what was necessary? Do you hear that, ʿUwaylī?

ʿUWAYLĪ (*uncertain all the while as to whether* ZAYNAB *is a human being or a genie, and listening very attentively to the conversation*): No more of your trickery, boy!

ʿUWAYS: You see, my lady, people of Cairo think that all the village chieftains are simple fools, too dim to see a joke.

ZAYNAB: Please accept our apologies, Your Excellency. Off you go, Nashashqī; get the bath ready, and let the gentlemen put their clothes and their money in the chest and give them the key! Hurry up and clean the large closet for them, the one which the Judge uses before he arrives! (*She sits on the sofa.*)

NASHASHQĪ: All right, my lady. By the Prophet, you're a marvellous person and you solve all problems! (*Exit.*)

ʿUWAYS: So you are not one of these genii, after all, good lady?

ZAYNAB (*laughing*): Whoever gave you that idea? I'm only the daughter of the owner of these baths.

ʿUWAYS: Daughter of the owner of these baths! Was it you who was singing just now, sounding like a nightingale?

ZAYNAB: Did you like my voice then?

ʿUWAYS: I was enchanted by it. You were singing such a lovely ballad that it would ensnare even a bird.

ZAYNAB: Oh, Sir! You are so courteous and say such sweet things to me. May the Lord protect you!

ʿUWAYS: Could you please tell me what you were singing?

ZAYNAB: A ballad about my life.

ʿUWAYS: Do please sing it, sweet lady. Happy is the man who has been blessed by your beauty! We, wretched country folk, are denied such lovely things. We only hear the mooing of cows and buffaloes in our village. God curse the countryside and all that there is in it! Boy, oh boy! So you are the daughter of the owner of these baths, sweet lady.

ZAYNAB: Yes, Sir.

ʿUWAYS: But where is your father?

ZAYNAB: He has gone to the Judge's house.

ʿUWAYS: And what is your ladyship's name?

ZAYNAB: Zaynab, at your service!

ʿUWAYS: What a lovely name! May the Lord protect you!

ʿUWAYLĪ: I say, isn't she a lovely thing, Your Excellency the ʿUmdah?

ʿUWAYS (*turning to him somewhat angrily*): You go in there, boy, take off your clothes and have your bath. I shall guard your clothes for you in the mean time. (*Shoos him with his stick, so* ʿUWAYLĪ *goes off and disappears inside the baths.*) Well, well! And what are you doing here now, good lady? Where is your mother?

ZAYNAB: I lost her.

ʿUWAYS: Oh, I am sorry! I too lost my mother.

ZAYNAB: Sorry to hear it.

ʿUWAYS: May God protect you! But who is this Nashashqī?

ZAYNAB: He is only the baths' attendant. He's a simpleton who understands nothing.

ʿUWAYS: A simpleton! And who keeps you company inside?

ZAYNAB: No one, Your Excellency. I'm all alone here. My father doesn't come home until late in the afternoon. I daren't come down here at this time of day in case there are men clients about. But I caught a glimpse of your face through the shutters, so I rushed downstairs at once to have a good look at you . . . I thought you were my husband returned to me. You have the same lovely eyes.

(pp.99–102)

During the altercation between the ʿUmdah and the bath attendant the latter, in his exasperation with the new clients, appeals for help from *Ahl al-Bayt* (i.e. (members of the holy family of the Prophet), but the ʿUmdah, as we have seen, understands the expression to mean the evil spirits that inhabit the house, and when Zaynab appears on the scene he is scared of her, thinking that she is a supernatural being and (to the delight of the audience) hides from her, fearing that she might do him some harm. She reassures him that she is only a human being but, as he will soon realize, she turns out to be no less harmful to him than an evil spirit could be. When playing the part of the Judge, Abū Ḥasan, who is illiterate, tries to raise the standard of his speech by the intrusion of what he thinks are classical Arabic expressions, thereby providing a rich source of verbal humour. But perhaps the most striking element in this outstanding comedy is the character of Zaynab, who is one of the most memorable portraits of the Egyptian *baladi* woman (traditional lower class townswoman). While being an invaluable help to her husband, she is not easily daunted by him or impressed by his harsh words. She is earthy and coquettish, shrewd and resourceful, and by an unerring instinct knows how to get what she wants. While remaining every whit an Egyptian and Muslim female, she is easily the strongest and most dominant character in the whole play. It is no wonder that the play proved a success whenever it was produced as Zakī Ṭulaymāt says in his introduction to the printed version of the play published in 1924.[26] It is significant that Ramzī's gifted contemporary, Muḥammad Taymūr, said in his praise 'It is enough praise that Ramzī wrote the play 'Admission to the Baths'.[27] No other Egyptian has written a play like it: a comedy with characters so fully portrayed and so deeply analyzed'.[28] In fact, Ramzī managed to leave his imprint on the Arabic language through this play for it is extremely difficult to mention the colloquial expression, which gave the play its title, without bringing to mind the action and plot.

By opting for the colloquial as the language of the dialogue in 'Admission to the Baths', Ramzī provided a neat but bold solution to the problem of diglossia (which has plagued many Arabic playwrights), thereby easily creating an effect of verisimilitude. Of course, because of the fairly homogenous, linguistic universe inhabited by his characters, unlike that of Faraḥ Anṭūn, he did not feel the need to create more than one level of discourse; the Cairene characters belong to the lowest orders of society who cannot be expected, even by a long stretch of the imagination, to communicate in classical Arabic and the same thing is more or less true of the uneducated, though rich ʿUmdah and his man from the village. When the manager of the baths poses as a *Sharia* judge, he is naturally expected to use the legal jargon of Islamic law, hence the need to observe rules of classical Arabic grammar which the actor breaks most of the time with hilarious results. In the second play we are going to discuss by Ramzī, *Abṭāl al-Manṣūra* ('The Heroes of Mansura'), the dramatist chose classical Arabic as his medium. 'The Heroes of Mansura' is a historical drama set in the Middle Ages and deals with events of the Sixth Crusade of 1248 led by Louis IX of France. The characters, therefore, come from either Islamic or European medieval history, so the problem of producing an illusion of contemporary Egyptian reality does not arise. In an article published in 1924[29] Ramzī wrote concerning the language of dialogue in drama:

> Spoken Arabic must be the language of modern plays, irrespective of the type of character speaking, for it is obvious that in today's spoken Arabic there are different levels, dialects and idioms. But for the grammatical inflections, some of these indeed resemble the written/literary language, depending on the situation, customs, the speaker's character, degree of perception and extent of education. As for making the élite use literary Arabic and the servants the spoken and so forth, this is a worthless device, an unacceptable falsehood which the stage cannot tolerate. But when a play happens to be historical, dealing with ancient times, or when it is about far-off peoples such as the Chinese, the Russians or the English, and it is serious drama, literary Arabic must be the language to use as it will help in giving meaning greater clarity and sharper definition, and because of its local characteristics spoken Arabic might damage the serious intent of foreign drama.

Obviously Ramzī felt that the distancing of the subject, whether temporal or spacial, made it easier for the audience to accept dramatic conventions, and enabled them to respond to a Frenchman, and certainly a medieval Frenchman, expressing himself in classical Arabic without feeling any absurdity in the situation.

However, it would be wrong to assume that 'The Heroes of Mansura' is a purely historical play without much relevance to contemporary Egypt at the time; it is very much the work of an Egyptian nationalist and, as the author himself informs us in the introduction to the printed text, it was inspired by nationalist sentiment and events in Egyptian history which resulted in the British forcing a change of ruler (Khedive) without paying any regard to the feelings of the Egyptian people. Following the declaration of war on Turkey in September 1914, Britain declared a protectorate over Egypt on 18 December 1914, removing the pro-Ottoman Khedive ʿAbbās, and replacing him with the more pliable Ḥusayn Kāmil as Sultan of Egypt. According to the author, the performance of the play was not allowed until 1918 when the troupe of ʿAbd al-Raḥmān Rushdī obtained permission from the censor to produce it in the provincial capital, Mansura.[30] The play was praised by leading personalities in Egypt such as the founder of the Bank of Egypt, Ṭalʿat Ḥarb Pacha, and Muḥammad Ḥusayn Haykal for its promotion of the cause of patriotism.[31]

'The Heroes of Mansura' is divided into four acts, but the acts are not subdivided into scenes. As we have seen in Ramzī's other play, the stage directions are extremely detailed, even more so than in 'Admission to the Baths', particularly in matters related to the stage sets and to the costumes to be worn by each character (see pp.28–9 on Shajarat al-Durr's costume).[32] Act I takes place in the royal palace in Mansura shortly after the invasion by the Crusaders led by King Louis IX who captures the city of Damietta. The courtiers, noblemen and generals are assembled in the state room, anxious about the state of health of the Sultan who is seriously ill; many of them have been summoned by the Queen, Shajarat al-Durr, for some undisclosed urgent matter. Others are keeping vigil because of the Sultan's condition, whiling away the time playing chess, reading the Koran or engaging in conversation. The atmosphere is tense. Aqṭāy, the Second-in-Command of the Army, asks Suhayl, the Queen's eunuch and private secretary, for news of the Sultan's health. On being told that his physician, Hibat Allah, has just been looking after him and rubbing his body with ointment, Aqtāy expresses concern that the Sultan is being treated by this doctor who is the son of a French Crusader, killed in battle. However, he is reassured that Hibat Allah has been the Sultan's private physician for many years and has been travelling with him wherever he goes and that everybody trusts him. But from the ensuing conversation we learn some facts which prepare us for what is going to happen later on: for instance, that Hibat Allah is passionately in love with the Queen's sister, Ṣafiyya, for whose hand in marriage he has unsuccessfully asked the Sultan, and that seventeen years previously he had a desperate and unrequited passion for a lady who later became Aqṭāy's wife. Another important fact we learn is that Ṣafiyya has just been taken prisoner by the French while on her way back from Syria. The news seems to disturb Baybars, Chief of the Mamluk Princes, who, as we shall see later, is deeply in love with her. However, he refrains from showing his feelings at this point. On the other hand, he makes abundantly clear his resentment of the presence of the Commander-in-Chief of the army, Prince Fakhr al-Dīn, whom he considers to be responsible for the surrender of the city of Damietta to the French and the retreat of his troops to Mansura. He accuses him of cowardice, provoking a quarrel which their friends try to compose. It is the appearance of the Queen, however, that puts an end to the argument, her speech upbraiding them for attacking each other when their enemy has just invaded. Fakhr al-Dīn is, in fact, a very dear friend of Baybars but, despite his close friendship, on such an important national issue the latter did not hesitate to fight him as he is clearly first and foremost a man of principle. Unlike the Sultan and the Queen he did not, however, know that the surrender was due to an act of treachery which resulted in false information being given about the whereabouts of the French forces and that Fakhr al-Dīn had acted the way he did in order to save his monarch and the city of Mansura. After this misunderstanding has been cleared up, the Queen explains in a statesmanlike indirect manner the reason for her summoning the notables of the land: the king has died without appointing a successor from his family and she is now seeking their advice. They propose that she should succeed her husband as their monarch, but she firmly declines the offer on the grounds that she does not think it proper for a Muslim nation to be ruled by a woman. During the discussion Baybars emerges as a born leader and his suggestion is that, considering the difficult circumstances of the war, the Sultan's son, Ṭūrānshāh (despite the weakness of his character), should be appointed Sultan, but since it would take four months for the messenger to reach him in Mesopotamia and return with him, the death of the Sultan should be kept secret lest the news should have a demoralizing effect upon the nation during the war. The Queen should in the mean time run the affairs of the state in consultation with them.

In Act II the scene changes from the court to a farm in Faraskūr which belongs to Shaykh Bernard. The contrast between the opulence of the glittering royal court and the simplicity of the village dwelling is most striking. Bernard is a seventy-year-old Frenchman who served during the previous Crusade, was taken prisoner by the Muslims but managed to escape and hide in a monastery. For the past thirty years he has been living on a farm in Egypt, outwardly adopting Egyptian ways, while remaining intensely loyal to his mother country. He is helped to run his farm by sixteen-year-old Maryam/Marie who is led to believe she is his daughter. It was she who, acting on Bernard's instructions, gave false information to Fakhr al-Dīn about the movements of the French forces, thus enabling them to capture Damietta without a fight.

Bernard is anxiously awaiting the weekly visit from the physician, Hibat Allah, whose real name is Philippe, and who is in truth a spy supplying Bernard with useful information to pass on to the French. Bernard confides in Maryam his true origins and early background as well as his intention to go back to France with the victorious King, leaving her behind in the care of Philippe. Maryam, disappointed and displeased at the thought of being deserted by the man she has come to regard as her father, confesses that she felt slightly guilty when she deliberately misled the Muslim general. This annoys Bernard who explodes angrily, cursing that the tie of kinship could be so strong, which prepares us for the information we are given later concerning Maryam's true parentage. Hibat Allah/Philippe arrives to convey the news of the impending death of the Sultan. From the dialogue we learn that Bernard has been providing the physician with the poisonous lotion with which he has been treating the Sultan. We also learn that during his early manhood Bernard used to work in the French court waiting on the Queen Mother, that he knew her son, King Louis, and that he is expecting his Majesty to visit him on his way to Mansura when he is planning to ask him to reward Philippe for his services. Philippe says that the thing he desires most in life is to be allowed to marry the woman he loves, Ṣafiyya, the Egyptian Queen's sister who, he knows, has been captured by the French. Bernard advises him to stop thinking about such a hopeless matter since the King's brother, Prince D'Artois, is also interested in her and has been entrusted by the King with the task of returning her to her sister. Because of his infatuation, however, he has disobeyed the King and brought her secretly to Bernard's house as his prisoner until the war ends. Sensing that Bernard dare not disobey the Prince for fear of his life, Philippe threatens to inform King Louis, to which Bernard reacts at once by threatening to unmask Philippe to Baybars and the Muslims. In this way we discover more facts about Philippe's dismal past: his hopeless passion for the Muslim noblewoman (who later married Aqṭāy) seventeen years previously and his resentment against her and her husband which prompted him to avenge himself on them by kidnapping their daughter, ʿĀʾisha, whom he subsequently gave to Bernard to place in a monastery under the name Maryam. Bernard still has the documents to prove it. This threat at once brings Philippe to his senses and he humbly begs Bernard's forgiveness and Bernard promises to speak to D'Artois on his behalf. At this point Ṣafiyya appears and scolds Bernard for holding her prisoner. Then Maryam rushes in asking for protection against D'Artois who has been chasing her intending to rape her, and is horrified to see that neither Bernard nor Philippe is willing to stand in the Prince's way. In the confusion caused, Ṣafiyya escapes but is soon recaptured by Prince Poitiers, the King's other brother, who recognizes her and brings her back whereupon the two brothers proceed to quarrel over her. Bernard, however, suggests that the brothers share the two women between them. Alarmed at the prospect of being raped, the women scream for help and Ṣafiyya calls out to Baybars who happens to be on his way to the French King to negotiate the release of the Princess. He hears the cries for help, comes into the cottage, releases the two women but is attacked from behind by the French Princes just as King Louis arrives; King Louis greets the Egyptian hero and expresses disgust at the unchivalrous conduct of his brothers. The act ends in a fight with Baybars refusing to forsake Maryam who has sought his protection. King Louis claims that, as Protector of Christianity, he cannot allow her to go while Baybars argues that she may be the King's sister in religion, but as an Egyptian she is Baybar's sister in *waṭan* (motherland) and that this is a much more important bond. In the end Baybars manages to leave unscathed, accompanied by the two women, having inflicted a wound on Poitiers.

In Act III we go back to Mansura, but this time to the palace of Fakhr al-Dīn, Commander-in-Chief of the army, where Ṣafiyya, Maryam and the Queen have been transferred from the King's palace for their own safety. Preparations for the decisive battle are being made. The Queen delivers a rousing and dignified speech to her generals who subsequently take leave of one another to go to battle. Here Baybars too bids farewell to his beloved Ṣafiyya in a scene in which Egyptian nationalism is eloquently expressed (pp. 104, 106–7). In this act Hibat Allah's character is further delineated; his resourcefulness and persuasiveness are amply illustrated. He comes in allegedly to convey some information to Fakhr al-Dīn, pretending not to know that the latter's palace has now been taken over as residence for the women. He is seen by Maryam who at first takes him to be Philippe, despite his Arab dress, but Ṣafiyya recognizes him as the physician who had treated her sister in Aleppo some years earlier. He asks for a drink of water to get Maryam out of the room so that he may be left alone with Ṣafiyya and reminds her of her promise to recompense him if he cured her sister. He now expects her to fulfil her promise. Hibat Allah tries to court her in a scene of consummate artistry where every word he uses has a double meaning which is lost on the innocent woman, and when for a fleeting moment she senses in alarm his true intention she is at once reassured by his skilful manipulation of words. Realizing that his attempt to woo her will only meet with failure he changes his tactics and resorts to cunning; he asks her to provide shelter for him for one night only in the palace and to keep it a complete secret, for having consulted his astrolabe he has learnt that his life will be in danger if anyone other than the person dearest to him knows where he is. Being innocent of his real intention she agrees to put him up in a room to which he asks for the key. In the mean time, he deals brilliantly with the problems posed by Maryam's recognition of him; he convinces her that he is the brother of Philippe and that she should not endanger his life by saying anything about his brother, otherwise he will reveal her secret to the Egyptian generals. Scared of the punishment she may receive, she agrees to do as he tells her and keep a close watch on her mistress, Ṣafiyya. He even promises to return her to her real parents if she strictly follows his instructions for a week.

During the battle some of the French break into the city. Bernard, disguised as a beggar, is let into the house. Stumbling on the doorstep he asks for help pretending to have hurt his leg. He grabs hold of Ṣafiyya, calls out to D'Artois who captures her. Maryam rushes in to ask for help, Fakhr al-Dīn comes to the rescue, fights and is stabbed in the back by Hibat Allah who comes from within. He drugs Ṣafiyya and takes her into his room. Soon Poitiers comes in to look for D'Artois who gleefully tells him that Fakhr al-Dīn has been killed. Poitiers is not pleased and scolds his brother for having disregarded their military plan because of his foolish passion for Ṣafiyya, thereby contributing to the total disarray and defeat of the French. The acts ends with Baybars, Muḥsin and others coming in to declare their victory, chasing away the French Princes and their men, killing D'Artois and taking many prisoners. The curtain falls amid the beating of drums and cheering of soldiers.

The final act of the play deals with the aftermath of the war; it takes place in the palace of the new Sultan Ṭūrānshāh in Faraskūr. The Queen and her secretary, Suhayl, discuss the absence of Baybars which they think is probably due to his being engaged in negotiation with the captured King Louis over the question of his ransom. They also express their concern about the inexplicable disappearance of Ṣafiyya and Maryam. The Queen would like to see Bernard in case he has any news but is dismayed to hear from Suhayl that against her express wishes Hibat Allah has ordered his death, despite his earlier promise to spare his life. Suhayl goes on to say that he has just seen Hibat Allah walking with the new Sultan by the Nile, and that for some time now he has been acting suspiciously. Baybars is then shown completely distraught on account of the disappearance of Ṣafiyya and is comforted by the Queen before he goes away to complete the ransom arrangements. In the mean time, Sultan Ṭūrānshāh, whose mind has been poisoned by Hibat Allah, comes in and addresses the Queen in insulting language, accusing her of concealing Princess Ṣafiyya whom she has promised to Baybars because she prefers Baybars to him. He also accuses her of having squandered his father's fortune, demands that she should surrender to him all the pearls and rubies his father had given her and orders her to go to her room at once and have no contact with anybody, including her private secretary, without his permission. When the Princes come in to ask his advice about the terms of ransom they have negotiated with King Louis, he roundly reprimands them for rushing into talks without his permission, pointing out to them that *he* is the King, the sole ruler of the land and that they are there only to receive orders from him or pass information to him. This angers the Princes, particularly as they have learnt that he has been plotting their death. Baybars reminds him in the strongest terms that it is they, and not his father, who have appointed him monarch, and that he has nothing to do with the victory since he arrived only after the war was over.

BAYBARS: Listen to me Ṭūrān, if you wish to live amongst us as our Sultan ruling over us then you have no choice but to consult us, for discussions

> will have to be communal . . . We have just about had enough. You assume that Egypt now is just as it was in the past: a country whose people are driven like sheep. No, Ṭūrān! You have been living away too long and do not realize that Egypt is now a different nation. Today the Egyptians know that they are entitled to a greater share than the Sultan himself, for they can do without you, the Sultan, while you cannot do without them. (p.153)

At this impressive show of resolution Ṭūrān gives in, but the Princes insist that he should offer his apologies to the Queen which he does. When they demand that he should show her further signs of respect, he feels he cannot bear any more humiliation and orders them to go, threatening not to receive the King of France in connection with the ransom terms as they have arranged. Led by Baybars, the Princes draw their swords and threaten to remove him from the throne and appoint someone else, even Suhayl, in his place. Once more Ṭūrān submits, receives Louis IX graciously and conducts the negotiations with him to their satisfaction. The act ends with the unmasking of Hibat Allah who is killed by Baybars, the rescue of Ṣafiyya and Maryam by the King of France, the reunion of Ṣafiyya and Baybars, and of Maryam and her father, Aqṭāy.

This lengthy account of the plot is meant to show how packed with action the play is. Yet, despite so much incident, 'The Heroes of Mansura' does not give the impression of being a confused, overcrowded work. On the contrary, the line of progression is clear; there are hardly any melodramatic surprises for at every juncture we are cunningly prepared for subsequent developments, an evidence of the strong, controlling mind of the dramatist behind the events in this remarkably well-constructed play. Our suspense is skilfully aroused and intelligently gratified. For instance, in Act I we hear of the retreat of Fakhr al-Dīn, the Commander-in-Chief, from Damietta, which prompts Baybars' anger and contempt and we are not given the reason for this setback until much later. Similarly, the Princes are summoned to the palace by Queen Shajarat al-Durr and for a while we are not told why but remain in a state of suspense, especially in the tense atmosphere of the court, waiting for an explanation. In Act I (p.19) a passing reference is made to the desperate passion which the physician, Hibat Allah (Philippe), developed for the woman who was to become Aqṭāy's wife, but it is not until the middle of Act II (p.62) that we are told about the outcome of that passion: namely that his desire for revenge and his jealousy of Aqṭāy drove him to kidnap their baby daughter, ʿĀʾisha, and place her under the name Maryam in the monastery where Bernard was employed.

Despite the obvious contrast between the world of the village and that of the Court, the characters who inhabit both of these worlds are interrelated. Bernard had been employed by the mother of King Louis IX, and had served in the previous Crusade and the King is going to visit him in Faraskūr on his way to attack the town of Mansura. The Sultan's physician, Hibat Allah, works in close co-operation with Bernard, whom he visits every Monday to keep him informed of the latest developments at the Court, and from him the physician obtains the poisonous ointment which he uses on the Sultan until he dies. The timing of the King's assault was suggested by Bernard in the light of the information received concerning the Sultan's illness and the quarrel that is likely to follow the Sultan's death. Maryam turns out to be Aqṭāy's daughter. Love is a further binding factor; Princess Ṣafiyya is loved not only by Baybars and Hibat Allah but is also desired by the brother of the French King, D'Artois, who keeps her prisoner in Bernard's farmhouse.

Naturally, to create such a closely-woven plot the author had to depart to some extent from the historical events. After all, he was writing not history, but historical drama, which has its own exigencies. He decided to mark the fictitious characters, which he introduced for the sake of the plot, by an asterisk in the list of *dramatis personae*. From it we learn that the princes and generals on both sides are historical and that he invented very few characters indeed: these include Hibat Allah, Philippe, Bernard, Princess Ṣafiyya and Maryam/ʿĀʾisha; they provide either the element of intrigue and treachery or serve the love interest, both elements designed to add liveliness and suspense to the action, emphasis to the political point Ramzī is trying to make, as well as colour and depth to his characters. Even in the portrayal of the historical figures some features are emphasized by the author, while others are suppressed to serve either his dramatic purpose or the thesis he wishes to advance. For instance, in the portrait of Baybars none of the ruthlessness of the historical figure is shown, because it would not accord with the idealized paragon of virtue and chivalry we are given here. The historical Queen Shajarat al-Durr did agree, although admittedly later on, to become ruler of Egypt after the assassination of Ṭūrānshāh but she was much more hungry for power than the noble figure presented in this play. The impetuosity of D'Artois's character is a historical fact, but he was not motivated by his passion for a woman. While Baybars is idealized the picture of Ṭūrānshāh is much darker than the historical figure. Apparently, there was considerable discussion amongst the leaders of Egypt and a loss of morale in the Egyptian army following the death of Sultan al-Ṣāliḥ Ayyūb and Sultan Ṭūrānshāh managed, at least temporarily, to dominate dissident factions in Cairo. Some Arab sources maintain that Ṭūrānshāh was present at the battle of Mansura and played a part in the liberation of Damietta, but Ibrāhīm Ramzī tells us (p. 131, footnote) that he deliberately chose the version which stated that Ṭūrānshāh arrived nine days after the battle and that he built his play around this fact. Obviously, it suited his nationalistic, democratic thesis to present a despotic, inglorious monarch who wanted to impose his will upon a politically conscious people.

The author also enforces the formality of his play by resorting to parallelism in structure. For instance, the quarrel between the Egyptian Princes in Act I is contrasted with a parallel quarrel in Act II in the French ranks, first between the spies, Philippe and Bernard, and then between the two brothers of the King, D'Artois and Poitiers. The point the dramatist wishes to make is that whereas the quarrel between the Muslim Princes is motivated by patriotism and a jealous concern for the fate of the country, the French quarrel is over who is to carnally possess Princess Ṣafiyya.

'The Heroes of Mansura' is pervaded by an intensely nationalistic sentiment; we notice that the treachery is perpetuated not by Egyptians, but by people of French origin: the physician, Hibat Allah (Philippe), the son of a French doctor captured in the previous Crusade, and Shaykh Bernard who uses as his tool the kidnapped, helpless Egyptian girl who wrongly believes she is simply obeying her father by supplying the Muslim general with false information about the French troops, thus enabling them to enter Damietta and capture it unopposed. The champions referred to are primarily Egyptians rather than Muslims, but 'The Heroes of Mansura' does not suffer artistically from cheap, facile nationalism. Not all the French characters are portrayed as vile and unprincipled. Unlike some plays by later dramatists, it does not present characters drawn in black and white. While the brothers of King Louis, D'Artois and Poitiers, are cowardly, lecherous and, particularly the former, lacking in chivalry, the King himself is painted as the personification of all the values of medieval chivalry (although he is superstitious enough to believe that Baybars' sword possesses magic qualities). When Princess Ṣafiyya is taken prisoner, King Louis decides to send her back in great honour to her family and entrusts his own brother, D'Artois, who is unfortunately captivated by her physical charms and betrays his trust, with this task. When the King learns what has happened he severely reprimands his brother (p.83) and Ṣafiyya herself testifies that Louis 'is a noble prince' (p.84). He is also instrumental in the final rescue of Ṣafiyya and her safe return to her people. The Egyptian Muslim leaders themselves are not all heroic or good. The newly-elected, young Sultan is painted as a drunkard and is shown as untrustworthy. He is *forced* by Baybars and the other noblemen to rule less like an authoritarian monarch and to honour the widowed Queen, Shajarat al-Durr.

Although most of the characters are sufficiently distinguished from one another there are three major ones in whose creation the playwright has particularly excelled. These are Baybars, Queen Shajarat al-Durr and Hibat Allah. Baybars is the nearest thing in Egyptian drama to the ideal knight. Our impression of him is formed not only by what we see him do and hear him say on the stage, but also from what other characters say about him. For instance, Suhayl, the Queen's private secretary, says of him 'He is the leader of this country without a doubt. Had I a say in the matter of succession I know whom I would have chosen' (p.94). He is a brave warrior whose virtues are acknowledged by the enemy and who, according to the Queen, has saved Egypt and therefore Sultan Ṭūrānshāh should be sufficiently grateful (p.144) to offer him Princess Ṣafiyya instead of competing with him over her. He is shrewd and intelligent; alone, of all the Princes present he is the one who realizes that the Queen is trying gently to break the sad news of the death of the ailing Sultan (p.37). He is affectionate as we see in the warmth of his embrace of the Commander Fakhr al-Dīn (p.102), yet on a matter of principle he is known never to let friendship stand in the way of his duty (p.31); he does not hesitate even to fight Fakhr al-Dīn when he thinks he is guilty of the cowardly surrender of Damietta (p.28). Despite his deep love of Ṣafiyya, which at times afflicts him almost to distraction, he feels Egypt should always come first in his thoughts (p.106) and he postpones his marriage to her until the war is over. His love inspires courage to the point of foolhardiness; after the battle of Mansura, in which he inflicts a heavy defeat on the French forces, he runs the risk of being killed in revenge by going over to the French in Damietta to ask the Queen of France about Ṣafiyya – an act which Queen Shajarat al-Durr considers utter folly.

It is perhaps inevitable that in a work dealing with such themes an element of romance should creep in. Once in distress Ṣafiyya calls out to Baybars for help who, true to the romance tradition, is ready at hand to oblige (p.76). The explanation he offers for being there is that he heard someone shouting for help while he was on his way to see the French King who was not far off, to ask him to be gracious enough to free Princess Ṣafiyya from captivity, having heard much about this great Frenchman (p.84). It must be admitted, however, that such improbable happenings do not occur again in the play, for there are several scenes in which the call of a lady in distress is not promptly answered by a hero conveniently available. Furthermore, Baybars is himself saved by the two women he rushed to rescue. Ṣafiyya wrenches his sword from a French soldier, who was about to use it against him, and stabs the soldier in the arm (in Act II) and Maryam warns him of enemies coming from behind to attack him.

The character of Queen Shajarat al-Durr is no less idealized. She too is held in the greatest esteem by her people. The new Sultan's man, Ṣabīḥ, says of her 'I have not seen such piety and resolution in any woman' to which her secretary, Suhayl, replies 'Nor in any man either!' (p.95). She has so much dignity and commands so much respect that she only has to appear before the fighting Princes for them to stop their quarrel at once. She is loved by the nobility, who dearly wish to elect her as their monarch after the death of her husband, but she declines the offer on the grounds that, according to the Prophet, no nation can prosper that allows itself to be governed by a woman (p.39). She discharges her royal duties so admirably that she inspires utter loyalty to her person and confidence in her ability. A courageous woman, she wishes to remain in Mansura, near the thick of battle, as she is supposed to be the ruler of Egypt until the arrival of the new Sultan (p.98). She makes a short but powerful speech quoting effectively from the Koran while addressing the army generals before the decisive battle at Mansura (p.99) and even appears fully armed, ready to take her part in the fighting (p.129). In the painful scene of confrontation with the new Sultan she conducts herself with the utmost dignity, and retains her noble self-composure despite his offensive language. Yet she is not without warmth of character which reveals itself in the scene where she provides comfort for Baybars, who, distraught by the disappearance of his beloved, pours out his heart to her.

As for Hibat Allah, he is a slightly more complex creature; although his evil is somewhat exaggerated, he cannot be said to suffer from motiveless malignity. He has had to embrace Islam, put on a false outward appearance and lead a double life in order to survive; he is short of stature and not particularly handsome; he has been insultingly spurned by the woman he loved, and he then discovers her married to another man whose public career and presence provide a powerful stimulus to his jealousy. Bernard accuses him of stupid, impulsive behaviour and to some extent he is capable of that; yet he is not merely a slave of passion, he can be cool and calculating and extremely persuasive. He is so plausible that he won the trust not only of the departed Sultan whose private physician and constant companion he remained on all his travels , but he soon became the trustworthy companion of the new Sultan and managed to turn his feelings not only against the Queen and Baybars, but also against the other Princes. All the Princes, with the possible exception of Aqṭay, trust him. We can see how resourceful and persuasive he can be in the scene where he manages to extricate himself from difficulty first with Ṣafiyya, then with Maryam:

PHILIPPE *disguised as* HIBAT ALLAH, *suddenly appears before* ṢAFIYYA *and* MARYAM. *The latter is at first taken by surprise, but soon she suspects he is* PHILIPPE:

MARYAM: Oh! Who are you? Heavens, it's Philippe!

ṢAFIYYA: No, Maryam. This is Hibat Allah, the physician. Don't be afraid!

MARYAM: My lady, I could have sworn he's...

HIBAT (*interrupting* MARYAM *and addressing* ṢAFIYYA): Good day Your Highness!

ṢAFIYYA: Welcome, Hibat Allah!

MARYAM: Surely this is Philippe who used to visit us at Faraskur.

HIBAT: How can you fail to recognize me? I'm Hibat Allah, the physician who looks after His Majesty, the Sultan, and his gracious wife. I treated Her Highness, the Princess, some years ago. Do you still remember those days, Your Highness?

ṢAFIYYA: Of course. It was in Aleppo, wasn't it?

HIBAT: Aleppo, indeed. Aleppo it was.

ṢAFIYYA: What has brought you here, Hibat Allah? (*She returns to her seat, followed by* HIBAT ALLAH.)

HIBAT: I really don't know. I did not wait to complete my prayers, but rushed to impart to Prince Fakhr al-Dīn some important information regarding the movements of the French. I couldn't find him where I thought he would be, so I came looking for him in his house. But I seem to have come to the wrong place.

ṢAFIYYA: No, you haven't. This is Prince Fakhr al-Dīn's house all right, but he and his family vacated it last week and we were brought here yesterday evening. How come you didn't know that?

HIBAT: I didn't. Is he camping on the bank?

ṢAFIYYA: And you didn't know that either? The bank is close enough for you to see. You work at the royal court and yet you are not aware of all this. Where have you been the past few days?

HIBAT: We physicians are only concerned with treating our patients, be they our own men or our enemy.

ṢAFIYYA: You do surprise me, Hibat Allah. Medicine is no more than a profession like any other. It's no different from being a secretary or a general. I shouldn't imagine anyone belonging to those professions would be totally unaware of his position in relation to this raging war. Didn't you say just now that you had come here to impart some important intelligence concerning the movements of the French to Fakhr al-Dīn?

HIBAT: True, my lady. Obviously I'm too preoccupied with my personal problems to know what I am saying. Where is Prince Baybars now?

ṢAFIYYA: He's gone to guard the royal palace, and he'll soon return to us safely. He's promised me to do just that, and he is not a man to break his promise.

HIBAT: May God bring him back safe!

ṢAFIYYA: Amen.

HIBAT (*swallowing*): May I have a drink of water, please? (*Turning round.*) I'm dying of thirst.

ṢAFIYYA: Bring the doctor a glass of water, Maryam. It's just like summer today, although it is midwinter.

MARYAM (*murmuring as she goes out*): I'm sure it's Philippe. My eyes never deceive me.

HIBAT: Now I can talk to you, my lady.

ṢAFIYYA: And what has been stopping you? Surely you don't fear Maryam?

HIBAT: Maryam? You mean the girl from Faraskur? Oh, no. But tell me, my lady! Can't you see how I stumble for words, not knowing what to say to you?

ṢAFIYYA (*laughing sarcastically*): It must be the excessive warmth of the winter, doctor.

HIBAT: It is indeed the warmth, the warmth of my feelings, the memory of that hour I spent in Aleppo two years ago. I was then in the company of a young lady of bewitching eyes, two years younger than you are now. Her sister was then very ill while her brother-in-law was engaged in the wars, and she was extremely concerned about her sister's health. This young lady of ravishing beauty promised to reward me well if I could cure her sister. I wanted to see how serious she was, so she gave me her solemn oath. I don't know whether or not this fair lady remembers her promise.

ṢAFIYYA: She does.

HIBAT: Do you know her then?

ṢAFIYYA (*laughing courteously*): Does it look as if I didn't know her (does it)?

HIBAT: God willed that her sister's cure was to be accomplished at my hands, thank Heaven! But she has not yet fulfilled her promise to me.

ṢAFIYYA: That was because she has been so far away, Hibat Allah.

HIBAT: I thank God for that.

ṢAFIYYAT: Why so?

HIBAT: It seems that God has planned that I should be more in need of her fulfilling her promise now than at any time in the past, so He delayed directing my steps to this place until today. Will the fair lady carry out her promise to me now?

ṢAFIYYA: Of course, if it is within her power.

HIBAT: What I ask of you is to conceal me in this mansion one whole day.

ṢAFIYYA: Conceal you in this mansion?

HIBAT: Yes, my lady.

ṢAFIYYA: And what for?

HIBAT: I've been examining my astrolabe lately, and I saw that today, Tuesday, will be a most critical date in my life: if anyone at all, other than the person dearest to me, was to know where I was at nightfall I would meet my certain death.

ṢAFIYYA: Am I the dearest person to you then? Thank you very much, Hibat Allah. You are certainly the one man everybody trusts at the palace, and it's no wonder that we all honour you and hold you dear.

HIBAT: Thank you, my lady. Only God knows the nature of the love I bear Your Ladyship. This heart and this eye! When I saw you in Aleppo it was as if I glimpsed a houri from Paradise. I nearly put an end to my life when I had to leave in the Sultan's retinue while you remained behind.

ṢAFIYYA: Oh! Why?

HIBAT (*confused*): Because you were then unwell, and I had hoped . . .

ṢAFIYYA (*somewhat relieved*): Thank you.

HIBAT: Because of you I suffered in silence, and like a desperate lover I endured my pains.

ṢAFIYYA: A desperate lover!

HIBAT: Yes, my lady. When I learnt that you had been taken prisoner by Count D'Artois I nearly died of grief, for I realized then that I had lost the last ray of hope which kept me alive.

ṢAFIYYA (*alarmed*): What hope do you mean, doctor?

HIBAT: Oh. I . . . I . . . Nothing. I only wished that . . . Well (*Scrutinizing her face, speaking slowly and bowing his head from time to time.*) I meant that if you remained in the Count's hands and I failed to find you on Tuesday (*Detecting in her eyes a look of revulsion, he speaks more hurriedly, glad to find a plausible way out.*) and you, the dearest person to me, were unable to find a secret place for me to hide that day, I would lose all hope of survival.

ṢAFIYYA (*as if relieved*): I see. Your request shall be answered. (*Rises and shouts.*) Maryam! Why do you take so long, Maryam? What's keeping you? (*she takes one step towards the door.*) I shall go and hurry her, and I shall also look for a suitable place for you to hide.

HIBAT: Thank you, my lady. (*He bends over to kiss her hand, but* ṢAFIYYA *walks on, unaware of his intention and goes inside.* HIBAT *remains standing, following her with his eyes, looking like a man desperately in love.*) I had hoped to kiss her hand, but she has denied me even that. Now my hopes are miserably dashed. But why can't this girl be my wife? Am I of less noble descent that she is? Why shouldn't I attain a higher position in this land? I am no less worthy or noble than anyone here. (*Sitting down after a pause.*) I must have her. I love her. I want her for myself. I desire her more than anything else in the world (*He bows his head for a while, then bursts out laughing.*) Really! Nothing surprises me more than my own ambitions. But I will get her somehow, and I think I am already on the road to success. I've shown them where to cross the river enabling them to enter the town of Mansura, and I must now carry out the rest of my plans. D'Artois will be coming here soon and so will Baybars. One of them is bound to kill the other when they meet and get him out of the way. The survivor I shall deal with in my own fashion when he least suspects me. But Mary, God curse her, has recognized me and no doubt will reveal my secret unless I act quickly. (MARYAM *enters and* HIBAT ALLAH *glowers at her, addressing her angrily.*) Come on, Mary. Give me the water quickly. Why were you so long fetching it? I've nearly died of thirst.

MARYAM (*frightened*): I didn't know where to get the glass or water from. I had to wait for My Lady to show me. We only came to this mansion this morning.

HIBAT: Ah! I'm grateful to you. (*Takes the glass from her and examines the water.*) I suspect this is as dirty and polluted as the water in Damietta. You do remember the Damietta water, don't you? (*He throws the water onto the ground.* MARYAM *looks scared.*)

MARYAM: I've never been to Damietta in all my life.

HIBAT (*laughs sarcastically*): Let me think. The first time you were there was seven months ago. You went there with an old man from Faraskur. Yes, he sent you to a certain Prince on a mission in which you acted like the Devil incarnate. No doubt you know what water tastes like there. (*He looks triumphantly at her.*)

MARYAM: O my God!

HIBAT: Isn't that true?

MARYAM: No. I have never been to Damietta.

HIBAT: Don't lie to me! You were sent by Bernard, the farmer, to Prince Fakhr al-Dīn who, incidentally, owns this mansion. Do you really think there is anything at all about you that I don't know? (*He laughs.*)

MARYAM: All right then. What's wrong with what I did?

HIBAT: Then why are you so scared if it was all innocent? Doesn't your heart tell you certain things?

MARYAM: Do you think they will punish me for what I did so long ago?

HIBAT: What makes you think they will not? They never forget a wrong done to them. Now look what *you* have done to them. You only caused the loss of a whole town with its men and property and the slaughter of fifty of its princes. You certainly deserve death more than they did.

MARYAM: So you think they will kill me now?

HIBAT: Do you seriously doubt that?

MARYAM: But who will tell them of my crime now that Bernard has been killed.

HIBAT: Bernard killed?

MARYAM: That's what I was told.

HIBAT: I don't think so. In any case even if he was killed my brother Philippe is still alive.

MARYAM: Is he your brother, Sir?

HIBAT: We're twins. He retained the faith of his forefathers just like Bernard, while I was converted to the good religion of Islam. But this has not driven us apart: he used to visit me often and confide in me. He's told me all about you, Mary.

MARYAM (*sighing sadly*): Oh!

HIBAT: Don't be frightened. It's a secret which shall never escape from my lips.

MARYAM (*kneeling*): I thank you, Sir. You are a true gentleman. Have mercy on me and protect me! I am a poor orphan who has lost both her parents.

HIBAT (*secretly smiling*): Have no fear! I mean no harm, at least for my brother's sake.

MARYAM (*kissing his hand*): I thank you, Sir. I'm much obliged to you. I've been in desperate straits and so unhappy. I have no father to turn to for safety and comfort, nor a brother to relieve me of my burden. If I remain here I'm in danger of my secret crime being revealed. And if I flee to the King of France he is sure to punish me for disobeying his order on the night of Faraskur. Please God have mercy on me! I crave your pity.

HIBAT: Comfort yourself. Don't be afraid. From now on I shall be in place of your father.

MARYAM: I thank you, Sir. (*she rises.*)

HIBAT: Stay with your mistress, Princess Ṣafiyya! Keep her company all the time! Don't leave her; this will be safer for you. But beware of mentioning to her my relation to my brother, Philippe. Don't talk about our similar looks, otherwise they might kill me by mistake.

MARYAM: I'll do exactly as you tell me, Sir.

HIBAT: Whatever I ask you to do by day or night you must do it at once.

MARYAM: I shall be completely at your service, Sir.

HIBAT: This is a pact between us for one week only. As soon as the war is over I shall return you to your father and mother.

MARYAM (*surprised*): My father and mother! Do I have a father and a mother? Are they still alive?

HIBAT: Yes. That is what Philippe has told me and he says he knows them. He did not wish to tell you lest you should leave his uncle, Shaykh Bernard, who needed you to look after him. Now that you have left him I promise to take you back to them.

MARYAM: If you really do so I shall for ever be your slave, even more obedient than your slave. Fancy returning me to my father and mother! I already feel life creeping back to my heart at the mere thought.

HIBAT: You shall be reunited with your parents, you may rest assured of that. But you must not breathe a word of all this to a soul.

MARYAM: I won't. I won't. I'm utterly at your command.

(pp.108–19)

In a subtle way the author makes Hibat Allah's presence dominate 'The Heroes of Mansura'. We hear of him at the beginning of the play and, although we do not see him in Act I, we are told so much about him that our interest and curiosity are aroused. Also the play ends with his death at the hands of Baybars when the true nature of his villainy is revealed. To pursue his own interest and to possess Ṣafiyya, the woman for whom he has developed a blind passion, he is prepared to stop at nothing; when it suits him he does not hesitate to order the death of Bernard, the man who has been helping him and working very closely with him for more than seventeen years.

'The Heroes of Mansura' is not simply a successful, historical play full of dramatic events and convincing characters. Its dialogue is written in a type of classical Arabic totally free from the artificialities, the bombast and the rhyming prose which characterized many of the plays that had previously been produced in the classical language. Indeed at times it attains great heights of poetry and lyricism, as in the speeches in which Baybars complains of his love for Ṣafiyya to the Queen or the Queen's victory speech. The poetic atmosphere is strengthened by strikingly formal, ceremonial and almost ritualistic action. For instance, Act I ends with a scene in which all the noblemen present, together with Queen Shajarat al-Durr, take a ceremonial oath by placing their hands on the open Koran with Baybars' sword drawn, swearing to keep the departed Sultan's death a secret until his son is back in Egypt (pp.45–6). Another example is provided by the procession which takes place at the beginning of Act III, when Queen Shajarat al-Durr is carried in a litter preceded by torchmen and flanked by the Princes Baybars and Fakhr al-Dīn in the splendour of their full armour (p.95). The playwright even resorts to symbolism. The play opens with a game of chess in which a pawn checkmates the king; Fakhr al-Dīn, feeling a little superstitious at this hour of crisis, considers this a bad omen. He is made fun of by the other Princes; yet his fears are realized because the Sultan soon dies. A further significance of the fall of the chess king at the hand of a pawn is that it points forward to the end of the play when the new Sultan is mastered by his people. The message the author wishes to convey to his audience, and which runs like a leitmotif throughout the play, reiterated at crucial moments such as the time of deciding the question of succession to the throne of Egypt in Act I, just before the decisive battle against the Crusaders in Act III and in the memorable speech which Queen Shajarat al-Durr makes in her final appearance in the play in Act IV (p.159), is that a nation is not judged by the quality of its monarch but by the quality of its people, for the age of absolute monarchy has gone. This was Ibrāhīm Ramzī's response to the crisis created by the British when arbitrarily they replaced Khedive Abbas by Sultan Husayn Kamil. Despite its medieval historical framework, and despite its poetic atmosphere and romance themes, 'The Heroes of Mansura' was therefore very much a contemporary Egyptian play about a nationalist theme. It is certainly one of the classics of modern Egyptian drama and it deserves more critical respect than it has generally received so far.[33] With it, together with 'Admission to the Baths', it can safely be said that modern Egyptian drama has come of age.

MUḤAMMAD TAYMŪR

Unlike Ibrāhīm Ramzī, Muḥammad Taymūr (1891–1921) wrote only a small number of plays, three in all. There were several reasons for this: he died tragically young; his literary output was not confined to drama; unlike many playwrights, he was not driven by financial considerations to turn out cheap, popular work speedily; according to his brother, the only *opéra bouffe* he collaborated on was motivated by the desire to raise the standard of the popular theatre.[34] Taymūr was born to a rich aristocratic family of Turkish origin with several distinguished members in the world of learning and letters. His father, Aḥmad Taymūr Pacha, was a renowned Arabic scholar who owned an excellent collection of Arabic books, many in valuable manuscripts which he donated to the Egyptian National Library, his aunt, ʿĀʾisha, was one of the earliest women writers of note in modern Arabic literature while his younger brother, Maḥmūd, became a leading novelist and dramatist in the Arab world.

Taymūr developed a keen interest in the theatre while he was still a schoolboy, but it was really after his departure from Egypt that his mature views on the Egyptian stage took shape. Shortly before the First World War he went to Berlin to study medicine but he gave this up after two months[35] and left for France where he spent three years studying law in Lyons and Paris. His study was interrupted by the outbreak of the War which made it impossible for him to return to France after a trip to Egypt. In France he was exposed to much French literature, particularly drama; it is reported that he occupied a room overlooking L'Odéon and that he went to the theatre in Paris practically every night.[36] It was in France that he felt the need for 'Egyptianizing literature' (*tamṣīr al-adab*), and the idea of producing literature which had an Egyptian character and a purely local colour took hold of him and became his guiding principle in writing plays for the rest of his life.

On his return to Egypt Taymūr joined *Jamʿiyyat Anṣār al-Thamthīl* (Society for Promoting Acting), an acting group with a catholic interest in drama which included English plays, amongst other things; Taymūr (with the help of a colleague) translated Shakespeare's *Timon of Athens* for them but the translation unfortunately is lost. The first of Taymūr's full length plays was *al-ʿUṣfūr fī'l Qafaṣ* ('The Bird in the Cage') performed in 1918. He first wrote the play in classical Arabic in three acts and then subsequently rewrote it in colloquial Arabic (adding a fourth act) because he found this medium better suited to the events and characters in the play. After a brief initial success, the play apparently could not compete with the more popular shows.[37] Appalled at the commercial failure of the serious theatre compared with the cheap revue, farce, operetta and melodrama, Taymūr began to publish his series of critical articles on the leading figures of the Egyptian theatre, actors and singers such as Salāma Ḥijāzī, Najīb al-Rīḥānī, Jūrj Abyaḍ, ʿAbd al-Raḥmān Rushdī, ʿAzīz ʿĪd and Munīra al-Mahdiyya. In the hope of wooing the audience with a more comical work he also wrote in colloquial Arabic *ʿAbd as-Sattār Afandī* ("ʿAbd as-Sattār Effendī') performed in 1918), which deals with the life and problems of a middle class, Egyptian family, but because of the absence of singing and sexual titillation, this play did not attain much popularity either. According to his brother, Maḥmūd, he was so dejected at this failure that he turned away from play writing altogether, concentrating on editing the periodical, *al-Sufūr*.

In *al-Sufūr* he published his amusing, as well as instructive, series of articles on contemporary Egyptian dramatists in the form of mock trials which take place within the framework of a dream. In his sleep Taymūr dreams that he dies and is transported to the next world where he witnesses contemporary writers (as well as himself) being summoned for trial by a panel consisting of Molière, Corneille, Racine, Goethe, Edmond Rostand and presided over by Shakespeare. These humorous articles undoubtedly afforded the best critique of Egyptian drama at the time. After a brief interval, however, Taymūr was tempted to try his hand at operetta. With the co-operation of Badīʿ Khayrī he produced *al-ʿAshra al-Ṭayyiba* ('The Ten of Diamonds'), a four-act *opéra bouffe* in colloquial Arabic verse and prose based on the story of Bluebeard and set in Mamlūk Egypt. The music for it was provided by the celebrated composer, Sayyid Darwīsh. Because it portrayed the tyranny of Mamlūk rule, the play was severely criticized which drove its author to utter despair feeling as he did that he had failed to attract the audience both in his serious and his light-hearted attempts at writing plays.

According to his brother again,[38] Taymūr's last play *al-Hāwiya* ('The Precipice', 1921) was written with no thought of an audience in mind.

Apparently he wrote it simply to please himself, driven by an inner compulsion to write what he believed to be a good drama irrespective of what the world of the Egyptian theatre wanted. However, it coincided with a relative decline in the tide of the cheap, popular revue and a slow rise of interest in serious drama exemplified in the creation of a new troupe called the Promotion of Arab Acting Troupe (ʿUkāsha & Co.) which performed in a new theatre set up by the founder of the Bank of Egypt, Ṭalʿat Ḥarb. But Taymūr, alas, was already suffering from the jaundice which proved fatal when the rehearsals of this play began and it was two months after his death that the play was performed with considerable success.

Zakī Ṭulaymāt reminds us that Taymūr wrote no fewer than forty articles on matters relating to the theatre, concerning a wide variety of subjects ranging from the birth and development of drama in France and, in less detail, in Egypt, as well as a summary critique of contemporary Egyptian dramatists and actors and actresses. Ṭulaymāt's fair judgment of Taymūr's work (in 1922) was that 'despite its limitations what Taymūr has left us is the best that has been written in Egypt on our theatre'. He pointed out that, unlike other writers who attacked the vogue of the popular theatre in general terms and largely on moral grounds, Taymūr had a clear vision of the principles of good drama and showed how popular theatrical entertainments fell short of them.[39]

Among the important subjects Taymūr tackles in his articles are the definition of a good play and the reasons for the low standard of the Egyptian theatre. In his view a good play must meet the following five criteria: 1. Characterization must be based on sound psychological analysis. 2. It must have local colour. 3. It must be well constructed so that the audience's attention is constantly aroused and no boredom is felt. 4. Its author should be following his natural bent, be it towards comedy or serious drama. 5. It should avoid *irrelevant* excitement arising from sexual titillation, strange happenings, melodramatic coincidences and the like. He dismisses from the category of a good play melodrama, *Grand Guignol*, vaudeville and revue, after providing short, clear descriptions of these four forms, which may be useful to include here to help us see what he himself is trying to do, or rather not to do, in his plays. A melodrama is a sad story in which the author tries to move the audience by resorting to surprises, absurd coincidences, tear-jerking situations contrary to all logic, and in which characters are inconsistent and not shown in depth, construction is non-existent and local colour is totally absent. A *Grand Guignol* is a shorter play based on a horrendous, hair-raising event. Vaudeville, on the other hand, is the comic equivalent of melodrama; it provides no character analysis, no local colour, no reasonable incidents, only crude jokes and shameful and immoral situations and it is, therefore, the most morally dangerous of all four kinds. Finally, a revue consists of few songs sung on the stage, accompanied by scenes or sketches unrelated to the songs, with an admixture of crude jokes and immoral situations.[40]

When he comes to discuss the reasons for the low standard of theatre in Egypt, Taymūr states that 'the first cause is that our serious troupes are anxious to put on translated plays which cannot be digested by an Egyptian and in which no Egyptian can identify his manners and customs'. 'We should not present to the audience valuable, well-made European plays, but produce for the public plays which discuss its current issues in order that it may derive useful lessons from them.'[41] It is easy to see the connection between this and Taymūr's desire to write specifically Egyptian drama. It will be noticed that the second of the five criteria of a good play is, in his opinion, the need to create local colour; in importance, it comes immediately after convincing characterization and before even plot or structure. Taymūr has, therefore, been justly described as one of the founders and advocates of the school of Egyptian Theatre which insisted upon the need to write contemporary Egyptian drama to replace the translations or adaptations of foreign plays which had foreign settings and dealt with foreign events.[42] Related to that is the question of the language of the dialogue; to produce convincing characters and a credible local colour the dialogue had to sound plausible. Taymūr believed that in plays dealing with contemporary Egyptian issues, unlike those dealing with ancient Arab or Egyptian themes or translations from foreign languages, a playwright should employ the colloquial language. With this solution to the problem of the language of the dialogue, Taymūr's brother, Maḥmūd, agreed wholeheartedly at one time, defending it on grounds of realism and even praising his older brother for the considerable courage and daring which this solution involved in those days: 'I do not exaggerate', he writes, 'when I say that he was the first to write for the serious theatre serious drama in the spoken/colloquial language'.[43] It is not an accident, therefore, that the second most striking quality which Zakī Ṭulaymāt found in Taymūr's plays (after their good construction), was their 'excellent dialogue'.[44]

For a first play, Taymūr's *el-ʿAsfūr fi'l-Afaṣ (al-ʿUsfūr fi'l-Qafaṣ)* is a remarkable piece of dramatic writing. It is a genuinely Egyptian play with a compact, well-constructed and fast-moving plot, lively dialogue and competent characterization. Furthermore, although it deals with a real social problem, it is not devoid of humour. The author describes it as an Egyptian comedy in four acts. The events revolve around an upper class, Egyptian family whose head, Muḥammad el-Ziftāwī Pacha, is a wealthy but miserly landowner. Having lost his seat on the county council, which meant so much to him both socially and financially, he moves to Cairo where he has been living for some time trying by all possible means to persuade those who hold high office in the government, especially Ḥasan Pacha Raḍwān, to use their influence to help him regain his seat. He rules his home like a tyrant; his wife, ʿAzīza, is scared of him and is reduced to a suffering non-entity; his only son, Ḥasan Bey, who is in his final year at school, is scandalously ill-treated and given very little pocket money; for fear of spoiling him his father never smiles at his son or even allows him to eat at the same table with him at home.

Being penniless and deprived of his father's affection, Ḥasan welcomes the interest taken in him by the tender-hearted, westernized, Levantine maid, Marguerite, whose pity for him turns into love. The father catches them kissing and immediately fires her. Despite a limited and momentary show of resistance, Ḥasan accepts his lot and continues to live unhappily at home though his studies suffer and he fails his examination. Five months later, Marguerite writes to tell him that she is pregnant by him and when he does not react she threatens to call on him and break the news to his father. Distraught, Ḥasan seeks help from his cousin and friend, Maḥmūd, who together with the mother make an unsuccessful attempt to avoid a confrontation between the father and Marguerite. However, Marguerite finally confronts el-Ziftāwī Pacha who, at the news of her pregnancy, threatens to strike her and orders her out of the house. This time Ḥasan finds sufficient courage to stand up to his father and he leaves the house with Marguerite. They get married and rent a small flat where they live together with the new-born baby on a small, monthly salary he receives from his employment as a junior clerk. They are visited by his cousins and also by his mother who calls on them once a week behind her husband's back and occasionally helps them financially. Their luck turns a year later when Ḥasan saves a gentleman from a near-fatal, tramcar accident. This gentleman turns out to be none other than the Pacha whom his father has been courting to help him regain his seat on the council. To show his gratitude the Pacha offers to have a cup of coffee with Ḥasan in his flat where he meets Ḥasan's cousin who tells him the story of the family quarrel. The Pacha decides to reconcile the father and the son and tactfully but firmly lays down three conditions for his help: the reconciliation, an allowance of sixty pounds per month to Ḥasan and the father's agreement not to go ahead with his plan to disinherit his son. The father agrees and when he sees his grandson he seems to suffer a real, though sudden, change of heart and fully accepts his son's marriage.

This play does not strike us as the work of a novice. All the information necessary for us to follow the action is given here indirectly in the course of the dialogue. Suspense is cunningly created and our interest is maintained throughout. The characters are presented dramatically; we are not, for instance, just told by other characters what they are like, but they reveal their true nature to us in their actions on the stage. Furthermore, with the possible exception of the mother, they are not painted in black and white but they have a measure of complexity which bestows upon them an air of credibility. This applies even to the father whose excessive meanness borders on the caricature. He has been described, with some exaggeration, as a mixture of Molière's Harpagon and Monsieur Jordain.[45] He is a miser, but he is also a social climber and does not mind spending money on appearances in order to increase his social standing and the chance of election. He buys expensive vases about which he knows nothing in an attempt to keep up with the wealthy aristocracy.[46] To impress his guests he displays in the drawing room the volumes of the Arabic Dictionary (*Lisān al-ʿArab*), which he admits he does not understand.[47] He gives formal dinner parties at which he wears a frock-coat in honour of the man whose help he is seeking,[48] yet he will not buy his son a dinner jacket to wear at a high class wedding on the grounds that it is what infidels wear.[49] He is so tight-fisted at home that the maid has to purchase the spot-remover she needs to clean his suits with her own money.[50] He will not pay the cab driver his full fare and nearly has a heart attack when he discovers that he has given a beggar a shilling instead of a twopenny piece by mistake. Any damage that occurs on his extensive farm has to be paid for by his employees even though it may not be their fault. He discourages his wife from receiving her female friends because they consume too much coffee and he even delights at the thought of having saved twenty pounds on food during the year since his son Ḥasan left the house. Though a ruthless tyrant in his relation to his family, he becomes a most docile creature when faced with the man who he hopes, will engineer his election. This bundle of contradictions is at heart a superstitious, old-fashioned, semi-literate man, despite the veneer of sophistication shown in his outward garb and the gilt French furniture of his expensive home. He is disappointed not to find any pictures in a book on Napoleon which his son is reading and does not believe in modern medicine which he thinks works against the will of God. However, his change of heart at the sight of his infant grandson at the end of the play is a trifle too sudden to be convincing.

Likewise, his son Ḥasan is by no means a flat character. He knows that he has been attracted to Marguerite largely because he is starved of affection, but he is at first too weak to rebel against his father and join her when she is turned out of the house. Even after he learns of her pregnancy he tries to shrug off his responsibility and it is only gradually, and when he sees a re-enactment of the scene of her dismissal, that he grows up and decides to stand by her. Ḥasan's companions are his two cousins, Maḥmūd and Amīn, who are meant to be a contrasting pair, serving partly as confidantes and partly as foils to his character. Maḥmūd is painted as a model of virtue, a successful and conscientious university student, yet even he is not all white, since on hearing of Marguerite's pregnancy his first thought is how to save not the girl but his own cousin. Similarly Amīn, who is shown as an irresponsible, young man-about-town, a dandy and a womaniser, wasting away the family inheritance on his own pleasures, has enough charm to render him a fairly sympathetic character despite his serious vices. Contrary to what a critic of Taymūr says, he is not all evil.[51] Even Fayrūz Aghā, the Sudanese eunuch and manservant, is depicted as a somewhat hypocritical and cunning person. He develops a passion for Marguerite who understandably, albeit somewhat cruelly, laughs at him and, when he is caught by Ḥasan and Maḥmūd soliloquizing about his love for her, he pretends to be reading aloud from a well-known book of Muslim prayers.[52]

The main theme of the play is not merely the conflict between the generations, but also the disastrous results of the restrictive, and excessively conservative, oriental way of bringing up children. Although it deals largely with a small section of Egyptian society, namely family life in the upper classes, much is revealed about the social questions of the moment, including the phenomenon of the village chief squandering the proceeds of the sale of his crop on women in the metropolis which, as we have seen, has been dealt with in other literary works.[53] The plot betrays the underlying state of flux of the social values at the time and the need to maintain the class distinctions, emphasized by the all too revealing advice given by Raḍwān Pacha to Ḥasan's cousins not to follow his example and marry beneath them. While wishing to do justice to the 'fallen' woman, the victim of the socially superior male, the dramatist clearly does not approve of socially unequal marriage alliances.

One final comment deserves to be made about the links in Taymūr's work, conscious or otherwise, with earlier Egyptian comedy. The appearance of the Sudanese/Nubian servant who provides humour not only because of his stereotyped character, but also verbally through his peculiar dialect of Arabic, has already been seen not only in Ṣannūʿ (the character of Abū Rīda) but even in Ibn Dāniyāl. Likewise, the lowly servant falling in love with the Europeanized maid has been encountered before in Ṣannūʿ's play, 'The Cairo Stock Exchange'. The ludicrous imitation of western manners was another theme favoured by Ṣannūʿ, and in Taymūr's play one of Amīn's serious problems is having to decide whether to wear a dinner suit or tails for the wedding which he is planning to attend![54]

Taymūr's second play, also described as an Egyptian comedy of manners in four acts, is *ʿAbd as-Sattār Afandī*. It forms an interesting contrast with *el-ʿAsfūr fi'l-Afaṣ*. It does not attempt to depict the life of the upper classes of Egypt but that of a middle class Egyptian family. Although it still deals to some extent with the conflict of generations, the situation is here reversed for it is the son who is the tyrant, bullying his father and mother and indeed the entire household. Despite the assertion of several critics to the contrary, including the dramatist's distinguished brother, *ʿAbd as-Sattār Afandī* does not merely attempt to show different 'psychological' types of characters, but it also treats several problems which confronted Egyptian society at the time, even though the dramatist does not offer a crudely-stated moral at the end of the play as he does in *el-ʿAsfūr*. As in the earlier play, what we are shown here is a society in transition in which values are in a state of flux. In the world of *ʿAbd as-Sattār*, traditional norms are threatened by a veneer of westernization, parental authority eroded and, for selfish reasons, a spoilt brother tries to force his older sister into marriage.

ʿAbd as-Sattār Afandī, a minor civil servant, is a henpecked husband, who, nevertheless, is capable of occasional spurts of courage and self-assertiveness. Unaware of his inadequacies and driven largely by his disappointment in his wife, he is given to flirting with younger women and of boasting of having indiscriminate affairs with females from the lower walks of life. His virtually illiterate, shrewish wife, Nafūsa, is in her turn, completely under the thumb of their spoilt, unemployed and good-for-nothing son, ʿAfīfī, who behaves as if he was a gentleman of leisure. Afīfī is an amateur actor. He keeps dogs and, because he is a member of the Society for the Prevention of Cruelty to Animals, bullies everybody for not devoting themselves utterly to the care of his dogs with the result that they allow one dog to fall ill. With his mother on his side and helped by the maid, Hānim, a young, lower class woman of enormous vitality and full of devilry with whom he has an affair, ʿAfīfī plans to marry off his sister, Jamīla, a quiet girl a few years older than himself, to his poetaster friend, Faraḥāt, a plausible crook and probably a pimp, who has led him to believe that in return for this marriage he will be able to arrange, through his connections, a lucrative marriage for ʿAfīfī to the daughter of a rich, aristocratic family.

In the mean time ʿAbd as-Sattār, who has no illusions about Faraḥāt, has chosen for his daughter, whom he loves dearly, a decent young man called Balīgh, a minor civil servant of modest means who is in love with his daughter and whom she wishes to marry. The action of the play consists in the attempt by ʿAbd as-Sattār, helped by the old servant of the family, ʿAmm Khalīfa, to thwart the plot hatched by his wife and son to marry Jamīla to Faraḥāt and to bring about a successful union between her and Balīgh. Thus the characters are divided into two camps: ʿAfīfī, Nafūsa, Hānim and Faraḥāt on one side and on the other ʿAbd as-Sattār, ʿAmm Khalīfa, Jamīla and Balīgh. The conflict rages particularly when, overhearing a conversation between her brother and Faraḥāt, Jamīla becomes convinced that the man her brother wishes her to marry is in truth no more than a criminal. She would, therefore, rather die than marry him. It is an unequal battle as ʿAbd as-Sattār lacks sustained courage and he is so keenly conscious of his cowardice that the external conflict, which provides the dramatic tension and several comic situations in the play, is in some measure paralleled by an inner conflict in ʿAbd as-Sattār's weak personality between his ardent desire to save his daughter and his fear of his wife and son. However, chance intervenes twice to lend ʿAbd as-Sattār a helping hand. First, Balīgh's rich uncle dies at the right moment leaving him a considerable fortune in land and money. The good news announced by ʿAbd as-Sattār momentarily sways Nafūsa but ʿAfīfī, more interested in the prospect of having a rich wife, persuades his mother not to give credence to her husband's story since, he tells her, he is a liar and has been an unfaithful husband. To prove his untrustworthiness ʿAfīfī manages to make her hide with him and to overhear a conversation (engineered by him) between her husband and the maid, Hānim, who has agreed to act seductively and to encourage ʿAbd as-Sattār to give expression to his lust for her and his hatred of his wife and to boast of his various affairs with women of her acquaintance. Shocked at the words and behaviour of her husband in this mock seduction scene (somewhat reminiscent of *Tartuffe*), Nafūsa proceeds to attack him with her shoes to teach him a lesson. She and her son have him locked up all night in a damp, dark room without a bed (while his loyal servant, Khalīfa, is made to spend the night in the lavatory), a punishment which seems to destroy his power of resistance and demoralize him utterly. In the morning Faraḥāt arrives accompanied by the marriage clerk to go through the marriage ceremony with Jamīla, but at the same time Balīgh turns up armed with the title deeds to prove his wealth and promises to give large presents to Nafūsa and ʿAfīfī in an attempt to win their approval. There follows an amusing scene in which the two suitors try to outbid each other in the size of their intended gifts although Faraḥāt, who pretends to be a rich man, makes the excuse that he has no money on him at present but promises to pay soon. However, at this moment chance intervenes for the second time: a police officer interrupts the proceedings and arrests Faraḥāt on a charge of forgery and deception. This incident, again somewhat reminiscent of the close of *Tartuffe*, finally saves Jamīla.

Like its predecessor, this is also a well-constructed play in which events move very fast indeed. Its humour arises from situations and characters as well as from verbal sources such as malapropisms. Many of the situations contain comic possibilities of which the author fully avails himself. In the opening domestic quarrel scene Nafūsa shouts at the porter, Khalīfa, then at the maid, Hānim, ʿAfīfī shouts at Khalīfa and then, when the servants have gone, at his own mother. The author's ironic treatment shows how everybody involved resorts to pretense and lying and is motivated purely by self-interest. The unemployed and impecunious ʿAfīfī accuses his mother of not showing him sufficient consideration and tries to assure her (and himself) that he is a respectable member of the community; after all, he is an amateur actor and a member of the Society for the Prevention of Cruelty to Animals, the two main sources from which he thinks he derives his social standing. His mother who dotes on him readily agrees with him, although she is too ignorant to pronounce correctly the words 'amateur actor' and naively describes him as a member of the zoo. He insists on giving her a demonstration of his acting which she at first welcomes. He chooses a scene from *Othello*, in his own translation, which is a sort of burlesque or travesty of the original, and he acts the part when Othello is about to strangle Desdemona using his mother as a substitute for the actress. He gets carried away, however, and presses her throat so hard that she thinks he has gone mad, screams for help and has to be rescued by her husband. Her husband scolds his son and criticizes his indolence and irresponsibility and his general way of life, but the son accuses his father of being an old-fashioned fogey incapable of appreciating his son's modern, sophisticated activities. The mother, far from being grateful to her husband for coming to her rescue, takes the son's side and proceeds to attack the father:

ʿABD AS-SATTĀR: What is going on here? What the hell are you doing, boy? (*Releasing* NAFŪSA.) Attacking your mother? Have you no shame?

NAFŪSA: What to you think you're doing, ʿAfīfī? You nearly killed me.

ʿAFĪFĪ: I'm only trying to show you what proper acting should be like.

ʿABD AS-SATTĀR: Proper acting, my foot! Have you gone mad, boy?

ʿAFĪFĪ: Watch your language, I'm warning you!

ʿABD AS-SATTĀR: Are you going to be impudent with me as well?

ʿAFĪFĪ: Do you hear him, Mother? He's picking a quarrel with me.

NAFŪSA: Bear with him, son! He's your father, after all.

ʿABD AS-SATTĀR: Isn't it enough that you were about to kill your mother?

ʿAFĪFĪ: Kill my mother? I was only acting, my dear man, acting.

ʿABD AS-SATTĀR: I've been telling you for so long to stop this nonsense and look for some decent job to earn you a living instead of loafing around as you're doing now, idle and unemployed.

ʿAFĪFĪ: Do you hear him, Mother? He calls me idle.

NAFŪSA: You idle! Never! You're a respectable, amateur Lesbian [Thespian] and a member of the zoo, to boot. You're never idle.

ʿABD AS-SATTĀR: Isn't it enough that he was about to throttle you? You still approve of his actions? I'm telling you, boy; you simply have got to find yourself a proper job and stop leading this sort of existence which pleases nobody. Your father is not a rich man and you cannot afford to go about doing exactly as you please, taking heed of no one.

ʿAFĪFĪ: Don't you call me 'boy'! I'm a grown-up man and everybody at the café addresses me as Sir.

ʿABD AS-SATTĀR: Don't you bandy words with me, boy, I'm warning you!

ʿAFĪFĪ: I hope you're listening to what your husband is saying, Nafūsa Hanim. By God, I'll make it a terrible day for you if you don't let off.

ʿABD AS-SATTĀR: Don't forget your manners, boy! Don't, I say! You're utterly without shame. Where were you dragged up, boy?

ʿAFĪFĪ: In your house, Father.

ʿABD AS-SATTĀR: And you have the impertinence to say it. It looks as if you're yearning for one of those thrashings I used to give you.

ʿAFĪFĪ: You dare! Just raise your hand and you'll see. I swear to God I'll make you see stars in broad daylight.

ʿABD AS-SATTĀR: Do you hear, Nafūsa, what this boy is saying?

NAFŪSA: Surely it is your own fault, provoking him to say such things. You tell me! What is it you have against your son? Why don't you leave him alone? It's you who have no shame.

ʿAFĪFĪ: Mother is right. You have no shame.

ʿABD AS-SATTĀR: How dare you talk to me like this? (*He rushes to strike* ʿAFĪFĪ, *but* NAFŪSA *grabs hold of his stick.*).

NAFŪSA (*shouting*): You are a worthless man! Striking your own son, and in my presence, too! Don't you have any respect for me? By heaven, if you dare raise your hand against him again you'll soon enough feel my slipper on your cheeks.

ʿABD AS-SATTĀR: (*calming down*): All right! All right! Why do you get so upset and excited? For God's sake don't get into such a temper!

NAFŪSA: Not get into a temper? Why shouldn't I if I want to? I am a free woman and can do as I like. What an old fogey you are!

ʿAFĪFĪ: Absolutely! Not at all civilized. Don't you realize that hitting someone is a crime punishable by law?

NAFŪSA: He certainly is the sort that deserves a prison sentence with hard labour, son. I swear to you, man, by the Prophet and all the Holy Saints that unless you behave yourself and watch every word you say and every deed you do you'll find me coming down on you like a ton of bricks. And this is how I'll start. (*Brandishing her slipper.*) Do you hear me? A ton of bricks, I say.

ʿABD AS-SATTĀR: All right! All right! It's all my own fault and I humbly apologize to you. Only don't get so upset, please.

NAFŪSA: I'm telling you, unless you mend your ways, I'll shed your blood and make mincemeat of your flesh, so beware!

ʿABD AS-SATTĀR: Why do you talk to me like this, Nafūsa? What wrong have I done to deserve all this?

NAFŪSA: What wrong indeed? Strike the boy in front of me and then ask what wrong you've done?

ʿAFĪFĪ: That's enough, Mother! He has admitted his guilt and will soon repent, thank goodness for that.

NAFŪSA: Do you already feel so sorry for him, ʿAfīfī?

ʿAFĪFĪ: Good God, Mother! Have you forgotten that I am a member of the Society for the Prevention of Cruelty to Animals?

ʿABD AS-SATTĀR: Thank you very much!

ʿAFĪFĪ: It's all over now, thank God! I'm going to change as I have to go out soon. (*Exit.*)

(*Mu'allafāt Muḥammad Taymūr*, vol. III [Cairo, 1974], pp. 120ff.)

In this topsy-turvy world with its reversal of values, the news of the dog's sickness fills the household with horror and makes the grief-stricken son weep:

ʿAFĪFĪ: (*shouting off-stage*): How come the dog has fallen ill? You must have neglected him. This is intolerable! Intolerable, I say!

ʿABD AS-SATTĀR: Who is shouting out there? It isn't ʿAfīfī, is it?

ʿAFĪFĪ (*still off-stage and addressing* KHALĪFA): By God, I'll pluck your beard, old man! I'll knock off your turban! I'll give you a drubbing you've never had the like of, unless you tell me how this dog has fallen ill.

KHALĪFA (*off-stage*): The dog is simply constipated.

ʿABD AS-SATTĀR: Nafūsa, I beg you! The boy seems to be in a foul temper and is sure to come here to make your life and mine a misery. Please stay here. You, too, Jamīla dear, don't go away! It looks as if your brother is rather angry.

JAMĪLA: Don't worry, Father.

ʿAFĪFĪ (*enters looking upset and agitated and casts a quick glance at those around him*): How come Fox has fallen ill, while you are all well? I've a pretty rough idea why he's fallen ill. (*To his mother.*) It's because you don't care for my dogs, do you? The only creatures in the whole wide world you want to remain alive are your rabbits. (*To his father.*) As for you you're always pretending you have serious business to attend to in your office. Always going to your office, coming back from your office, without ever bothering to enquire about the dogs. (*To his sister.*) And you are only concerned about one thing and one thing only, your marriage prospects. All you say is 'Yes, I would like this man for a husband' or 'No, I don't want that man for a husband'. You are all, every one of you, utterly devoid of mercy. The dog is suffering from constipation, I tell you.

NAFŪSA: Have you given him an enema, son?

ʿAFĪFĪ: What enema, woman? I've given him a purge.

ʿABD AS-SATTĀR: Salts or castor oil?

ʿAFĪFĪ: He's far too delicate for either.

NAFŪSA: I've told you, son. It's an enema he needs.

ʿAFĪFĪ: No, madam! I've given him milk of magnesia. Let's wait and see how he'll react to it. Please God make Fox better soon.

NAFŪSA: Answer his prayer God, please.

ʿAFĪFĪ: I tiptoed into the room, afraid lest I should disturb his sleep. I found the poor wretch lying on the floor, utterly motionless. His condition was pitiable and I nearly wept.

NAFŪSA: Poor, poor Fox!

ʿAFĪFĪ: The poor creature! Then he had an attack of colic, he writhed in pain, kicking with his legs, moaning and howling as if he was asking me for help. I rested his pretty head on my arm and kept gazing at him, and the poor thing gazed back at me while still kicking. It was such a moving sight! Such a moving sight!

NAFŪSA: Would that the pain were in my own stomach instead, dear Fox!

ʿABD AS-SATTĀR (*to himself*): Would it were indeed!

ʿAFĪFĪ: Don't say that, mother! Don't! The dog's condition is now absolutely heart-rending. I fear he's going to die. (*He weeps.*)

NAFŪSA: Poor darling Fox! Fifī, my love, don't upset yourself. God is sure to cure him soon.

ʿAFĪFĪ: No, Mother. The dog is sure to die. Dear God, please cure our beloved invalid. He's the sole object of our love!

JAMĪLA (*softly to her father*): This is balmy!

ʿABD AS-SATTĀR: Child, we've been condemned to live in a loony-bin.

(*Ibid.* pp. 164–6)

The play contains some amusing scenes in which the eavesdropper takes advantage of what he hears, the best example being when ʿAfīfī and Nafūsa overhear the father trying to make love to the maid servant, Hānim. Locking the father up in a dark room for the night and Khalīfa in the lavatory gives rise to humour, albeit of a somewhat crude variety, and the auction-like bidding by the two suitors for Jamīla is also comical.

It is the author's power of characterization, that gives the play its ultimate value.[55] Interestingly enough the two female characters in the play are the most memorable: the mother, Nafūsa, of whom everybody except the son is scared and who conveniently justifies her bad temper by claiming that she is possessed by evil spirits and, more particularly, the maid servant, Hānim, one of the liveliest characters in Taymūr's work. Aware of her charms, she flirts her way through life. She behaves seductively not only towards ʿAbd as-Sattār from whom she extorts money in return for her silence, but also towards the old servant, ʿAmm Khalīfa, who, as a result of her wiles, falls in love with her and is made a fool of by her. She constantly teases him and mocks him. She makes no secret of her love for the son of the family, ʿAfīfī, who leads her to believe that he loves her, but in reality makes use of her and borrows money from her which he never pays back. Her love for him is, therefore, her weakest spot, but as soon as she realizes that he is hoping to marry somebody else, she becomes such a formidable rival that no one else, not even her mistress Nafūsa, is a match for her. However, she is not the only person deceived in the play; practically everybody, however strong-willed and selfish, seems to entertain illusions about someone else: Nafūsa, who believes that she rules her husband, is in fact deceived by him, ʿAfīfī is deceived by his friend Faraḥāt, Balīgh and Jamīla have clandestine meetings unknown to the rest of the family, ʿAbd as-Sattār and even the elderly servant, ʿAmm Khalīfa, are deceived by Hānim, just as Hānim herself is deceived by ʿAfīfī.

Just as we have seen in the earlier play, here too Taymūr combines foreign drama with elements from traditional and even folk entertainments; while the influence of Molière is still visible, the henpecked husband who is ill-treated and even beaten up by his shrewish wife is a theme to be found in *Qaraqōz*, and in Sannūʿ's play, 'The Alexandrian Princess'.

By general consensus Taymūr's last work, *al-Hāwiya* ('The Precipice'), is the best play he ever wrote. In 1922 his brother went as far as to write, perhaps with some slight exaggeration, that it was the best drama ever produced for the Egyptian stage. The author described it as '*comédie-drame*' in three acts, but it is really a bourgeois tragedy which ends with the death of the hero. The term was explained by Taymūr in one of his articles[56] as denoting a comedy of manners dealing with the playwright's times and society and mixed with sad or 'dramatic' events such as we find in the work of the French dramatists, Victorien Sardou, Paul Hervieu, Henri Bataille and Henry Bernstein. Clearly the comedy Taymūr had in mind was drama with a serious moralizing strain. Taymūr's play, the events of which take place in Egypt soon after the end of the First World War, is a frontal attack on a problem of contemporary Egyptian society at the time, namely drug addiction and its destructive impact, particularly on marriage.

In 'The Precipice' Taymūr returns to the world of 'The Bird in the Cage', to the upper classes of Egyptian society of which he had first hand experience. The hero, Amīn, bears some resemblance to ʿAfīfī in ʿ*Abd as-Sattār Afandī* in that he has been thoroughly spoilt by his mother. Because he lost his father at the age of six[57] his mother decides, in her overwhelming desire to make up for the loss of a father's affection, not to deny him anything or thwart his wishes, with the result that as a young man he soon acquires many of the vices to which youth is vulnerable: alcoholism, womanizing and gambling. In the hope that marriage might reform his character the mother and his uncle, Aḥmad Pacha Yusrī, encourage Amīn to marry, but to their utter disappointment he chooses for a wife, Ratība, a heavily made-up, westernized, young woman far from the strict, traditional type they had wanted for him. In any case, marriage in no way changes his way of life and, as a result of being neglected by her husband, Ratība spends her time reading modish novels, buying expensive clothes of the latest fashion or going alone to the opera. Act I opens in Amīn's richly furnished house where he lives with his wife and mother. His mother, Ḥikmat, has sent for her brother to tell him of her anxieties about Amīn, who has now added cocaine addiction to his other vices, and whose behaviour is giving her cause for alarm as he spends whole nights out and when he comes home he is often drunk or in a querulous mood and hardly ever dines at home. We also learn that Amīn is squandering his wealth and has begun to sell up his farms. At this point Ratība comes home with a servant laden with expensive clothes and a vase she has bought, and disappears for a while to change. Yusrī Pacha goes out briefly on business but says he will return later to talk to Amīn. In the mean time, Amīn himself comes home accompanied by his friends Magdī and Shafīq. The women withdraw from the lounge. The young men are shown exchanging jokes, indulging in their trivial chat about their silly pursuits, amorous adventures and taking cocaine. Amīn reminds his friends that he has promised to introduce his wife to them – a daring act, regarded at the time as the ultimate expression of westernization since no Muslim was supposed to show his womenfolk to males not closely related to the family. He brings in the apparently reluctant Ratība who, however, soon loses her shyness, and begins to talk freely with the men about fashionable boutiques in Cairo, the opera, horse-racing and gambling. Yusrī Pacha returns and is shocked to find Amīn's wife in the company of strange men and does not hide his disapproval. He sends Ratība out of the room on some pretext. Amīn's friends take their leave and Yusrī proceeds to scold Amīn for his recklessness and to warn him against his false friends, only to be told by the angry Amīn to mind his own business and subsequently to clear out of his house. Amīn even tells his mother, who has come in to find out what is going on, to get out too. The act ends with Amīn, agitated and angry, taking more cocaine to sooth his nerves.

In Act II, which we learn from the dialogue takes place four months later, the scene shifts to the drawing room in the villa of Amīn's friend, Shafīq. Shafīq has just penned a note to Amīn, apologizing for not being able to join him and his female friend that day because of a headache and kidney trouble. The real reason, we are told, is that Ratība, on whom Shafīq has been working very hard, has at long last yielded and agreed to pay him a visit in his house that day. To ensure privacy he sends his manservant with the note to Amīn and dismisses him for the day. Shafīq anxiously awaits Ratība's arrival with a bottle of champagne and two glasses in front of him, having given instructions to a servant boy to sit by the front door and not to allow any male visitor to come in and to say that his master is out. To encourage the boy to keep guard he gives him a piastre, with which the foolish boy at once decides to buy sweets and leaves the door unattended long enough for Magdī and later Yusrī to walk in. Shafīq asks Magdī to leave as he has an assignation with a married lady, but Magdī is naturally curious to find out who 'that honourable and respectably married lady' is and, therefore, turns a deaf ear to Shafīq's entreaties for him to go. When at last he makes a move to go they hear footsteps so he hides in the bedroom which Shafīq promptly locks. It is not Ratība, however, but Yusrī who has come to ask Shafīq not to take advantage of Amīn's weakness and folly by buying one of his rich farms from him at a ruinously low price. He appeals to his friendship and generosity but Shafīq takes no notice of Yusrī, tells him that he has no time to pursue the matter further and orders him out of his house. Yusrī goes and Magdī reappears and insists that Shafīq give him three pounds to buy himself some cocaine. On his way out he sees Ratība entering the house and makes a meaningful remark as a parting shot. Ratība is shocked to see him but is soon talked out of her anger by Shafīq, who proclaims his love for her and reassures her that he can always buy Magdī's silence. He offers her a glass of champagne but before they touch the drink, the drunken voice of Amīn is heard telling the servant boy to let him come in as he knows his master is not out but ill at home. In alarm, Ratība is rushed into the bedroom and the door is locked, but in her confusion she has forgotten her fan, one of an unusual pair, the other belonging to Magdī's married sister. This little touch (reminiscent of Oscar Wilde's *Lady Windemere's Fan*) further complicates the situation and becomes a rich source of dramatic irony. Amīn, whose woman friend has failed to turn up, has been spending the time drinking and taking cocaine and has now decided to call on his sick friend. Shafīq tells him that he pretended to be ill in order not to intrude on his friend and suggests they go out for a walk, but Amīn, noticing first the champagne and then the fan, senses Shafīq's anxiety to get him out of the house and becomes convinced that his friend has a woman visitor in his bedroom and is curious to find out who she is. Shafīq declines the offer of cocaine on the grounds that he has given it up and refuses to disclose his visitor's name as she is a married lady. He does not, however, contradict Amīn when he assumes she must be Magdī's sister, whereupon Amīn proceeds to scold Shafīq for having an affair with his friend's sister and ironically keeps on saying that he only feels sorry for her husband who is being fooled by her. When he finally goes, Ratība appears shocked and scared; she cannot believe her good fortune at having had such a narrow escape and realizing now the enormity of the crime she was about to commit, she decides to put an end to her relationship with Shafīq. When he attempts to embrace her before she leaves she slaps him in the face and calls him a base coward.

Act III takes place the following day when the scene shifts back to Amīn's house. Ratība in a depressed state, wishes to be left alone to read her book and is unable to put up with Amīn's tomfoolery. Yusrī Pacha comes to see his sister in order to report on his unsuccessful attempt to make Shafīq change his mind about fleecing Amīn. Magdī calls on Amīn and surprises him by unintentionally revealing that he was with Shafīq at his house the previous afternoon. They both take large quantities of cocaine and become querulous and unguarded in their conversation, revealing they know the identity of the lady who was in Shafīq's house and making insinuating and taunting remarks about one another. Finally Amīn forces the truth out of Magdī who, when thrown out of the house, swears never to step into it again. Amīn, shocked and incredulous, takes another huge dose of cocaine and confronts Ratība who, angry at Amīn's manner of questioning her, admits the truth and proceeds to put some of the blame on him for having nearly succeeded in driving her into the arms of Shafīq, who he himself has introduced her to in the first place, because of his shameless neglect of his duties as her husband. Amīn, now hopelessly full of cocaine, falls into a fit of impotent rage which proves fatal to him. Like the Greek chorus, here as in other places in the play, Yusrī seems to step out of his character and make a direct comment on what is taking place, saying that 'such is the end of those who neglect themselves, their home and their honour, the end of those who take the road from which there is no return.'[58]

Like the rest of Taymūr's work 'The Precipice' is a well made play, in which every word serves a purpose either to advance the plot or further delineate a character. Taymūr did not refrain from using strong language, which later critics found a little too crude,[59] if he felt it was necessitated by the exigencies of character and situation. Except perhaps for Ḥikmat who is rather a pale image of the traditional, doting, long-suffering mother, the main characters are well realized and sufficiently distinguished from one another. The uncle is a rich, old-fashioned landlord, an adherent to traditional values and anxious to protect the interests of his nephew and the family. Not wishing his property to fall into the hands of anyone outside the family, he buys the land his nephew has put up for sale with the intention of returning it to him after he has repaid himself the purchase price from its produce (although the nephew, and indeed some critics,[60] suspect that he is motivated by self-interest and a desire to acquire land for his own children). As has been shown, he sometimes steps out of his character to make a moral comment on events which, at the end of the play, makes him sound as if he has no feelings for his dead nephew. Amīn's two friends, despite their common interests, are quite different from one another; Magdī seems to be a rather tiresome playboy, living for the moment and always short of money, while Shafīq is a strong, though unprincipled, character out to make use of Amīn's weaknesses, unscrupulously scheming to steal his fortune and his wife.

By far the most vividly portrayed characters are Amīn and his wife, Ratība. They are both convincing creations who undergo considerable development in the course of the play. Amīn deteriorates rapidly, his rebellion against the traditional family values and his mistrust of his uncle, along with his increasing dependence on cocaine, drive him towards self-destruction. Under the pressure of events Ratība grows from a spoilt, superficial, middle class girl, interested only in social life and women's fashions, into a more liberated, Egyptian woman who just in time saves herself from falling into the trap set up for her by Shafīq. She stands up against the husband who has neglected her, refuses to give an account of her movements because he is not prepared to do the same thing; and she regards herself as in no way inferior to him, does not allow him to raise his hand against her, and even threatens to strike back if he does. Although she does not belittle her own guilt she tells him that he is partly to blame for her misadventure on account of his outrageous behaviour towards her. In this sense it can be said that, in portraying her character, Taymūr has struck a blow for the emancipation of the Egyptian woman and 'The Precipice' may be described as a plea for responsible relations between marriage partners:

AMĪN (*making an effort to suppress his anger*): Ratība, I want to ask you a question.

RATĪBA: What about?

AMĪN: I want to know where you were yesterday afternoon.

RATĪBA: You are not exactly in the habit of letting me know your movements, why then do you want to ask me about mine?

AMĪN: Ratība, please tell me where you were yesterday afternoon.

RATĪBA: All right, you too. Please tell me where you were yesterday afternoon.

AMĪN: I was with a friend.

RATĪBA: I too was with a friend, a female friend.

AMĪN: Liar!

RATĪBA: Am I really?

AMĪN: Of course you're a liar.

RATĪBA: If you say so. (*She makes a move to go.*)

AMĪN: (*goes after her, shouting*): Where do you think you're going?

RATĪBA (*stopping*): I take it that my business is over.

AMĪN: What do you mean?

RATĪBA: You said I was lying, didn't you? You seem to know where I was yesterday afternoon. What more do you want from me?

AMĪN (*suppressing his anger*): So you don't intend to tell me where you were yesterday?

RATĪBA (*staring at him courageously*): No, I don't intend to tell you.

AMĪN (*in obvious anger and shaking as a result of the large dose of cocaine he has taken, bangs the table with his fist*): Ratība, you've got to tell me where you were yesterday. I insist.

RATĪBA (*unimpressed*): No, I won't.

AMĪN (*growing more angry, shaking and banging the table three times and shouting*): Ratība, you've got to tell me! You've got to tell me! You've got to tell me!

RATĪBA: Are you threatening to hit me? I am not going to tell you. (*She takes three steps to the inner door to go inside.*)

AMĪN (*screaming*): Ratība! (*He runs after her and intercepts her, raising his hand.*) I won't let you go! I won't!

RATĪBA (*taking a step towards him*): Let me go! I say let me go!

AMĪN (*shaking more visibly and his anger mounting*): You wish to go without telling me where you were yesterday? I won't let you. I simply won't. You are intent on fooling me, aren't you? (*Laughing sarcastically*) I must know where you were. I must know everything. (*charging at her, dragging her to the middle of the stage, squeezing her hand*) Come over her! Come over here! (*he tightens his grip on her hand.*).

RATĪBA: My hand, my hand! Let go of my hand!

AMĪN (*shaking her hand furiously*): Tell me where you were yesterday! Tell me!

RATĪBA (*brought down to her knees by pain*): Let go of my hand! Let go!

AMĪN: (*squeezing harder and staring at her eyes*): Where were you?

RATĪBA (*in spite of her pain, defiant and angry*): Do you really want to know where I was yesterday afternoon?

AMĪN (*still holding her hand tight*): Yes, tell me!

RATĪBA: I was with the man you called on yesterday. I was there when you arrived drunk and incapable of coherent speech.

AMĪN (*releasing her hand, screaming*): So you were with Shafīq. You were being unfaithful to me?

RATĪBA (*rising to her feet*): Yes, I was with Shafīq, but I wasn't unfaithful, thank God!

AMĪN (*in a state of great agitation, rushing towards her, raising his hand to strike her*): You adulterous harlot!

RATĪBA (*takes a step towards him so that he dares not strike her but he drops his hand and stands facing her, uncertain as to what to do*): Take your hand away! I'm not your servant. Yes, I was with Shafīq, your close friend whom you trusted and allowed to control your affairs and run your life; the man you chose to introduce to your wife and who was bent on deceiving and dishonouring you.

AMĪN (*shaking more violently and showing even more clearly the symptoms of a cocaine fit*): Unfaithful woman! Adultress! Deceiving me, deceiving your husband, soiling my honour! You have besmirched my honour!

RATĪBA (*with a sarcastic laugh*): Your honour, your honour indeed! Since when have you known about honour? For God's sake don't talk to me about your honour! Let me weep over it, rather. I suppose you think honour is no more than a toy. Or perhaps you assume that if you bring firewood close to a fire it won't ignite. (*Sarcastically.*) Your honour! I am amazed to hear you talk about your honour now, for the first time. I suppose we should be grateful that you have now come to recognize such a thing as honour. But, alas, it is too late now! If only you had been able to see the value of your honour earlier.

AMĪN (*His shaking much increased and his eyes flashing, he charges at her, raising his hand and screaming*): Adulterous whore! Adulteress whore! Adulterous whore!

RATĪBA (*confronting him, undaunted*): Take your hand off me! (*He pauses and drops his hand.*) I'm not your servant that you may strike me. Well, well! You certainly know how to defend your honour! You wanted to hit me because I was about to be unfaithful to you? Don't you know why I nearly deceived you? If you had only an ounce of brains you would have forgiven me for what I was about to do.

AMĪN (*agitated*): Forgiven you? How the hell could I have forgiven you?

RATĪBA: Of course you would have forgiven me.

AMĪN (*laughing sarcastically*): Forgiven you indeed! You obviously wish to clear yourself of the sin you have committed.

RATĪBA: Don't worry! I admit that I've contemplated committing something for which I deserve to die. Death is the least punishment for a woman who tries to deceive her husband. But I also declare that the guilt is not mine alone. There is another person who was pushing me with his own hands to the edge of the precipice into which I was about to fall.

AMĪN: Rubbish! Rubbish! I don't want to hear such utter rot.

RATĪBA: Yes, yes! You must hear it! You must realize that that person is none other than yourself.

AMĪN (*shaking*): Me! Me! Nonsense! You're mad! You're out of your mind!

RATĪBA: I suppose that you've forgotten about all those nights you stayed out enjoying yourself, coming home at dawn, drunk and totally incapable of speech. I suppose you've forgotten how many times you told me, laughingly, that you had lost no less than a hundred pounds in gambling the previous night. You've forgotten how you never spent more than three or four hours a day in my company. You've forgotten too all that secret correspondence you received from your numerous mistresses. And who were those women? Common prostitutes who sold their honour and virtue for money, prostitutes utterly devoid of all conscience or decency. Yet you preferred them to your wife who wanted to lead an honest and honourable life with you.

AMĪN: Prostitutes? Ha! Ha! Yes, prostitutes, so what? I suppose you too have forgotten that now you've become one yourself. Like them you have neither conscience, nor virtue left. Like them you forfeited your honour.

RATĪBA: Thanks to your guidance, my dear husband!

AMĪN (*shaking more violently and deeply agitated*): But my honour, my honour, you harlot! You've soiled my honour with Shafīq! My honour!

RATĪBA: I've told you I have not been unfaithful to you with Shafīq. Strange to find you harping on about your honour! Thank God that you feel sorry about the loss of your honour! Thank God that you now realize that I was on the point of soiling it! But you must remember that your honour was sacrificed by both of us. We were both responsible.

AMĪN: Rubbish! You're mad, mad and deserve nothing less than death. Death, I say! (*Suddenly breaking down and crying.*) Adulteress! Deceiving your husband, your own lawful husband! Even supposing I was wrong how could you allow yourself to deceive your husband. I... I'm your husband, your husband!

RATĪBA: You never made me feel that you were my husband. It's true I was a foolish woman, and I didn't realize the full meaning of marriage. But I wasn't blessed with a husband who could point out my duties to me. It was your duty to guide me, instead of letting me go astray while you were engrossed in your gambling, drinking and whoring, doing all those things that damaged your honour and your standing in the world.

(*Mu'allafāt Muḥammad Taymūr*, vol. II [Cairo, 1973], pp. 397ff.)

'The Precipice' was produced on the stage in 1921 and published in 1922 in volume II of the author's complete works with a critical introduction by Zakī Ṭulaymāt. For many years, however, it was neglected by students of Egyptian drama. It was not until 1959 that the Egyptian critic, Muḥammad Mandūr, wrote about it in some detail in his rather brief study of the Egyptian prose theatre *al-Masraḥ al-Nathrī*, and although he praises it for its good construction and lively and economic dialogue, he regrets the fact that this gifted young dramatist did not live long enough to change his views on dialogue and write in classical Arabic instead of the Egyptian colloquial, just as his younger brother Maḥmud was to do.[61] In 1973 another Egyptian scholar, ʿAlī al-Rāʿī, praised it unstintingly in his more extended discussion:[62] 'it is a serious social drama, written with warmth and realism',[63] although his analysis of it, in which he finds a subconscious presentation of 'the crisis of Egyptian feudalism', is not totally convincing. He finds Amīn an incomplete rebel against feudal values and regards his one-sided rebellion as the cause of his downfall. Another writer considers Amīn merely an example of a class of people who ape the superficial aspects of westernization in the mistaken belief that they are being 'modern'.[64] But this diversity of interpretation of Amīn's character is really a tribute to the dramatic genius of Muḥammad Taymūr, whose untimely death certainly robbed the world of Egyptian drama of a figure that held so much promise.

ANṬŪN YAZBAK

Perhaps colloquial Egyptian Arabic was most expressively employed in serious drama in Anṭūn Yazbak's play *al-Dhabā'iḥ* ('The Sacrifices') which was performed by the troupe of Yūsuf Wahbī with tremendous success in 1925.[65] Yazbak, a lawyer by profession, had tried his hand at writing domestic, tearful melodrama in an earlier work, *ʿĀṣifa fī Bayt* ('A storm in a House'), which was produced by the troupe of Jūrj Abyaḍ at the Cairo Opera House in 1924. But it is in the later play that Yazbak managed to produce the most moving drama in the colloquial Egyptian after Taymūr's 'The Precipice'. Muḥammad Mandūr goes as far to say of it that 'For the first time we see a play in the colloquial composed in an artistic language, capable of expressing the deepest emotions and subtlest ideas which are generally beyond the reach of colloquial speech'.[66] He finds the dialogue to be 'so precise, deep and rich in dramatic movement, employing to its full all the potentialities of imagery and figurative expression in a manner until then thought impossible to achieve in the spoken language'.[67]

Describing *al-Dhabāʾiḥ*, Mandūr writes that it deals with the social problems that arise from Egyptians marrying European women. But surely the play is about much more than just mixed marriages. The story, in brief, is the following: Hammām Pacha, a retired Egyptian army general who, after a brief marriage to Amīna the daughter of a prosperous merchant, meets and falls in love with a European woman, Noreska, whom he marries after divorcing his first wife. His second marriage proves to be a disaster although it lasts twenty years and the union produces a son, ʿUthmān, who is eighteen years old when the play opens and in his final year at school. In the same household lives the Pacha's niece, Laylā, an orphan who has lost both parents several years before. Hammām, whose unhappy marriage we are told has turned him into a nervous wreck, is now a sick man suffering from rheumatoid arthritis; he is looked after by Ḥafīẓa, the nurse.

The play opens with the nurse giving instructions to the servant who seems to resent this interference from a newcomer to the house. From the dialogue, however, we learn something about Hammām's unhappy domestic life, and we also suspect that Ḥafīẓa may be more than just a nurse newly arrived on the scene; this is economically written by the author and with considerable artistic tact. Hammām is visited by his older brother, Muḥammad, who works as a bailiff to an estate and who in the course of the conversation reveals that his son, recently returned from Europe where he has been studying, is resolved to marry a European woman. This alarms Hammām who at once bursts into a tirade against European wives, strongly advises his brother to stop his son's marriage and try to learn from the sad example of his own mixed marriage. He also talks nostalgically about the happy days he enjoyed with his first wife. In the course of the conversation he confides to his brother that certain papers relating to a secret, army plot, in which several of his protégés are involved and which he has quietly removed from the investigator's file, seem to be missing from his study. As he continues to search for them his brother asks if all his servants are trustworthy, to which Hammām replies in the affirmative since, with the exception of the nurse who has just arrived, they have been in his service for a long time. After his brother has left to attend the wedding of the daughter of a family friend, Hammām proceeds to find out more about the new nurse. He is overwhelmed to discover that she is none other than Amīna, his ex-wife, who, having fallen upon evil times, has had to start nursing to support herself, and when she learnt from Hammām's sister of his illness she decided to come, incognito, to look after him. Moved by her kindness and conscience-stricken for his past cruelty to her, for which he now feels he has been punished by God in the form of his unhappy marriage to Noreska, Hammām decides to make amends for his wicked past and sends for the marriage clerk to marry them. He now has two wives and two households; he walks out of Noreska's house where he leaves his son and sets up home with Amīna, taking his niece, Laylā, with them to save her from the corrupting influence of his liberated European wife. ʿUthmān is now doubly unhappy on account of this rupture between his parents and on account of his having to part from Laylā, for whom he obviously entertains a passion which is requited by the girl. On a visit to his father, ʿUthmān is seen by Hammām courting Laylā. In the mean time, Noreska calls first to discuss the situation with the new wife and then to face Hammām, who, in his fury caused by their confrontation, declares Noreska divorced and removes ʿUthmān from her custody. ʿUthmān witnesses the closing moments of the angry scene between his parents and this has a devastating effect upon him. When his father resolves to send Laylā away to live with her aunt, safe from the tempting company of her cousin, the young man commits suicide in a fit of despair and the shock unhinges Laylā's mind. Now the contrite Hammām unable to face the consequences of his actions, decides to put an end to his own life, particularly as the missing documents implicating his friends in the army have been made public thanks to Noreska who has stolen them and given them to her journalist cousin. Hammām makes a will in which he leaves half his fortune to Amīna and the other half to Laylā, but the sight of Laylā, distraught and incapable of looking after herself, makes him change his mind. However, at this point Noreska, who has just received a telegram bearing the news of her son's death, arrives in a state of uncontrollable rage and shoots Hammām dead as a punishment for all the harm he has caused to so many people.

This brief account of the plot may seem to emphasize the melodramatic character of 'The Sacrifices', yet it would be unfair to regard the play merely as a melodrama. Admittedly, it does contain melodrama especially at the conclusion in which the dramatist is clearly intent on squeezing every drop of emotion out of the situation, but the play is generally free from the sensational surprises and the flat stereotype characters which are usually the hallmark of melodrama. Indeed, the dramatist carefully prepares us for what is to come and the leading characters have sufficient complexity to render them credible and therefore capable of enlisting our genuine sympathy. Furthermore, 'The Sacrifices' is so well constructed that, more than any previous Arabic play, it is permeated by tragic irony. The four main characters are Hammām, Noreska, ʿUthmān and Laylā (in comparison Amīna plays only a minor role.) Of these the most forceful are the first two.

Hammām's character is drawn on a grand scale. He is dominant, indeed domineering, and his explosive anger has terrifying proportions. Because of the superior rank he has attained in the army he expects to be obeyed, even by his older brother, and cannot brook having his wishes crossed. His fatal flaw, his *hamartia*, is his lack of self-knowledge. He assumes that all his troubles are the result of his marriage to a European woman and of his having foolishly divorced his first Egyptian wife. Yet he would not have been happier if he had been married to an Egyptian woman who was not prepared to be his doormat and suffer meekly and in silence. The interesting thing is that he divorces his first wife who was prepared to be the doormat, having fallen in love with an European woman, who, because of her difference in temperament and background, clearly holds considerable fascination for him. What he evidently wants is the control of her mind as well as her body, and that is precisely what she does not allow him to have. He is genuinely incapable of understanding her need to think for herself and he attributes it to her being European. However, as she points out to him, this is a universal need which even Egyptian women are bound to feel soon if they do not already do so. Why he has allowed himself to suffer this unhappy marriage for so long is not very clear; obviously, given the Islamic context, it is not because of his difficulty in obtaining a divorce for he was able to divorce his first wife after only a brief marriage. His own explanation is that he kept the marriage going for the sake of their son, ʿUthmān, and his orphan niece, Laylā, who needed to be cared for by his wife even though eventually it became clear to him, as the girl was growing to womanhood, that his wife's influence was not a healthy one. As already mentioned, in the end Hammām impetuously divorces her in a fit of extreme anger.

The scene of confrontation with her counts among one of the most memorable scenes of the war between the sexes in Egyptian drama; the intensity of the conflict between them, which is colourfully described by the servant Marzūq in the opening scene of the play, is somewhat reminiscent of the work of Strindberg:

HAMMĀM: I know why you've come today, Noreska. I've been expecting this visit for a long time, and I've been preparing myself for it. I realize that a woman like you isn't likely to take what I've done quietly. You too are aware that a man like myself will never go back on something he's done, which he thinks is right.

NORESKA: So you think what you've done is right, do you?

HAMMĀM: Absolutely. You were stifling me. You had been stifling me for twenty years, in the end I could no longer bear it. I found myself gasping for breath, almost dying. Then a woman came my way whom I had wronged twenty years ago, at the time you got your grip on my throat.

NORESKA: So you immediately decided to make amends to her, to ease your conscience.

HAMMĀM: Yes, to ease my conscience.

NORESKA: And where was this conscience of yours all those twenty years? Was it asleep? Or perhaps it was dead?

HAMMĀM: I can assure you it was wide awake and troubling me every day.

NORESKA: Well, so now you've made amends to her. But in the mean time you've done me wrong.

HAMMĀM: Not I. You have brought it upon your own head. If only you had given me peace of mind even for one day during our life together.

NORESKA: Then you wouldn't have wronged me, no doubt.

HAMMĀM: I certainly wouldn't have.

NORESKA (*sarcastically*): But you would have continued to wrong the other woman, Amīna, I mean. You wouldn't have heard then the voice of your conscience which you say has been worrying you for twenty years, would you?

HAMMĀM: I would have found another way to do justice to both you and her.

NORESKA: Really? What would have been that other way, I wonder? The way to reconcile water and fire, I presume. Did you ever consider if that other way was at all possible? You needn't answer me, Hammām. I've heard enough. You're talking like a man who never thinks of the consequences of his actions. For God's sake leave your conscience alone! Stop babbling about your desire to do us justice and hurling your accusations at me! You can't prove to me today, after what you've done, that you have a conscience; what conscience is that which changes overnight? You have no desire to do justice to anybody either; justice doesn't mean making amends to one person while wronging another. You're like a thief who steals to dispense charity. I suppose you can accuse me of all sorts of things; you say it's my European nature which doesn't agree with your Eastern character. But that wasn't my fault. Do you wish to hold me responsible for the sins of all the Europeans in the world?

HAMMĀM: Didn't you hold me responsible for the sins of all Orientals? Didn't you know that I was Oriental when you married me? Why did you marry me then?

NORESKA: I didn't propose to you, Hammām. You proposed to me. You are the man, and a man chooses first. In marriage, alas, unlike love, it is the man who has the initiative.

HAMMĀM: I married you on the understanding that you should obey me, not that I obey you. You were supposed to become part of me, and not the other way round.

NORESKA (*nodding in assent*): True.

HAMMĀM: I took it that you were to live as I did, and not the opposite.

NORESKA: Correct.

HAMMĀM: And that you should eat and drink the way I ate and drank, and you should dress in the manner I liked you to.

NORESKA: That too I grant you.

HAMMĀM: And that you should think as I wanted you to think.

NORESKA (*angrily*): Oh, no! Never! That was out of the question. I didn't mind very much that you should want to enslave my body, but that you should want to enslave my mind too, that was never on. Never, I say!

HAMMĀM: But that is the way my people think. We want our women to be our willing slaves (as you put it), in body and mind.

NORESKA: You would never find a woman prepared to be that, neither among my people nor yours.

HAMMĀM: But I have found such a person.

NORESKA: That is what you think. You've only found a silent slave, never a contented one. Silence is not the same thing as acceptance, Hammām. Because your woman is silent you assume that you managed to enslave her mind as well as her body. But you are wrong there. The truth is that her mind is rebelling against you all the time. (*She raises her voice.*) One day your women will feel they have had enough and then they will raise their voices. When that happens you will never be able to silence them again.

HAMMĀM (*angrily*): You only say these things to excuse yourself. For twenty years you have been raising your voice and no one has been able to stand up to you.

NORESKA: Not at all. I say these things because I am a free woman.

HAMMĀM (*sarcastically*): A free woman, indeed! And where did you learn that freedom of yours? From the works of your philosophers? From the novels and the fiction you read? To you freedom means shamelessness.

NORESKA: And to you it means license and the pursuit of pleasure.

HAMMĀM (*in a deluge-like outpouring*): The moment you entered my house you stuck your nose up in the air and looked down upon us. You liked none of us and none of us liked you. Only my poor brother, Muḥammad, could put up with you. And even he did not meet with your approval. As for our womenfolk neither did you tolerate them, nor they you. My own mother went to her grave without ever setting foot in my house. When my sister Saniyya, Laylā's mother, died you did no more than pay one single visit to offer your condolences, just for appearance's sake. My sister, ʿĀʾisha, paid us one visit which to this day she has not let me forget. You've not been unfaithful to me, or dishonest with my money, I grant you that. But what you've done to me is much worse. You've despised me. You've set yourself up as a deity and wished to create me anew. You've opposed me in my habits and my character. You've tried to convince me, by bullying me, that you are superior to me. You've changed everything in this house, even the furniture hasn't escaped your interference. You lived with me for twenty years, swollen by your pride. You did not share with us our joys or our griefs, our comfort or our trouble. A stranger you entered my house and a stranger you've remained. To this day your sole concern has been to change our ways, our manners and customs on which we were brought up, us and our ancestors for hundreds of years.

NORESKA (*angrily and scornfully*): That's because those ancestors of yours died so long ago and are now no more than dust and decayed bones. Yet to this day you wish to behave like them. You admire no one but them. Why don't you look forward and leave all those bones behind you?

HAMMĀM: My ancestors, whom you describe as decayed bones, often thrashed yours and with their swords chased them and forced them to flee the land, swimming across the salty seas.

NORESKA: But my ancestors' descendants came back. My God! For twenty years I have been trying to teach you the way to chase them out of your country again. But I've failed.

HAMMĀM: Teach me? I don't want any of this teaching of yours which is accompanied by scorn and bullying. We're not such barbarians here that we merit your scorn. We're not slaves for you to drive us with a stick. Keep your teaching to yourself!

NORESKA: I don't need to be taught. The truth is that you don't want a woman to share your life. You are only after someone to be your servant, to give you her body, and cheat you over the rest.

HAMMĀM: Here we need a woman who is prepared to obey us and, in return, we look after her and cherish her. We don't want a woman who hates us while we are kind to her.

NORESKA: Kind? You, kind?

HAMMĀM: Yes, I am. My house is still yours to this day. I've done justice to Amīna, but I've also been fair to you.

NORESKA: What did you say? Fair and just? You, Hammām, fair and just? (*she paces up and down in a state of fury.*) Listen to him, O Lord! Hammām Pacha, General Hammām, says he is fair and just. He's just like you, Lord! Hammām Pacha feeds and clothes me and houses me in a mansion. But he has trampled on my heart, as a man treads on stone. He doesn't understand that my heart too is full of blood, just like that of the servant, Amīna.

HAMMĀM (*in considerable anger*): Shut up, will you! Won't you stop behaving like a wicked, depraved woman.

NORESKA: Which of us is wicked and depraved? You could call me that only if I took on another man to share me with you, just as you've done to me.

HAMMĀM (*in a low, rough voice*): Shut your mouth! I've committed no adultery. Don't you know that I…

NORESKA (*interrupting*): Yes, I do, I do. God has privileged you, men, with your right to marry and to marry. But let me tell you this: God has not told us women to be silent, silent. We have been let loose to speak our minds.

HAMMĀM (*in extreme anger*): Be quiet, I tell you!

NORESKA: I won't, not till you yourself are quiet.

HAMMĀM (*in a thunderous voice*): Get out! Out of this house! (*He pulls her by the hand and tries to push her out.*)

NORESKA: Before you touch me you'd better remove these swords stuck on your epaulettes, hide the shiny decorations on your chest. A brute! That's what you are, a brute wearing gold braid!

HAMMĀM (*in a thunderous voice*): Go, you are divorced!

NORESKA (*laughing as if out of her mind*): Ha! Ha! Ha! (LAYLĀ, ʿUTHMĀN *and* AMĪNA *enter in a state of alarm.*)

LAYLĀ: What on earth is going on?

NORESKA: Of course, a peasant beats his wife with a stick, but a civilized man slaps her face with the threat of divorce.

HAMMĀM (*foaming*): I'm telling you again: you're divorced!

LAYLĀ (*hanging on to* HAMMĀM): Uncle! You can't do that, uncle, you can't do that to ʿUthmān's mother!

NORESKA: Divorced! Ha! Ha! Ha! I have not looked upon you as my husband for the past twenty years.

HAMMĀM (*in a superhumanly loud voice*): I say it for the third time: you're divorced!

(ʿUTHMĀN *and* AMĪNA *collapse on chairs.*)

NORESKA: My son! I'll take my son. (*She throws herself upon her son, as if demented.*)

HAMMĀM: Your son? Where is your son? This is not your son, Noreska. Look at him closely! Does he remotely resemble you? His eyes, his hair, his features, his general appearance are totally different from yours. Neither does his mind resemble yours. Have a good look at him, Noreska, for you won't be able to set eyes on him again, not after today.

(NORESKA *is utterly defeated and speaks in a sad voice.*)

NORESKA: My son, my own flesh and blood.

HAMMĀM: Now you've quietened down. Now you are silent, dead, dead! I tell you, you are divorced! Do you hear me? You are divorced! I repeat it as many times as there are graves dug from the time of Adam to this day, as many times as there are stars in the sky, or grains of sand in the sea. Now you're dead, you've lost your tongue!

LAYLĀ: Please, uncle, enough! I beg you, have mercy on her! (*She tries to push him away.*)

HAMMĀM: Out of my way, child! Let me tell her once more. (*In a thunderous voice.*) You are divorced, divorced, divorced! (*He goes inside, his voice resounding 'You are divorced, divorced!'* ʿUTHMĀN *is in a state of shock,* NORESKA *holding him on the seat,* LAYLĀ *hanging on to her uncle's clothes and* AMĪNA *totally frozen. The curtain falls slowly.*)

(Yazbak, *al-Dhabāʾih*, pp. 42–7.)

The dramatist maintains his objective stance throughout; he does not take sides, but portrays both antagonists equally impartially. Hammām is shown as a senior military man of considerable dignity; he cares for his son and niece so much that he is prepared to endure an extremely unhappy marriage rather than deprive them of the care and affection they receive from his wife. He wishes to save his nephew from a possible disastrous marriage at any cost. He is also loyal to his friends and junior colleagues implicated in a secret army plot; he goes to any length to protect them, even to the extent of removing some dangerous documents from the investigation file. But the author also shows him as a tyrant, an extremely conservative *paterfamilias*; unlike his brother, Muḥammad, he does not accept the fact that his 22-year-old nephew is an adult and should, therefore be free to choose any woman he wishes to marry. His is a typical, tidy, military mind; his vision is clear but limited, and he is inclined to think in terms of sharply defined categories and neat solutions. He is totally unaware of the emotional complexities of life that make human beings unique individuals and impel them to take somewhat irrational action. It is easier for him to think of his wife as a western woman than as the individual Noreska. He cannot understand how young people can commit suicide because of failure in love or in important school examinations, which makes his brother, Muḥammad, accuse him of being hard-hearted.[68] Hammām is totally unaware of the emotional needs of his son and ruthlessly forbids him to see his mother and, equally heartlessly, decides to send away Laylā, the young woman he loves, once he has become aware of the true nature of the relationship between the young couple. In order to save the skins of his guilty friends in the army he does not mind using his position to steal the incriminating evidence, even though the loss of the documents means that the innocent, humble clerk in whose charge they were placed is unjustly punished by dismissal and loss of livelihood (p. 32).

Yet Hammām does not fail to gain our sympathy; when we first encounter him we find him an ailing invalid, already having suffered for many years, who welcomes his suffering as penance for his folly in divorcing his first wife so many years back. This sense of guilt, even though somewhat exaggerated as his sensible brother keeps reminding him, coupled with his readiness to atone for it, contribute no doubt to soften any harsh judgments which we may form on his behaviour. Furthermore, in the course of the play any dogmatic positions he may have held are thoroughly undermined, causing him enormous mental anguish. The overbearing pride and the cocksureness which we encounter at the beginning give place to humility, doubt and uncertainty which drive him to contemplate suicide. His son does commit suicide because of his thwarted love, his niece goes mad for the same reason and his confident attempt to cover up his friends' misdemeanours proves a failure; the whole world around him seems to collapse. At first suicide appears to be the easiest way out, but he later learns true humility and accepts his responsibility in continuing to live in order to protect his vulnerable, insane niece. It is, therefore, truly tragic that when he has painfully learnt humility he is cut down by Noreska's bullet.

According to Hammām, Noreska has never been able to adapt to the oriental way of life, but surely we must not accept his view of her as an impartial judgment on her character. What we see of her is somewhat different; she has been able to adapt in several ways, but she is not prepared to accept the traditional, submissive role of the Muslim Egyptian woman which her husband has been endeavouring to force on her. Intellectually she is a liberated woman, whose ancestry can be traced back to Ibsen's *Nora*.[69] In this sense, she is no more ready to compromise than Hammām. She makes fun of her husband's attempt to make his niece adhere to the custom of wearing the veil. She tries to make Amīna realize that she is as much a victim of Hammām as she is herself although unfortunately Amīna is both too old and too conventional to accept any position for woman other than that of subservience to men and, because she was divorced, she suffered many of the serious disadvantages of a divorced woman in traditional Egyptian society of the time:

NORESKA: You and I have been wronged. That is why we should be friends, not enemies. I know you thought that I had taken your husband away from you twenty years ago, and for twenty whole years you have hated me for that reason. Are you now suddenly going to like me? Of course not! That would not be possible. I too imagined that you had taken my husband away from me. Yet the truth is that I never took your husband. It was he who took me. You have not taken my husband. He has taken you. Today I have come to exact justice from him for you and for me.

AMĪNA (*extremely alarmed*): Exact justice for me? What on earth do you mean? What do you propose to do?

NORESKA: No, no, don't be scared! I'm not one of those European women you are thinking of. I don't walk about with a revolver hidden in my clothes ready to shoot at people. No, my dear friend, I'm not such a woman. I just can't suffer in silence when a man, who holds a whip in his hand, keeps hitting me with it. I can't turn the other cheek, or kiss the hand that strikes me. I can't bring myself to bless the mouth that digs its teeth into my heart.

AMĪNA: Neither can I, Madam.

NORESKA: You see, we are really in complete agreement. Yet a moment ago, when I told you that we should not hate each other because we both have been wronged, you shrugged your shoulders as if you mistrusted me.

AMĪNA: Not at all. It's only that I am convinced it is all a matter of fate. This is our lot and we have to endure it. What else could we do? We must resign ourselves to our fate.

NORESKA: Our lot indeed! This is exactly what has encouraged men to treat us the way they do. When we talk about our lot in their presence, they think that their unjust treatment of us is fair justice because it has been preordained for us to suffer it. No, my friend. Don't talk about our lot! Nobody has been pre-ordained to suffer injustice, nobody. When a man does wrong, he obeys the command of no one but himself. No one has told him to wrong others, neither God nor man. When Hammām wronged me he was a free agent, totally responsible for his actions. If a man runs over a dog in the street, the dog's owners pounce on him to make him pay the price. You don't say then it is only the dog's lot; it was destined to die this way. But when the same man runs over his wife who has given him her youth and her body, when he throws her to the ground and presses hard with his feet on her chest until she nearly spits out her heart, do you mean to say when this woman staggers to her feet again, she should look kindly at her husband and say: 'It's only my lot, please kick me again'? Oh, no! We won't accept that, ever.

(Yazbak, *al-Dhabā'ih*, pp. 38ff.)

Noreska, an idealist to the core, from the start has set out to liberate Egypt, its men no less than its women, so that they might throw off the yoke of the European imperialist (p. 45); but the people are too tied to the past and she is too impatient to reform them to make a success of it. The result is unhappiness not only for her husband, but for her son as well. However, to say that Hammām and Noreska are primarily individuals, and not merely oriental and western types, does not mean that they do not at the same time embody certain conflicting attitudes to life: to the past with its traditions, to women's freedom and the conception of a good wife. Because of their sharp differences and given their extremist dispositions, tragic conflict is bound to result.

Yazbak's conscious craftsmanship is admirably revealed in the way he constructs his play. Each of the four acts builds up into a crescendo ending in a dramatic event. Act I ends in Hammām's decision to remarry Amīna, Act II in his repudiation and divorce of Noreska, while ʿUthmān's suicide concludes Act III and the shooting of Hammām, Act IV. Despite the relatively quiet interlude in Act II, presenting Amīna's resumption of happy, domestic life, the whole play moves ruthlessly towards its climactic end. The time of action is clearly indicated, though always indirectly, in the course of the dialogue: Act I takes place in December, Act II begins four months later, while Acts III and IV are set in June. The timing is important; for example, speaking with unwitting foresight, Hammām declares half-jokingly that young men's suicide occurs only in June or July when school examinations are held and the results are published (p. 13).

The play is highly organized; there is so much talk about suicide and shooting that the audience is unconsciously prepared for both events later. Likewise, there is considerable premonition. ʿUthmān tells Laylā that he fears the strained relationship between his parents is bound to snap one day with disastrous results both for himself and for her (p. 33). He feels that the days of happiness have gone, never to return, and that Laylā will be forced to go away:

(ʿUTHMĀN *is seen sitting at his desk as if asleep with his head buried in his outstretched arms, while* LAYLĀ *is knitting a tie for him.*)

LAYLĀ: Goodness! You're asleep. Wake up, ʿUthmān! Fancy you falling asleep with all your clothes on! (*She goes up to him and shakes him gently, displaying the tie.*) Wake up, and have a look at your tie! It's nearly finished. (*She holds his hand and shakes it.*) I say, you do have a temperature. (ʿUTHMĀN *raises his head a little and looks at her.* LAYLĀ *looks surprised and dismayed.*) You've been crying? Whatever for? You're not a little child! (*She helps him to get up.*) Come on, get away from that desk! You must not cry! You must never let things get you down like that, never! (ʿUTHMĀN *moves away from the desk with her.*) You're not a child any more. Making yourself so unhappy, and ill with grief! You've already run a temperature. Why, what's the matter? It's not the end of the world!

ʿUTHMĀN (*his anger mounting*): What more do you want to happen, Laylā? Isn't what has happened enough? When my father returned to aunt Amīna I felt that our days of happiness were over and different days were to follow. And I was proved to be right. The first thing they did was to say, 'Laylā must not continue to stay with Noreska, who is sure to corrupt her. She must move in with us'. And they brought you here. I was then left alone with my mother, who was thoroughly miserable and in her unhappiness took it out on me. But I bore that too, telling myself that she is my mother after all, and she is so unhappy. Then my father broke with her, and how? You saw and heard them yourself... Then he insisted that I also should leave her. I put up with that too, determined to visit her secretly from time to time. Then he forbade me to see her. That too I was prepared to endure.

LAYLĀ (*playfully*): Oh, you exaggerate so! Don't you slink away and visit her behind his back? When they ask me where you have gone, I lie to them and tell them you have gone to the school to see if the exam results are out.

ʿUTHMĀN (*sadly*): If it hadn't been for you, Laylā, I wouldn't have been able to live one minute longer in this house.

LAYLĀ (*playfully*): And why not, pray? Is there anything you lack here? Perhaps you want to go back to play hide and seek and chase me in the garden as we used to do in the past? Or is it perhaps you want us to amuse ourselves with the camera and take photos? Let's do that then, if it pleases you. Just tell me what you want!

ʿUTHMĀN: Do you think that they would now let us do any of these things in the garden? I bet you one day they will tell you that you too have to leave this house.

LAYLĀ (*haughtily*): Let them dare!

ʿUTHMĀN: Do you think you would be able to stop them? They already exchange meaningful glances about us.

LAYLĀ: Let them do what they like, who cares?

ʿUTHMĀN: I don't know, Laylā. But I feel that our days of happiness have now gone for ever.

LAYLĀ: What are you talking about? Whoever told you that? You are not quite eighteen and lots of happy days lie ahead of you. What nonsense you talk! Just because your father left your mother you let yourself lose all hope like that? How about me then, and I'm a girl? I was orphaned ten years ago. I lost both parents and yet I never gave up hope and the good Lord looked after me.

ʿUTHMĀN: I too am an orphan. Yet both my parents are alive. Surely it is easier to be an orphan like you.

LAYLĀ: What rubbish you talk! Easier to be an orphan like me, indeed! All right then, we are both orphans. Only an orphan can understand another orphan.

ʿUTHMĀN: At least you've found those who have given you love and kindness.

LAYLĀ (*giving him a sweet look*): And you haven't found anyone to love you? (*She looks at him again.*) No? Never?

ʿUTHMĀN: You are about the only one who actually talks to me in this house.

(Yazbak, *al-Dhabāʾih*, pp. 48ff.)

Another symptom of the organic unity of the play's structure is the frequency of tragic irony. Only a few of the numerous instances will be mentioned here. When Muḥammad expresses his and his wife's reluctance to put too much pressure on their son lest, crossed in love, he might take his life, Hammām dismisses his brother's fears as groundless, so certain is he that no one is going to commit suicide. 'Tell his mother', he says to Muḥammad, 'not to worry but sit back and relax; no one is going to kill himself' (pp. 13–14). Again Hammām is absolutely sure that in the war raging between himself and his wife he 'will never be the first person to fall' (p. 17). Looking back nostalgically upon his marriage to his first wife, now very much idealized, Hammām is asked by his brother whether or not he could recognize her if he saw her now after the passage of some twenty years. With characteristic assurance he declares that he would be able to tell her at once were she to be placed among twenty women (in some sort of identification parade), her face, body and hands completely covered (p. 19). He says these words while Amīna, dressed as Nurse Ḥafīẓa, is in the same room without his being able to identify her. Similarly, Noreska assures Amīna that she is not the sort of European woman who hides a revolver in her clothes with which to kill people (p. 39). Yet she proves to be precisely that kind of person in the end. Such instances of tragic irony show not only that in the act of writing the author was able to hold the entire play in his mind as one interrelated whole, but they also hint at the presence of some hidden, almost supernatural power directing men's actions and controlling their destinies, a power besides which human beings seem to be limited, pathetic creatures.

The author of 'The Sacrifices' is skilful in his use of devices designed to create pathos, ranging from powerful contrast and reversal of situation to verbal contrivances. For instance, at the very moment of announcing the joyful news of ʿUthmān's passing his important examination and while everybody around him is congratulating him and promising him all kinds of gifts, ʿUthmān is quietly contemplating putting an end to his life and the joy turns into the shock of his suicide. The dead ʿUthmān who has been in the habit of falling asleep fully clothed is told off by Laylā (who is keening over his body in her lap) for not listening to her last words to him, namely her advice to him that he should take off his clothes before falling asleep (p. 64).

Because of his decision to use the colloquial language the author has no difficulty in making his characters express their thoughts and feelings without creating the slightest effect of artificiality. Not a word is out of place in this remarkable play; the dialogue moves forward spontaneously revealing the character of the speakers while at the same time advancing the action of the play. Fortunately the author has not been side-tracked into an attempt to make the European Noreska express herself naturalistically in broken Arabic, but he wisely makes her use the same level of spoken Arabic as other characters. And because of the intensity of her feelings and the credibility of her character, the dramatist makes a successful use of basic, dramatic conventions; we do not find her language any more strange than that of Othello describing himself in most eloquent verse as 'rude am I in speech'.

Occasionally, the Egyptian colloquial rises to truly poetic heights, as has been noted by critics.[70] For instance, this is how Hammām repudiates Noreska, 'I tell you you are divorced! Do you hear me? 'You are divorced! I repeat it as many times as there are graves dug from the time of Adam to this day, as many times as there are stars in the sky, or grains of sand in the sea' (p. 47). ʿUthmān, who seems to suffer from hypersensitivity, often expresses himself in poetic language with Koranic quotations, to the extent that the more practically-minded Laylā teases him about his poetic temperament (p. 51). The result, however, is that a poetic atmosphere is created in which certain objects become potent symbols crystallizing or embodying states of mind and feeling as, for instance, in ʿUthmān's description of the little garden of Amīna's house to which he is made to move by his tyrannical father, in comparison with the spacious garden of Noreska's house where he spent his happier childhood days. In this little garden, he complains to Laylā 'plants wither away and die, the Jasmine bush is sickly and incapable of climbing up the wall, even the stars in the sky do not shine above this house' (p. 51).

Finally, the strength of 'The Sacrifices' lies in the fact that, while it is firmly set in a specific social context with references to several problems of Egyptian society ranging from the position of women in Egypt to the tyranny of fathers and even the stifling effect of artificial conventions in modern Arabic love poetry (p. 30), it is primarily a play about individual, human relationships. It depicts the destructive impact of the self-absorbed, older generation upon the lives of the impressionable and sensitive young, who are often thoughtlessly sacrificed by their elders caught up as they are in the clashes between them. Even bearing in mind its melodramatic ending, 'The Sacrifices' remains one of the most significant achievements of serious Arabic drama in the Egyptian vernacular.

CONCLUSION

With the work of Ibrāhīm Ramzī, Muḥammad Taymūr and Anṭūn Yazbak it can safely be said that Arabic drama reached its maturity. Certain norms had been more or less established. As far as the language of dialogue was concerned, plays set in modern Egypt which were designed to be produced on the stage and not simply read in the study were written in the colloquial, while the classical language, or a simplified form of it, was used in those dealing with serious, historical themes. The preceding discussion, it is hoped, has shown that in the second and third decades of this century Egyptian dramatists were able to write plays, both in the classical and the colloquial language, which, despite their minor imperfections, deserve the serious attention of the literary critic. Whether in social satirical comedy, *drame*, tragedy or historical drama, the imperfections were no longer the result of teething troubles, but the concomitants of all fallible human endeavour. Convincing characters revealed their natures in crisp, natural dialogue and they developed within the framework of reasonably well-constructed plots. The world they inhabited, their preoccupations and problems were all recognizably Egyptian. It is interesting to see the large space occupied in some of these plays by the pressing problems and controversial issues of the time, from the question of women's emancipation and the relationship between the sexes, to the conflicts between the generations within the family, in a period of transition during which society was passing from tradition to modernity and certain values were in a state of flux. Economic and political problems such as those created by the First World War or the nationalist struggle for independence are there to see although discreetly kept in the background. The perennial tension between town and country was also presented, albeit in a light-hearted, almost farcical manner.

Just how far ahead of the rest of Arabic drama Egyptian plays were at the time can be gauged if any of the works discussed above is compared with the best known, non-Egyptian play of the period. One of the very few works listed by Landau under the heading *Dramas* and described as 'good drama'[1] is *al-Ābā' wa'l-Banūn* ('Parents and Children') which the distinguished Syro-American poet and man of letters, Mīkhā'īl Nu'ayma, first published in 1917 and which has been reprinted several times since.[2] 'Parents and Children', a full length four-act play, is the work of an intelligent writer, who, as the introduction to his play amply illustrates, not only stresses the important role drama should play in modern Arabic literature and society, but who is also keenly aware of the acute problem of the language of dialogue given the diglossia of modern Arabic. 'Parents and Children' reveals many serious weaknesses, however, even in the version which its author revised in 1953.

The play is set in a small, Lebanese town at the beginning of the twentieth century and the action revolves around a Christian family. Umm Ilyās, a strong-willed widow of fifty, is an old-fashioned, tyrannical mother who expects and demands blind obedience from her children of whom there are three: two sons, Ilyās, who is thirty-years-old, and Khalīl who is twenty-four, and a twenty-year-old daughter, Zayna. Umm Ilyās is trying to force her daughter to marry the forty-year-old Naṣīf Bey, the titled son of Mūsā Bey, an old friend of her dead husband, because he comes from the same social class as herself. What she does not realize is that, despite their pretence to the contrary, both Naṣīf and Mūsā are now utterly penniless and deeply in debt and that Naṣīf is a worthless person who spends his time gambling and drinking and is under the illusion that he is a gifted poet. Zayna falls in love with Ilyās's friend, Dāwūd, who is an intelligent, but impecunious school teacher the same age as Ilyās, but who comes from a lower social stratum. Dāwūd returns Zayna's feelings. Similarly, Ilyās meets and falls in love with Dāwūd's sister, Shahīda, also a school teacher, who too develops a liking for him. The immediate problem facing the young people is how to stop the mother, Umm Ilyās, from making her daughter marry Naṣīf against her will, after Zayna has decided to break off her engagement because of his unkind remarks to her about Dāwūd. Umm Ilyās beats her daughter in a vain attempt to make her change her mind. Naṣīf plots to kill Dāwūd, but the plot miscarries and Dāwūd escapes with a few minor injuries. Umm Ilyās also strongly opposes Ilyās's intention to marry Shahīda when she hears about it not only because Shahīda is a mere school teacher but also, much more importantly, because she is of the Protestant faith (pp.90ff.).

Meanwhile, the wicked old man, Mūsā, anxious to see his son married to Zayna because of her money, schemes with Naṣīf to destroy her chances of marrying Dāwūd. He manages to blacken Dāwūd's image by falsely accusing him of bigamous intentions since he claims that he has been lying about his relationship to Shahīda, who is in reality his wife and not his sister. Naṣīf also announces the shocking (false) news that Dāwūd is suffering from incurable consumption and is, therefore, unfit to marry Zayna as he is bound to pass the fatal illness on to her. The trick seems to work. The disappointed Zayna, unable to cope with the shock, takes poison to end her life but is saved in time and nursed back to health by Shahīda. Zayna's imminent death makes her mother begin to relent and for a while contemplate allowing her to marry the man she loves, but she is soon swayed back by Mūsā, who assures her that it is in Zayna's best interest to bring in a priest (a corrupt man who will do as he is told) to marry her to his son as soon as possible. Only the news of Naṣīf's sudden arrest by the police for his failure to repay a debt and the discovery of his and his father's bankruptcy saves the situation in the end. Eventually and reluctantly Umm Ilyās becomes reconciled to the idea of her daughter and son marrying the persons of their choice.

According to the Preface, the author's intention is to dramatize the conflict between the generations and to show the need for the young to rebel against the cruel and outworn traditions of the old, a need which is reiterated time and again by the young characters themselves. Dāwūd discusses with his sister the appalling oriental custom of parents forcing their daughters to marry against their wishes. He is the one who inspires the rebellion against the tyranny of the old and preaches to Ilyās the necessity of the struggle to change and modernize society. His words, we are told, encourage Zayna to change from a docile daughter, who is prepared to blindly obey her mother, into a person of independent judgment (p. 68). But instead of the characters living the conflict, and by their actions dramatically revealing the theme of the play, they engage in rational discussion and merely analyze their predicament. For instance, Ilyās discusses his mother's character with Dāwūd with remarkable lucidity as if, far from being one of the characters in the play himself, he is a literary or dramatic critic, viewing the scene from the outside and attempting a character analysis (p. 35). Despite their incessant talk of the need for rebellion, they all seem to be singularly weak and ineffectual. Only Zayna has the courage to disobey her mother and she does not do that all the time. The rest of the young people remain extraordinarily passive. The happy end of the play, in which the two pairs of lovers are allowed to marry, is not brought about by their own rebellious behaviour but as a result of an event that lies outside their power, namely the arrest of their enemy, Naṣīf. The plot of the play therefore fails to bring out the author's point.

As for the author's power of characterization, it is very limited indeed. The lovers are pale, shadowy and unconvincing figures. Zayna and Dāwūd confess their love for one another in a naively contrived, totally unrealistic manner. Characters faint. They contemplate suicide at the slightest provocation; this is true not only of Zayna, but also of Ilyās and Dāwūd, which is rather incongruous since Dāwūd is supposed to be the advocate of struggling to change society. They discuss big philosophical issues such as the meaning of life, human happiness and sorrow all too easily, even when they meet for the first time (as Ilyās and Shahīda do) (pp. 50ff.). Khalīl, the younger brother, is an unamusing clown who lacks motivation for he seems to change sides suddenly and for no apparent reason. Naṣīf is an impossible bore and his unprincipled father a pure stage monster straight from the world of melodrama, and it is difficult to see how the mother, Umm Ilyās, could have taken to either of them or been deceived by them. Umm Ilyās is clearly meant to be the strongest character in the play. To be sure, she is not an uninteresting creation. She is full of contradictions and social and religious prejudices. She boasts of the number of men her dead husband killed and treasures the swords with which he proved his manly courage. Yet she scolds her older son bitterly for his free thinking and for not going to church and is pleased with her younger one because he attends church on Sundays even though, unlike his older, more sensitive and better educated brother, he is no more than a thug and a drunkard. Yet one feels that all these features of Umm Ilyās are artificially put together and her character does not come to life.

But perhaps the most serious defect of the play lies in its dialogue. Instead of opting for either the colloquial or the classical language for his dialogue, Nuʿayma resorts to the method advocated by Faraḥ Anṭūn of making his educated characters speak in the literary idiom, while putting the colloquial in the mouths of the rest. This is an unwise decision for the result is not only very artificial, but at times downright absurd, particularly when in a single conversation each of the interlocutors expresses himself in a totally different idiom. It is ridiculous that even the two brothers Ilyās and Khalīl do not speak the same language; the former speaks in classical, while the latter speaks in colloquial Arabic (pp.36ff.). Naṣīf uses the classical even when he is drunk (pp.42ff.). Far from flowing smoothly, the speech of those who use the classical often sounds stilted and studied and it is even studded with quotations of apposite lines of verse as if the speaker was reading a literary essay aloud (pp.28, 35). Far more damaging is the author's inconsistency in this respect. Mūsā converses with his son Naṣīf in the classical, but with Umm Ilyās in the colloquial (cf. Act III Scene II with Scene III), and at other times he uses the colloquial with his son himself (e.g. Act III Scene VI). Naṣīf talks to Khalīl sometimes in the classical (Act I Scene VI) and at other times in the colloquial (Act III Scene V). This uncertainty and constant shifting of the level of the language of dialogue may be due to the author's inexperience in drama (as far as we know 'Parents and children' was his sole experiment in play writing), but it is certainly a serious defect in one of the most important elements in the play.

From this brief discussion it is all too easy to see how superior the Egyptian plays by Ramzī, Muḥammad Taymūr and Yazbak are when set beside 'Parents and children', which, despite its author's good intentions, is no more than a slight work of a dubious dramatic value: a melodramatic story with an unsatisfactory plot, shallow and unconvincing characterization, excessive discussion in the abstract and a seriously flawed dialogue. It is ironic that the text of Nuʿayma's play is much more easily available than that of many of those Egyptian plays which were published in the twenties only once and are now, alas, out of print.

From the late 1920s the Egyptian government began to take steps to promote the cause of the serious, Egyptian theatre which was facing a real threat from a popular, commercial theatre that was sweeping the market, relying as it did upon the money-spinning mixture of singing, dancing, farce, slapstick comedy, Arabized cheap French vaudevilles referred to as *Franco-Arabe* revues and titillating shows with easy humour arising from mixing Egyptian and European characters. The aid that the government provided ranged from offering prizes for play writing to granting scholarships to study drama and acting in Europe, culminating in the setting up of a school of dramatic arts in 1930 under the direction of Zakī Ṭulaymāt, who had received his serious training in Europe.[3] Clearly, by the 1930s, drama and acting had attained a measure of respectability, at least officially, in Egypt. No doubt this was helped by the fact that no lesser figure than the doyen of Arabic letters, the highly esteemed author, critic and educationalist, Ṭāhā Ḥusayn, was keenly interested in drama and had written extensively about, and translated specimens of, ancient Greek as well as modern French plays. Ṭāhā Ḥusayn's enthusiastic reception of the appearance of the first serious and mature play by Tawfīq al-Ḥakīm remains one of the most memorable pieces in the whole body of his literary criticism.[4] Also the fact that a great poet like Aḥmad Shawqī, who wrote within the classical Arabic tradition, turned to writing verse-drama during the last four years of his life (1928–32) when his reputation as a supreme Arabic poet was still at its highest throughout the Arab world helped enormously to render drama an acceptable mode of writing.

Other factors contributed to the rise in the status of actors and acting. One was the increasing number of well-educated or highly born individuals who became involved in the theatre, often despite their parents' wishes, either as actors such as ʿAbd al-Raḥmān Rushdī who was a law graduate, and Yūsuf Wahbī who was an heir to a large fortune, or as dramatists and drama critics such as the gifted Muḥammad Taymūr who came from one of the leading aristocratic families in Egypt, or Tawfīq al-Ḥakīm who was the son of a distinguished man in the legal profession. Another factor was the growth of theatre criticism which was published first in the columns of daily newspapers or weeklies and then in magazines devoted almost exclusively to the theatre. The story of the development of theatre criticism in Egypt was told in some detail not long ago in a book which, despite its ideological bias (revealed in the author's unfair treatment of several writers), contains some useful information on the subject.[5] From it we learn that around 1924 a spate of weekly or monthly magazines concerned with matters relating to the theatre began to flood the market.[6] They included, for instance: *al-Tiyatru al-Muṣawwara* (Illustrated Theatre, 1924), *Nūnū Magazine* (1924); *al-Tamthīl* (Acting, 1924), *al Masraḥ* (The Theatre, 1925); *al-Mikruskūb* (The Microscope, 1925), *Rūz al-Yūsuf* (1926/7); *al-Nāqid* (The Critic, 1927) and *al-Masāriḥ* (Theatres, 1930). Important daily newspapers which were concerned with the theatre included *al-Ahrām, al-Siyāsa, Kawkab al-Sharq, al-Balāgh, al-Akhbār, al-Muqaṭṭam* and *al-Ṣabāḥ*. It must be admitted that not all that was published in them about dramatists, actors and plays was in any way serious dramatic or literary criticism. Much of it was no more than gossip or even personal abuse. Nevertheless, these newspapers and magazines seemed to place the world of the theatre constantly before the eyes of their readers, thereby helping to make it part of the national scene. And it is perhaps no wonder that the authors of the best dramatic criticism in the first quarter of the century, Faraḥ Anṭūn and Muḥammad Taymūr, were also among the most distinguished Egyptian playwrights during that period.

For a while the commercial theatre proved a financial success as was seen in the activities of Yūsuf Wahbī's Ramsīs troupe which served in the main Arabic adaptations of French melodrama. For instance, it was estimated that his play *Awlād al-Fuqarā* ('Children of the Poor') alone netted as much as £75,000 during the 1931 season, a considerable amount of money in those days.[7] But the success was to be short-lived. Like other services, Egyptian theatres, even the more successful ones, were severely hit by the world economic crisis and the dramatic fall in the price of cotton, Egypt's main export. Companies, including Yūsuf Wahbī's Ramsīs, disbanded themselves. In 1933 while some actor/managers like Yūsuf Wahbī had their savings to live on, most actors and actresses found themselves unemployed and penniless having been dismissed from their jobs without any compensation at all. In an attempt to defend their rights in the future, they formed an association and appealed successfully to the government for financial aid. The aid was a modest sum, but it enabled them to form a troupe and they began their activities with a production of Victor Hugo's *Hernani*, to be followed by some indigenous plays including Ibrāhīm Ramzī's *Ṣarkhat al-Ṭifl* ('The Baby's Cry').[8] However, the Actors Association Troupe did not last very long due to a number of factors which, according to Fattūḥ Nashāṭī, included their use of an unsuitable, badly-situated theatre (al-Hambra), ill-management, internal squabbles, nepotism, bad casting, poor sets and insufficient rehearsing. The result was the resignation of many distinguished members.

In 1935, the dream of many enlightened theatre lovers came true when the government decided to set up the National Theatre Troupe from the leading actors and actresses of the day under the directorship of the poet, Khalīl Muṭrān.[9] In retrospect the formation of the National Theatre Troupe was not an unmixed blessing, for the government laid down for it a policy which, although it enlisted the help of many distinguished men of letters such as Ṭāhā Ḥusayn, Aḥmad Amīn, Muḥammad Ḥusayn Haykal, ʿAbd al-ʿAzīz al-Bishrī on its three committees for reading, administration and supervision, stipulated that the plays chosen for production should include proper translations of the masterpieces of world theatre but not a single play in colloquial Arabic. This policy confirmed and legitimized, as it were, the already existing rift between the colloquial and literary Arabic theatre. Drama in the colloquial had to wait for nearly a quarter of a century before it began to acquire official approval and respectability in the literary establishment and that is in spite of the fact that, as we have seen, excellent plays had already been written in it. The first play the new National Theatre Troupe performed, in 1935, was Tawfīq al-Ḥakīm's *Ahl al-Kahf* ('The Sleepers in the Cave'), which was followed by Shakespeare's *King Lear* in Ibrāhīm Ramzī's translation. Although it has changed its name more than once and despite the derisory salaries received by its members, the Egyptian National Theatre Troupe has continued to function bravely to this day.

It is fitting to end this survey of early Arabic drama with the mention of Tawfīq al-Ḥakīm, easily the best known and most important figure in the history of Arabic drama, for although his career as a dramatist really belongs to a later and more sophisticated stage in the development of the genre, al-Ḥakīm had his first experience of the Egyptian theatre during this period. For a detailed study of his work, however, as well as that of the still best known Arab verse dramatist, Aḥmad Shawqī, I refer the reader to my book on *Modern Arabic Drama in Egypt*.

NOTES

I THE INDIGENOUS DRAMATIC TRADITION

1. Edward William Lane, *The Manners and Customs of the Modern Egyptians* (Everyman's Library, n.d.), ch. VIII.
2. *Ibid.* p. 395.
3. *Ibid.* pp. 397–8.
4. R. Strothmann, *Shorter Encyclopaedia of Islam* (1961), p. 590.
5. Matthew Arnold, *Essays in Criticism* (Leipzig, 1887), vol. II, pp. 59–60.
6. Strothmann, *Shorter Encyclopaedia*, p. 590.
7. Arnold, *Essays*, vol. II, p. 59.
8. This should become immediately clear from the following rather colourful account by Arnold, based upon Gobineau, which seems, nevertheless, substantially true: 'Confraternities go in procession with a black flag and torches, every man with his shirt torn open, and beating himself with the right hand on the left shoulder in a kind of measured cadence to accompany a canticle in honour of the martyrs. These processions come and take part in the theatres where the Seyids are preaching. Still more noisy are the company of dancers, striking a kind of wooden castanets together, at one time in front of their breasts, at another behind their heads, and marking time with music and dance to a dirge set up by the bystanders, in which the names of the Imams recur as a burden. Noisiest of all are the Berbers, men of a darker skin and another race, their feet and the upper part of their body naked, who carry, some of them tambourines and cymbals, others iron chains and long needles. One of their race is said to have formerly derided the Imams in their affliction, and the Berbers now appear in expiation of that crime. At first their music and their march proceed slowly together, but presently the music quickens, the chain and needle-bearing Berbers move violently round, and begin to beat themselves with their chains and to prick their arms and cheeks with the needles – first gently, then with more vehemence; till suddenly the music ceases, and all stops. So we are carried back, on this old Asiatic soil, where beliefs and usages are heaped layer upon layer and ruin upon ruin, far past the martyred Imams, past Mahometanism, past Christianity, to the priests of Baal gashing themselves with knives and to the worship of Adonis.' *Ibid.* vol. II, pp. 62–4

   It is illuminating to contrast this with the account given by Lane of the quiet prayers recited at the shrine of Ḥusayn in his Cairo mosque in moderate Sunni Egypt on tenth of Muḥarram. (Lane, *Manners and Customs*, p. 258.)
9. See Introduction, p. 4 above.
10. See below, p. 14.
11. See below, p. 24.
12. Lane, *Manners and Customs*, p. 507.
13. Aḥmad Amīn, *Qāmus al-ʿĀdāt waʾl-Taqālīd waʾl-Taʿābīr al-Miṣriyya* (Cairo, 1953), p. 288.
14. Aḥmad Rushdī Ṣāliḥ, *al-Masraḥ al-ʿArabī* (Cairo, 1972), pp. 41–2.
15. Muḥammad Yūsuf Najm, *al-Masraḥiyya fīʾl-Adab al-ʿArabī al-Ḥadīth* (Beirut, 1956), pp. 73–4.
16. See Jacob M. Landau, *Studies in the Arab Theater and Cinema* (Philadelphia, 1958), p. 50.

17. Lane, *Manners and Customs*, pp. 395–7.
18. For a fuller discussion of Ibn Dāniyāl's work see M.M. Badawi, 'Medieval Arabic drama: Ibn Dāniyāl', *Journal of Arabic Literature*, 13 (1982), 83–107.
19. Ibrāhīm Ḥamāda, *Khayāl al-Ẓill wa Tamthīliyyāt Ibn Dāniyāl* (Cairo, 1963), p. 158.
20. *Ibid*, p. 185.
21. Alfred W. Pollard, ed., *English Miracle Plays, Moralities and Interludes* (Oxford, 1950), p. 8.
22. Enid Welsford, *The Fool* (London, 1968), p. 51.
23. *Ibid*, p. 300.
24. *Ibid.* p. 45.
25. *Ibid.* p. 299.
26. C.E. Bosworth, *The Mediaeval Islamic Underworld: the Banū Sāsān in Arabic Society and Literature* (Leiden, 1976), vol. I, pp. 30, 60ff.
27. Landau, *Arab Theater*, p. 19.
28. Again the mock preacher has a distinguished ancestry in Arabic literature of humour from the work of al-Jāḥiẓ to that of the authors of *maqāmāt*. See Bosworth, *Medieval Islamic Underworld*, vol. I, pp. 24ff.
29. ʿAbd al-Ḥamīd Yūnus, *Khayāl al-Ẓill* (Cairo, 1965), p. 21.
30. *Ibid.* p. 22.
31. Mohamed Mostafa, ed., *Die Chronik des Ijas* (Cairo, 1961), vol. V, p. 192.
32. J.M. Landau, *Shadow Plays in the Near East* (Jerusalem, 1948), p. xliii.
33. Aḥmad Taymūr, *Khayāl al-Ẓill* (Cairo, 1957), p. 19 and Yūnus, *Khayāl* pp. 29–30.
34. Landau, *Shadow Plays*, p. xlv.
35. The German scholar E.R.E. Prüfer assumed that there were originally two schools of writing and performing shadow plays: 'The one represented by the works of Ibn Dāniyāl was palatable to higher society, but in the course of generations and following the severe persecution suffered by the shadow play, the second popular kind became more accepted by the mass'. See Landau, *Shadow Plays*, p. xliv.
36. Yūnus, *Khayāl*, p. 83.
37. See Paul Kahle in *Nachrichten von der Königlichen Gesellschaft der Wissenschaften zu Göttingen Philologisch-historische Klasse aus dem Jahre 1915* (Berlin, 1916), p. 317, 343.
38. Yūnus, *Khayāl*, p. 89.
39. Kahle, *Nachrichten* (1920), p. 284.
40. Paul Kahle, *Der Leuchtturm von Alexandria, ein Arabisches Schattenspiel aus dem mittelalterlichem Ägypten*, with contributions from Georg Jacob (Stuttgart, 1930).
41. *Ibid.* p. 2.
42. ʿAbd al-Raḥmān al-Jabartī, *ʿAjāʾib al-Āthār* (11 Shaʿbān, 1215 A.H.).
43. Najm, *al-Masraḥiyya*, pp. 19ff.

2 THE FATHER OF THE MODERN EGYPTIAN THEATRE

1. To the bibliography of books and articles in the useful, though not always accurate, study of Ṣannūʿ by Irene L. Gendzier, *The Practical Visions of Yaʿqub Sanuʿ* (Cambridge, Mass., 1966), may be added the more recent article by Matti Moosa, 'Yaʿqūb Ṣanūʿ and the rise of Arab drama in Egypt', in the *International Journal of Middle East Studies*, 5 (1974), 401–33.
2. Muḥammad Yūsuf Najm, ed., *al-Masraḥ al-ʿArabī Dirāsāt wa Nuṣūṣ*, no. 3, *Yaʿqūb Ṣannūʿ (Abū Naḍḍāra)* (Beirut, 1963), p. 211.
3. Gendzier, *The Practical Visions*, p. 34.
4. Jacob M. Landau, *Studies in the Arab Theater and Cinema* (Philadelphia, 1958), p. 68.
5. *Ibid.* p. 66.
6. ʿAbd al-Ḥamīd Ghunaym (in *Ṣannūʿ Rāʾid al-Masraḥ al-Miṣrī* [Cairo, n.d.], p. 52) assumes that in calling his piece *Luʿba (liʿba) Tiyātriyya*, Ṣannūʿ was translating the English term 'play'. However, we must bear in mind the continued use of the term *liʿb* in the popular tradition of shadow theatre, see above, p. 25.
7. Najm, *al-Masraḥ al-ʿArabī*, p. 203.
8. *Ibid.* p. 193.
9. Muḥammad Yūsuf Najm, *al-Masraḥhiyya fi'l-Adab al-ʿArabī al-Ḥadīth* (Beirut, 1956), p. 434.
10. Matti Moosa, 'Yaʿqūb Ṣannūʿ and the rise of Arab drama in Egypt'. *International Journal of*

Middle East Studies, 5 (1974), 428. For a detailed discussion of Ṣannūʿ's debt to Molière in all his work see Atia Abul Naga, *Les Sources Françaises du Théâtre Egyptien (1870–1939)* (Alger, SNED, 1972), pp. 91–104.

11. For an intelligent discussion of the skilful use which Ṣannūʿ makes of *sajʿ* to produce a comic effect, see Attia Amer, *Lughat al-Masraḥ al-ʿArabī* (Stockholm, 1967), vol. 1, pp. 95ff.

3 THE SYRIAN CONTRIBUTION

1. Muḥammad Yūsuf Najm, ed., 'Mārūn al-Naqqāsh', *al-Masraḥ al-ʿArabī Dirāsāt wa Nuṣūṣ*, Beirut (1961), 11–12.
2. See Jacob M. Landau, *Studies in the Arab Theater and Cinema* (Philadelphia, 1958), p. 57.
3. See Najm, ed., 'Mārūn al-Naqqāsh', p. 20, Matti Moosa, 'Naqqāsh and the rise of the native Arab theatre in Syria', *Journal of Arabic Literature*, 3 (1972), 109 and Mohamed A. al-Khozai, *The Development of Early Arabic Drama (1847–1900)* (London, 1984), p. 44.
4. The page numbers in brackets in this discussion refer to Najm's edition of 'Mārūn al-Naqqāsh'. See n. 1 above.
5. Najm, ed., 'Mārūn al-Naqqāsh', p. 25, Moosa, 'Naqqāsh and the Arab theatre', p. 112.
6. Al-Khozai, *Early Arabic Drama*, p. 55.
7. Muḥammad Mandūr, *al-Masraḥ al-Nathrī* (Cairo, 1959), p. 4.
8. See the chapter 'The Arabs and Shakespeare' in M.M. Badawi, *Modern Arabic Literature and the West* (London, Ithaca Press, 1985).
9. The page numbers in brackets in this discussion refer to Najm's edition of 'Salīm al-Naqqāsh', *al-Masraḥ al-ʿArabī Dirāsāt wa Nuṣūṣ*, Beirut (1964).
10. Muḥammad Yūsuf Najm, *al-Masraḥiyya fi'l-Adab al-ʿArabī al-Ḥadīth* (Beirut, 1956), p. 66.
11. Najm, ed. 'Salīm al-Naqqāsh', pp. 247–8.
12. See his article 'Fawā'id al-Riwāyāt', in *al-Jinān*, Beirut (11 August 1875).
13. Najm, *al-Masraḥiyya*, p. 104.
14. On the mystery that surrounds al-Qabbānī's introduction to the theatre and his early theatrical activities see the good discussion in Atia Abul Naga, *Les Sources Françaises du Théâtre Egyptien (1870–1939)* (Alger, 1972), pp. 129ff.
15. On the fortunes of al-Qabbānī, see Najm, *al-Masraḥiyya*, pp. 61ff and 115ff.
16. Muḥammad Yūsuf Najm, ed., 'al-Shaykh Aḥmad Abū Khalīl al-Qabbānī', *al-Masraḥ al-ʿArabī Dirāsāt wa Nuṣūṣ*, Beirut (1963), 401–2.
17. *Ibid.* p. ḥ.
18. *Ibid.* pp. 337–9.
19. *Ibid.* pp. 168–176.
20. On the possible European source of *ʿAfīfa* see Naga, *Les Sources Françaises*, pp. 153ff.
21. Najm, ed., 'al-Qabbānī', p. 155.
22. Naga, *Les Sources Françaises*, p. 144. (The translation from the French is mine.)
23. *Ibid.* p. 158.
24. Najm, *al-Masraḥiyya*, p. 374.
25. See Najm, ed., 'al-Qabbānī, pp. 3, 8, 20.
26. *Ibid.* p. 204.
27. Mandūr, *al-Masraḥ an-Nathrī*, pp. 8–11.
28. ʿAlī al-Rāʿī, *Masraḥ al-Damm wa'l-Dumūʿ* (Cairo, 1973), p. 110. This play is described as the first, fully-fledged, Egyptian melodrama, *Ibid.* pp. 96–7.
29. The Arabic titles are *al-Ghayra al-Waṭaniyya, Abṭāl al-Ḥurriya*. For a discussion of the theatre and politics in Egypt in the period up to 1919 see Dr Ramsīs ʿAwaḍ's *al-Tārikh al-Sirrī li'l-Masraḥ qabl Thawrat 1919* (Cairo, 1972) and *Ittijāhāt Siyāsīyya fi'l-Masraḥ qabl Thawrat 1919* (Cairo, 1979).
30. Najm, *al-Masraḥiyya*, pp. 491ff.
31. For a plot summary see Nevill Barbour, 'The Arabic theatre in Egypt', *Bulletin of the School of Oriental Studies*, (1935–7), 996ff.
32. Landau, *Arab Theater*, p. 87. For an enthusiastic article on al-Rīḥānī see L. Abou Saif, 'Najīb al-Rīḥānī: from buffoonery to social comedy', *Journal of Arabic Literature*, Leiden, 4 (1973), 1–18. One obvious source of Kish Kish Bey, which Dr Abou Saif surprisingly does not mention, is of course Ibrāhīm Ramzī's play *Dukhūl al-Ḥammām* ('Admission to the Baths'), see pp. 76ff.

4 THE SEARCH FOR EGYPTIAN IDENTITY

1. See M.M. Badawi, *Modern Arabic Literature and the West* (London, 1985), pp. 191–204.
2. *Ibid.* p. 195.
3. *Ibid.* p. 196.
4. In his *Studies in the Arab Theater and Cinema* (Philadelphia, 1958), p. 109, Jacob M. Landau wrongly states that Jalāl translated the tragedies into modern literary Arabic.
5. See Luwīs ʿAwaḍ, *Dīrasāt fī Adabinā al-Ḥadīth* (Cairo, 1961), p. 145.
6. Landau, *The Arab Theater*, p. 109.
7. See Fattūḥ Nashāṭī, *Khamsūn ʿĀm fī Khidmat al-Masraḥ* (Cairo, 1974), vol. II, p. 165.
8. Muḥammad Yūsuf Najm, *al-Masraḥiyya fī'l-Adab al-ʿArabī al-Ḥadīth* (Beirut, 1956), p. 280.
9. See the perceptive analysis of Jalāl's translation of Molière in ʿAlī al-Rāʿī, *Funūn al-Kūmīdya min Khayāl al-Ẓill ilā Najīb al-Rīḥānī* (Cairo, 1971), pp. 122ff.
10. See especially his article 'al-riwāyāt wa anfaʿuhā lanā' (On plays and which of them are most useful for us) in *Mukhtārāt min Faraḥ Anṭūn Silsilat Manāhil al-Adab al-ʿArabī*, Beirut, 29 (1950), 45.
11. See his article 'al-kātib al-sharqī wa ḥājātuhu al-jadīda' in *Faraḥ Anṭūn: Ḥayātuh, Adabuh wa Muqtaṭafāt min Āthārih*, Beirut (1950), 9–10, 32, 37ff. See also *Mukhtārāt min Faraḥ Anṭūn*, p. 59.
12. See *Mukhtārāt min Faraḥ Anṭūn*, 42 and al-Sayyid Ḥasan ʿĪd, *Taṭawwur al-Naqd al-Masraḥī fī Miṣr* (Cairo, 1965), pp. 100ff.
13. Najm, *al-Masraḥiyya*, p. 334, n. 34. For a sympathetic discussion of this play see Najm, *Ibid.* pp. 327–31.
14. See the convincing discussion by ʿAlī al-Rāʿī in his book *Masraḥ al-Damm wa'l-Dumūʿ* (Cairo, 1973), pp. 78ff.
15. Muḥammad Mandūr, *al-Masraḥ al-Nathrī* (Cairo, 1959), pp. 53–4.
16. See Badawi, *Modern Arabic Literature*, p. 94.
17. *Ibid.* pp. 54, 73.
18. Ibrāhīm Dardīrī, *Adab Ibrāhīm Ramzī* (Cairo, 1971), p. 281.
19. *Ibid.* pp. 104ff.
20. Muḥammad Taymūr, *Mu'allafāt, Ḥayātunā al-Tamthīliyya*, Cairo, (1973), vol. II, p. 132.
21. Dardīrī, *Ramzī*, p. 130.
22. *Ibid.* pp. 125ff.
23. Al-Rāʿī, *Funūn al-Kūmīdiya*, p. 136, n. 1.
24. The page numbers in brackets in this discussion refer to the version of the play reprinted in the periodical *al-Hilāl* (July, 1971).
25. The expression is *ʿadam ṭalāq al-ghā'ib*. See Dardīrī, *Ramzī*, p. 298.
26. *Al-Hilāl* (July, 1971), p. 91.
27. *Ibid.*, p. 91.
28. Taymūr, *Mu'allafāt*, p. 168.
29. In *al-Hilāl* (March, 1924), quoted by Dardīrī, *Ramzī*, p. 240.
30. See Ibrāhīm Ramzī, *Abṭāl-Manṣūra* (Cairo, n.d., the author's introduction dated February 1939), p. 3. The page numbers in brackets in this discussion of the play refer to this edition.
31. *Ibid.* p. 4.
32. Muḥammad Mandūr regards this feature as an expression of Ramzī's highly developed sense of theatre (*al-ḥāssa al-masraḥiyya*). See *al-Masraḥ al-Nathrī*, p. 45.
33. J.M. Landau does not discuss a single play by Ibrāhīm Ramzī in his book *Studies in the Arab Theater.*
34. See the introduction by Maḥmūd Taymūr, 'Muḥammad Taymūr ḥayātuh wa aʿmāluh' to *Mu'allafāt Muḥammad Taymūr: Wamīḍ al-Rūḥ* (Cairo, 1971), vol. I, p. 38.
35. In his long, serious introduction to *Mu'allafāt Muḥammad Taymūr Ḥayātunā al-Tamthīliyya* (Cairo, 1973), vol. II, p. 17, Zakī Ṭulaymāt states that Taymūr had spent a year in Germany. However, in this brief biographical account I am following his brother's introduction to vol. I, which incidentally seems to be the main source of ʿAlā' al-Dīn Waḥīd's, *Masraḥ Muḥammad Taymūr* (Cairo, 1975).
36. *Mu'allafāt*, vol. II, pp. 17, 20.
37. *Mu'allafāt*, vol. I, pp. 35ff.
38. *Ibid.* pp. 40–1.

39. *Mu'allafāt*, vol. II, pp. 44–9.
40. *Mu'allafāt*, vol. II, pp. 88–94.
41. *Ibid.* p. 95.
42. *Mu'allafāt*, vol. I, p. 62.
43. *Ibid.* p. 63.
44. *Mu'allafāt*, vol. II, p. 61.
45. Al-Rāʿī, *Funūn al-Kūmīdiya*, p. 144.
46. *Mu'allafāt*, vol. III, p. 52.
47. *Ibid.* p. 56.
48. *Ibid.* p. 68.
49. *Ibid.* p. 42.
50. *Ibid.* p. 25.
51. ʿAlā' al-Dīn Waḥīd, *Masraḥ Muḥammad Taymūr*, p. 100.
52. *Mu'allafāt*, vol. III, p. 30.
53. *Ibid.* p. 36.
54. *Ibid.* p. 37.
55. Nevill Barbour felt that 'the delineation of almost all the characters is admirable' and found 'Abd as-Sattār himself 'unforgettable' and his worthless son 'another excellent study'. See 'The Arabic theatre in Egypt', *Bulletin of the School of Oriental Studies*, 8 (1935–7), 1002–3.
56. *Mu'allafāt*, vol. II, p. 92.
57. *Mu'allafāt*, vol. II, p. 380. There is some inconsistency in the play on this point. Elsewhere (p. 315) we are told that Amīn got married barely a year after his father's death.
58. *Ibid.* p. 405.
59. See ʿAlā' al-Dīn Waḥīd, *Masraḥ Muḥammad Taymūr*, p. 160, where the author objects to the use of the word *sharmūṭa*, a totally justified and appropriate word to use in this context in my opinion.
60. Such as Mandūr in *al-Masraḥ al-Nathrī*, p. 78 and al-Rāʿī in *Masraḥ al-Damm wa'l-Dumūʿ*, pp. 119–121.
61. Mandūr, *al-Masraḥ al-Nathrī*, pp. 82–3.
62. Al-Rāʿī, *Masraḥ al-Damm wa'l-Dumūʿ*, pp. 115–28.
63. *Ibid.* p. 127.
64. ʿAlā' al-Dīn Waḥīd, *Masraḥ Muḥammad Taymūr*, p. 160.
65. Fattūḥ Nashāṭī, *Khamsūn ʿĀm fī Khidmat al-Masraḥ*, (Cairo, 1973), vol. I, pp. 26ff.
66. Mandūr, *al-Masraḥ al-Nathrī*, p. 71.
67. *Ibid.*
68. Anṭūn Yazbak, *al-Dhabā'iḥ: Maʿsāh ʿAṣriyya fī Arbaʿat Fuṣūl, Sharikat Maṭbūʿāt al-Qirṭās* (Cairo, n.d.), p. 14. The page numbers in brackets in this discussion of *al-Dhabā'iḥ* refer to this edition.
69. On the possible influence of Ibsen on this play see the interesting discussion by al-Rāʿī in *Masraḥ al-Damm wa'l-Dumūʿ*, pp. 144–6.
70. See particularly Mandūr, *al-Masraḥ al-Nathrī*, p. 71.

CONCLUSION

1. Jacob M. Landau, *Studies in the Arab Theater and Cinema* (Philadelphia, 1958), pp. 117–18.
2. The edition used here is the fourth, Mīkhā'īl Nuʿayma, *al-Ābā' wa'l-Banūn* (Beirut, 1962). The page numbers in this discussion refer to this edition.
3. Landau, *Studies in the Arab Theater*, pp. 91–4.
4. See M.M. Badawi, *Modern Arabic Literature and the West* (Ithaca Press, 1985), p. 189.
5. Al-Sayyid Ḥasan ʿĪd, *Taṭawwur al-Naqd al-Masraḥī fī Miṣr*, (Cairo, 1965).
6. *Ibid.* pp. 228ff.
7. Fattūḥ Nashāṭī, *Khamsūn ʿĀm fī Khidmat al-Masraḥ* (Cairo, 1973), vol. I p. 71.
8. *Ibid.* p. 81.
9. *Ibid.* p. 90.

INDEX